TYPOGRAPHY BEYOND BORDERS

DESIGN WITH MULTISCRIPTUAL TYPOGRAPHIC ELEMENTS

Sherry Muyuan He

BISPUBLISHERS

BIS Publishers
Timorplein 46
1094 CC Amsterdam
The Netherlands
bis@bispublishers.com
www.bispublishers.com

ISBN 978 90 636 9943 7

Copyright © 2025 Sherry Muyuan He and BIS Publishers

All rights reserved. No part of this publication may be reproduced or transmitted in
any form or by any means, electronic or mechanical, including photocopy, recording
or any information storage and retrieval system, without permission in writing from
the copyright owners. Every reasonable attempt has been made to identify owners
of copyright. Any errors or omissions brought to the publisher's attention will be
corrected in subsequent editions.

ar٩(｡•́ w•̀｡)۶ab⊠ic□arm٩(￣、￣〃)ԏueni♥an NOGLIPH bur⊠⊠me
c(-(I)-)ɘse⊠chт (ʘ 益 ʘ т)in SORRY DUDE! □ese⊠cyr♥ ⊠il ヽ(`Д´*)ノ
lic⊠devana ⸾o(ҹ╲ҹo)gari□⊠ge'ሓ(￣^￣)ሓez⊠geo⊠ NO GLYPH rg(ღ
˘ - ˘ღ)ian♥ greΣ(°△°|||)ek⊠heb 0°ロ°)ש re NOGLIPH w⊠jap(つ ˘ω˘
ς)ane⊠se⊠khm(୨^_^୨)er⊠⊠kor⊠(눈_눈)ean⊠?lao(ງ̊ ̊ຈ)ɔ□
mon♥go٩(ԏ˘^˘)lia⊠n NO GLYPH per□?٩(ˊᗜˋ*)۵ و si⊠□an♥thฅ(=ω
=)ฅai⊠ OK! □ar٩(｡•́ w•̀｡)۶ab⊠ic□arm٩(￣、￣〃)ԏueni♥an NOGLIPH
bur⊠⊠mec(-(I)-)ɘse⊠chт (ʘ 益 ʘ т)in SORRY DUDE! □ese⊠cyr♥ ⊠il
ヽ(`Д´*)ノlic⊠devana ⸾o(ҹ╲ҹo)gari□⊠ge'ሓ(￣^￣)ሓez⊠
geo⊠ NO GLYPH rg(ღ˘ - ˘ღ)ian♥ greΣ(°△°|||)ek⊠heb 0°ロ°)ש re NOGLIPH w
⊠jap(つ ˘ω˘ς)ane⊠se⊠khm(୨^_^୨)er⊠⊠kor⊠(눈_눈)ean
⊠?lao(ງ̊ ̊ຈ)ɔ□mon♥go٩(ԏ˘^˘)lia⊠n NO GLYPH per□?٩(ˊᗜˋ*)۵وsi⊠□
an♥thฅ(=ω=)ฅai⊠ OK! □ar٩(｡•́ w•̀｡)۶ab⊠ic□arm٩(￣、￣〃
)ԏueni♥an NOGLIPH bur⊠⊠mec(-(I)-)ɘse⊠chт(ʘ益ʘт)in SORRY DUDE! □ese⊠

to all the people who write in

ARABIC

ARMENIAN

BURMESE

CHINESE

CYRILLIC

DEVANAGARI

GE'EZ

GEORGIAN

GREEK

HEBREW

JAPANESE

KHMER

KOREAN

LAO

MONGOLIAN

PERSIAN

THAI

INTRODUCTION

The Latin alphabet has remained the same for eight centuries, while other writing systems, such as Chinese, have undergone periods of significant—even radical—changes as recently as the twentieth century. These changes have ranged from eliminating letters and changing the reading direction to redesigning characters and even inventing entirely new alphabets. This book addresses how historical, cultural, and political shifts have altered letterforms and native speakers' relationship with type.

Before computer, handwritten letters played a prominent role in communication. People had more physical relationships with writing and access to the tools and practices of literacy was deeply tied to social status and gender. The ubiquity of handwriting—by chisel, quill, or brush—in early written communication resulted in an abundance of manuscript styles. A literate person with the physical writing tools could create "fonts" merely by writing in their own style.

The first books were produced by hand-copying content onto a surface—be it animal skin, bamboo, silk. European moveable types in the Early Renaissance era sped up printing and increased distribution, revolutionizing writing. Gutenberg's moveable type famously changed the fifteenth-century Western world in this way, but Chinese printers were already working to accommodate the thousands of characters of their own extensive language eight hundred years before Gutenberg, and the technologies they deployed were quite different from those of their European counterparts. Due to the large number of characters in Chinese writing, inserting type into a frame was not significantly faster than carving a block of passages for one page. Printers occasionally inserted the wrong type, because a character frequently shared the same components as others, and the intricate details in each character could easily get distorted when pressed. Despite the attempts to cast types in various materials, moveable types had never dominated printing in China until the twentieth century. These printing histories are just as intriguing as those of contemporary font design; equally fascinating, is how political, religious, and economic factors have shaped publications and technologies.

There is a clear distinction between a script and a language. Arabic is a language, but Arabic script is also used in Persian, Urdu, and other languages. Persian and Urdu use a few more letters than Arabic does, but most are the same. Likewise, Chinese script is used in many languages, both Chinese (e.g., Mandarin, Cantonese, Taishanese, Hakka, Hokkien) and others, such as Japanese (**kanji**) and Korean (**hanja**). Because this book concentrates on the diversity of scripts and similarities among languages using the same scripts, I refer, unless otherwise specified, to **scripts** rather than **languages**. For example, the word **Arabic** in this book denotes the Arabic script used in writing Arabic-, Persian-, and Urdu-language texts; **Chinese**, the script used for various languages across mainland China, Taiwan, Hong Kong, Japan, and Korea; and **Latin**, the script used for English, Spanish, German, and many other languages.

To research more widely accessible non-Latin scripts like Arabic, I studied language instruction books. By experimenting with writing in different scripts and typing in different fonts, I analyzed how letterforms transformed from one style to another. To complete such in-depth typographical and calligraphical research, I also purchased research-based books for specific writing systems. Scripts in some countries, such as Japan and South Korea, use native descriptive terminologies, but for comparative analysis, this book avoids highly localized words and instead emphasizes the evolution of type cross-culturally.

A **typeface** is a family of fonts that may include regular, bold, and italic forms, which is a specific style within that family. For example, Helvetica is a typeface, but Helvetica Italic is a **font** that explicitly refers to the italic style of the Helvetica typeface. This book uses both terms because complicated scripts can sometimes have only one typeface due to the large number of characters. Chinese, for instance, has more than four thousand characters, while Japanese has about eighty hiragana characters, eighty katakana characters, and more than two thousand kanji characters; Korean uses more than two thousand characters.

AMHARIC
ARABIC
ARMENIAN
BAYBAYIN
BERBER
BURMESE
GEORGIAN
GREEK
HEBREW
HINDI
KOREAN
MONGOLIAN
PERSIAN
RUSSIAN
TAMIL
THAI

INTRODUCTION

As a violin maker creates the instruments that a violinist plays, type designers create typefaces that graphic designers use in their work. Type designers invest time designing individual letters, punctuation, numerals, and ligatures. Other essential duties include embedding kerning pairs (i.e., the adjustment of spacing between two glyphs) and finetuning anchor points in each glyph. The author does not identify as a type designer but as a type researcher who analyzes the similarities and differences among typographic elements in various scripts. Therefore, this book is intended to help graphic designers appreciate the labor and understand current technological limitations involved in designing and displaying non-Latin types so that they can use them correctly and creatively.

Most typography books focus on the anatomy of the Latin alphabet, with additional quick overviews of other popular scripts like Japanese. Books dedicated to other scripts tend to target native users, and the creative treatments of type are complex for readers who cannot read the scripts to digest. This book proposes a new method of comparatively exploring typographic elements across different scripts.

Whereas standard typography books move from the micro to the macro—beginning with letterform details (e.g., serifs) and moving on to each line of text until ultimately reaching the paragraph—this book moves from the macro to the micro. Much like how we get to know a person—first remembering how they make us feel, then how they dress, and, after some time, their peculiarities and preferences—this book first introduces specific writing systems, then dives into the details of each letter.

In some countries, writing scripts is like drawing pictures, though most other parts of the world have developed alphabets for writing. Besides the most common left-to-right orientation of text, there are also other possibilities for text direction, some of which are compromised in digital devices. Inside each line of text, some scripts have tall heads and long feet that require more line space to be displayed correctly. The many methods of setting character space depend on the construction of the letters. Letter shape also determines the spacing between individual letters. Combining letters and constructing new glyphs is essential to type design, even though ligatures are not the priority in designing Latin type. Stretching is atypical in Latin but quite common in Arabic. Likewise, the style for displaying emphasis is not always italic as in Latin but can include letter spacing as in Greek.

Throughout the book are interactive exercises. I invite readers to experiment firsthand with non-Latin writing to facilitate a deeper relationship to the concepts covered and to enable the reader to imagine new design possibilities and goals for cross-cultural collaboration. In learning about these diverse writing systems, readers should develop their own take on good, non-Latin type design.

01 | ACCESSIBILITY

In US higher education and in tandem with diversity, equity, and inclusion (DEI) efforts, there have been many discussions, panels, and trainings related to accessibility. Such work has expanded the understanding of accessibility from the wheelchair icon to other forms of support in classrooms, such as screen-readable course materials and descriptive alternative text. This chapter analyzes how type design assists various communities in different languages. The unique features and histories embedded in some scripts affect their level of accessibility in type. Therefore, it is possible to discover more creative problem-solving moments in our world through the lens of script.

EXAGGERATED FORMS

Different writing systems train their readers' brains to identify distinct parts of letterforms they need to pay attention to as well as those they need to ignore.

Which one of the sentences below is easier to read?

1   a lazy but quick dog jumps over the brown fox

2   a quick brown dog jumps over the lazy foxes

Adobe Garamond Pro

For English readers, Number 2 is generally more legible. In the Latin alphabet, lowercase letters have more diverse forms on their top halves. So, when readers scan a page, they focus more on the top of each sentence. This is not the case in every language.

Consider the two lines below, written in Traditional Chinese script. Which one is more legible? If you do not read Chinese, venture a guess.

3   陰險的狗堅決不讓飛馳的狐狸跑過去

4   陰險的狗堅決不讓飛馳的狐狸跑過去

Source Han Serif SC

The outer contours are more distinct than the details inside each character, making the characters in Number 4 easier to interpret. In Numbers 1 through 4, readers of different scripts, such as Latin and Chinese, are trained to focus on different parts of letters. This indicates that linguistic accessibility is distinct for each writing system's community of users.

Atkinson Hyperlegible is an example of a Latin typeface designed for accessibility. Commissioned by the Braille Institute of America and designed by Applied Design Works (Elliott Scott, Megan Eiswerth, Linus Boman, and Theodore Petrosky) in 2019, the typeface aimed to be friendly to people with various vision impairments, including macular degeneration, retinitis pigmentosa, cataracts, and diabetic retinopathy. After extensive research, the designers learned that different parts of a patient's vision could be reduced, depending on their specific eye disease. As a result, the exaggeration of the forms for each letter became necessary so that there would be no confusion, for example, between the letter **B** and the number **8**, **O** and **0**, or **I** and **1**.

Atkinson Hyperlegible

B 8   O 0   l 1

Equipped badass

Ijuice loaded in 1 Macbook, 0 spillage

In the **b**, **d**, **q**, **p** group, each stem ends differently. Likewise in the **l**, **j**, **I**, **I** group, the lowercase **l** has a serif so that it cannot be confused with an uppercase **I**. The lowercase **i** also has a serif to distinguish it from lowercase **j**, which could otherwise be perceived as **i** by readers who have difficulty seeing text below the baseline.

Atkinson Hyperlegible

Comic Sans was not designed to be widely used as a body type (i.e., the text forming the main content as opposed to the titles). Vincent Connaire instead created Comic Sans to replace Times New Roman for the Microsoft Bob software, which was designed to make computers charming to learn.[1] In fact, Connaire did not even want to call it a typeface.[2] After Microsoft Bob was abandoned, Comic Sans was used internally for party invitations and externally in Microsoft MovieMaker.[3] Wider usage began when it was added as a bonus product with Windows 95, because there were no other typefaces like it.[4]

By the early 2000s, it had been so frequently in schools and, at times, even on funeral invitations that hatred toward Comic Sans exploded. Now, Comic Sans is used primarily as a joke or, occasionally, with attitude (i.e., "I made this bad design intentionally, but are you smart enough to get it?"). Another side of the story, though, is that it is one of the most dyslexia-friendly typefaces.[5]

Comic Sans

b d q p   t f a o l

1. Simon Garfield, *Comic Sans: The Biography of a Typeface* (W. W. Norton & Co, 2024), 36-39.

2. Garfield, *Comic Sans*, 42.

3. Garfield, *Comic Sans*, 42.

4. Garfield, *Comic Sans*, 44.

5. Simon Garfield, *Just My Type: A Book About Fonts* (Avery, 2012), 19.

Like Atkinson Hyperlegible, Comic Sans's lowercase **b** is not a direct reflection of lowercase **d**; neither is lowercase **p** of lowercase **q**. The stem of the lowercase **t** is shortened, further distinguishing it from lowercase **f**. The circle in the lowercase **a** also differs from that in the lowercase **o**. This approach to design is like having multiple keys to a locked room. Even if you lose one key, you still have another that allows entry; even if one part of vision or image processing does not work, other parts will still be able to recognize text typed in Comic Sans.

Connare also designed MS Trebuchet, another dyslexia-friendly typeface. Though lacking the personality and handwritten qualities of Comic Sans, MS Trebuchet retains the distinct features of each letter, as shown below with the lowercase letter groups **b**, **d**, **p**, **q** and **l**, **j**, **i**, **l**.

Trebuchet

In non-Latin writing systems, dyslexia-friendly fonts follow the same design philosophy. In his memoir **My Life with DX Dyslexia**, architect Takanao Todo writes about his experiences being dyslexic in Japan. Some of Takanao's confusion when reading Japanese resulted from the direction of the characters' final strokes.[6] **Re** and **ne**, for example, are only different on the bottom right. The same goes for the pair of **me** and **mu**. The characters for **open** and **close** share the same contour, with only one stroke in the center that distinguishes between the two.

6. Takano Todo, *My Life with DX Dyslexia* (Shufunotomosha, 2011), 29.

Yu Mincho

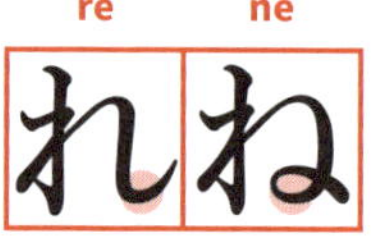

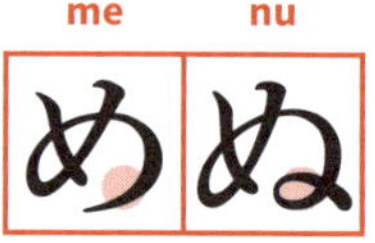

7. Todo, *DX Dyslexia*, 28.

U and **ra** are also very similar. Like the Latin **b**, **d**, **p**, and **q**, the Japanese **chi** and **sa** appear as reflections of one another.[7] Additional confusing pairs are show below.

Yu Mincho

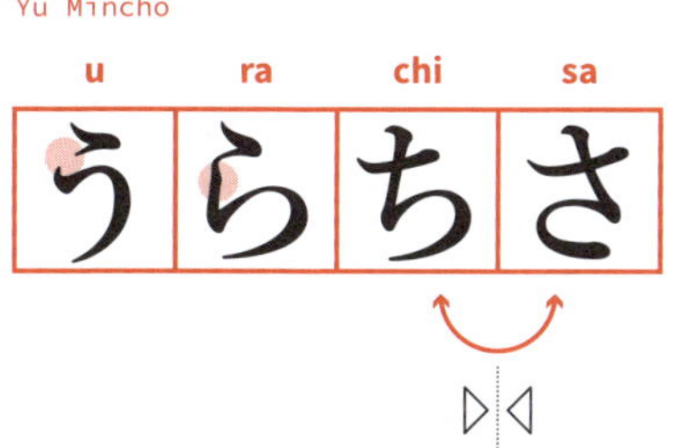

こいり

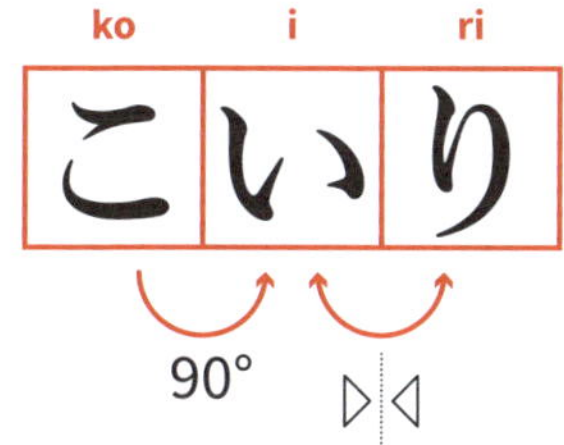

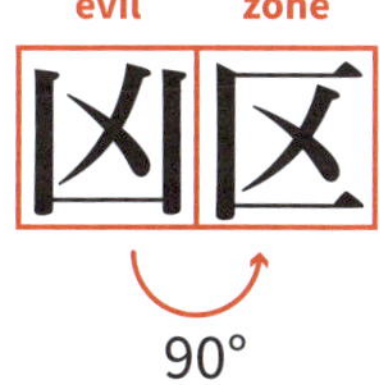

Traditionally, Japanese books are printed in typefaces like Mincho, the Japanese equivalent of Times New Roman. To resolve accessibility issues, schoolbooks have begun adopting Japanese Universal Design (UD) font families. UD fonts apply similar techniques of form exaggeration while maintaining a handwritten quality.

This clear distinction between graphically similar characters can be applied to any script. Tamil—which is used for the Tamil language in India, Sri Lanka, Malaysia, Singapore, and Indonesia—used to be engraved on palm leaves. These leaves tore easily when words were written on them in straight lines, so the script adopted a system of many circles in letters. When designing Tamil typefaces for wayfinding, it is better to make similar letters more distinctive.[8]

8. Aadarsh Rajan, "November Tamil: Designing with Purpose," *Typoteque*, November 18, 2021, https://www.typotheque.com/articles/november-tamil-designing-with-purpose.

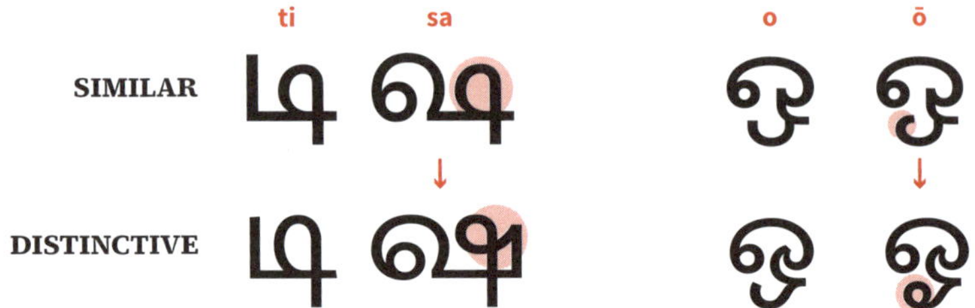

Hind Madurai, Catamaran, Mukta Malar

Ge'ez is the script for the Amharic language spoken in Ethiopia. In some Ge'ez typefaces, pairs of letters exist in which the only difference is either the serifs or the angles of one stroke. To increase the contrast between the two letters, a typeface can apply both serif difference and angle difference to increase the distinction.

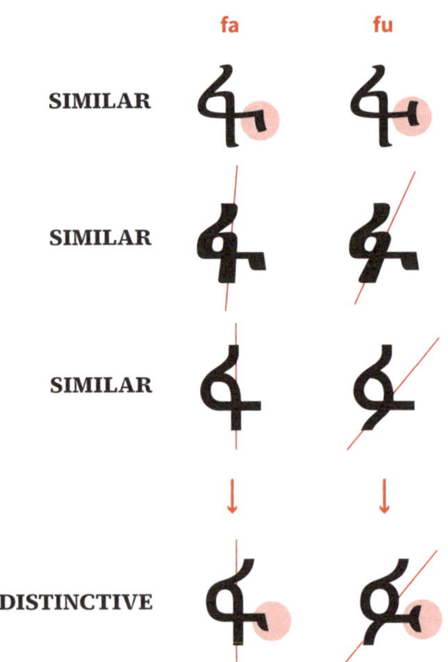

Kigelia Ethiopic, Tayitu, Shiromeda, Noto Sans Ethiopic

READING PACE

Everyone reads differently. Some skip, some skim, and some prefer reading every word. Research shows that reading comprehension improves when students read slowly because they have time to think. Comprehension can therefore be improved by intentionally making reading more difficult and compelling so that a reader requires more time with the text.

Yale professor Shane Frederick invented the Cognitive Reflection Test (CRT), the world's shortest intelligence test, to measure the deep analytical skills with which people pass impulsive judgments. Reading a true black, non-italicized body text font, a group of Princeton students scored 1.9 out of 3, but when he typed the same test questions in 10 percent grey, 10-pt italic Myriad Pro font, the average score increased to 2.45.[9]

9. Malcolm Gladwell, *David and Goliath* (Penguin, 2015), 104–05.

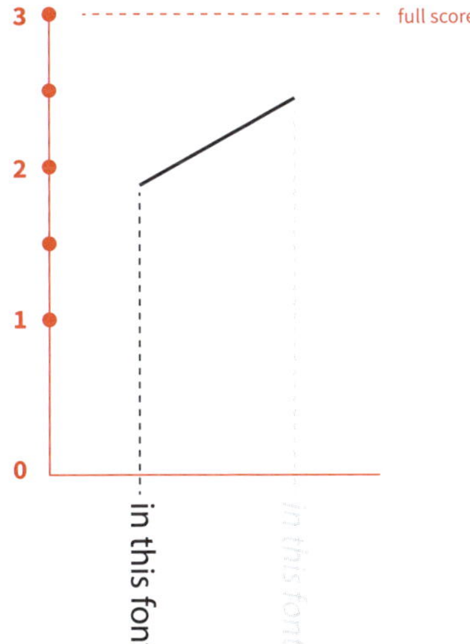

When the goal is to make people ponder and wonder, a block of clean, evenly textured, and readable text may not yield the best result. Below is a question adapted from Frederick's test, and likewise typed in 10-pt, italic Myriad Pro font.

If it takes 10 Sherrys 10 months to write 10 books, how many Sherrys does it take to write 100 books within 100 months?

INVENTING A NEW ALPHABET

In Japan, people still use **kanji** (Chinese characters). Chinese characters were also once used in Korea but learning to write in Chinese script was a luxury at a time when paper and brushes were expensive commodities. The inaccessibility of these essential writing tools was, therefore, a significant barrier to fluency. The presence of sounds in Korean, which do not exist in Chinese, presented Korean readers with another level of difficulty. Sejong the Great, the fourth king of the Joseon dynasty, created Hangeul—a unique alphabet explicitly designed for the Korean language—in the 1440s. Sejong made several notable contributions to Korea, but he is additionally respected as a graphic designer for his influence on the Korean writing system.

Hangeul consonants are modeled on the shape of the mouth, mimicking pronunciation. This design consequently eases memorization.

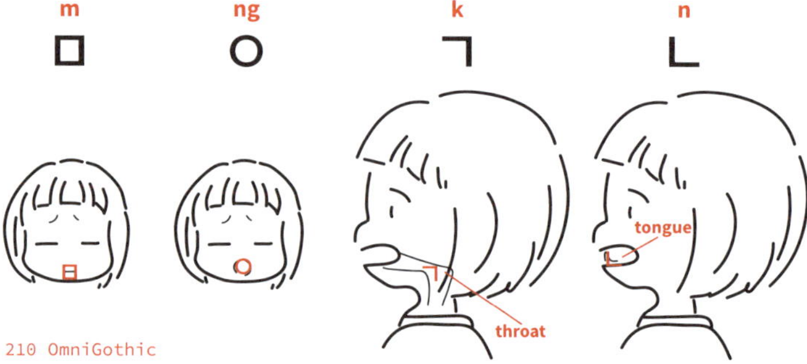

210 OmniGothic

Hangeul vowels were built from three basic shapes that represent the sky, earth, and human.

The initial design of the vowels consisted of straight lines and dots. The modern version, however, has replaced the dots with short lines.

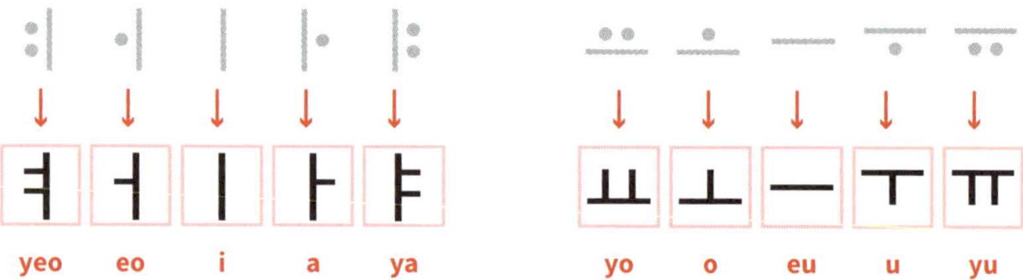

210 OmniGothic

To compose a word, you simply combine consonants and vowels like building blocks.

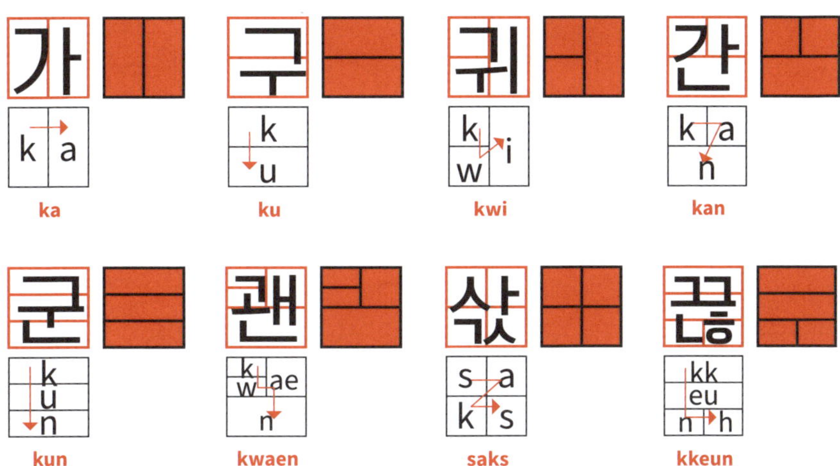

exercise ○○○

Can you guess the sound of the following words?

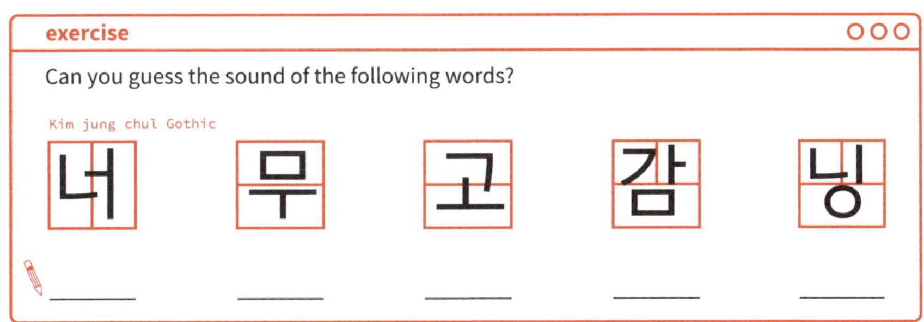

10. Jeongming Kwon, "Hangul," in *Bi-scriptual Typography and Graphic Design with Multiple Script Systems: Arabic, Cyrillic, Greek, Hangeul, Hanzi, Hebrew, Devanagari, Kanji/Hiragana/Katakana*, ed. Ben Wittner, Sascha Thoma, Timm Hartmann (Niggli, 2019), 166.

11. Christopher Calderhead and Holly Cohen, *The World Encyclopedia of Calligraphy: The Ultimate Compendium on the Art of Fine Writing: History, Craft, Technique* (Sterling, 2018), 239.

The development of Hangeul made Korean writing much more accessible, as the new script could be written with simpler tools—even with just a stick in the sand. As a result, Korean literacy improved throughout the fifteenth century. However, Hangeul met resistance from the educated high class, who called it a "vulgar alphabet" and continued using Chinese characters.[10] Many elite scholars, worried that their status would be threatened by rising literacy rates, discouraged the use of Hangeul for official, government documents. It was not until 1894 that Hangeul became the exclusively official script in Korea.[11]

UNIFYING LETTERS

In Arabic, even though there is only one direction in which to connect the letters—contrary to the building-block style of Hangeul—the shape of a letter can vary according to its position within a word.

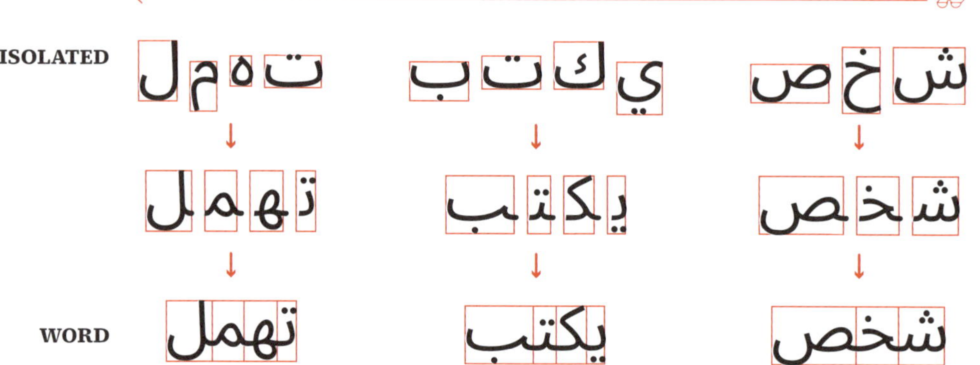

ISOLATED / WORD

Noto Sans Arabic

Some letters only require remembering the number of "teeth" (as in **s** in the figure below), the number of dots (as in **t** below), and the position of the dots, be they above or below. Nevertheless, some letters are not as predictable when they change their positions (as in **k**, **h**, and **ay** below). This requires extra memorization work to fully master the script.

	isolated	final	medial	initial	
s	س	ـس	ـسـ	سـ	2 teeth, 0 dot
t	ت	ـت	ـتـ	تـ	1 tooth, 2 dots above
sh	ش	ـش	ـشـ	شـ	2 teeth, 3 dots above
b	ب	ـب	ـبـ	بـ	1 tooth, 1 dot below
k	ك	ـك	ـكـ	كـ	
h	ه	ـه	ـهـ	هـ	
ay	ع	ـع	ـعـ	عـ	

Microsoft Sans Serif

Nasri Khattar was a Lebanese architect and type designer who devised a way of unifying Arabic letters so that each would appear the same if it were isolated or at the beginning, in the middle, or at the end of a word. Khattar's method is known as **Unified Arabic**. Frank Laubauch, a missionary and supporter of "Khattar letters," wrote to Khattar that after only half a day of instruction in Unified Arabic, one of his young students could already read any easy book printed in the system.[12] The example below is not the same as Khattar's original design, but it does take the same approach to unifying the shapes of each letter in all four positions.

12. Yara Khoury Nammour, *Nasri Khattar: A Modernist Typotect* (Khatt Books, 2014), 24.

individual letters

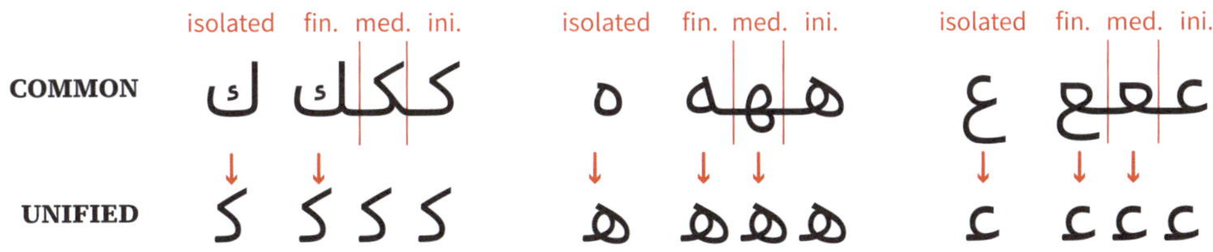

in a word

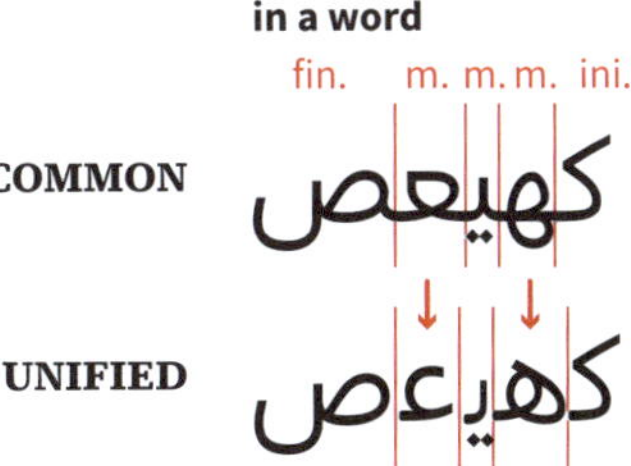

Another accomplishment that Unified Arabic achieved is the consolidation of keys on an Arabic typewriter, which has made typing Arabic faster and cheaper.[13] Some critics recognized this reform as "a surrender to Western standards" and "a rejection of Arabic heritage," not only because of the detachment of letters and homogenous letter heights but also because of his relocation to New York and the involvement of IBM and the Ford Foundation.[14] Khattar's vision did not become as widespread as Hangeul has.

13. Nammour, *Nasri Khattar*, 72.

14. Nammour, *Nasri Khattar*, 50.

UNITING THE MARGINALIZED

A much lesser-known writing system is Nüshu, best translated from Mandarin Chinese as "women's script." Nüshu is a secret writing system shared and used only by women in an ethnically diverse village in the Hunan Province of China. It was developed in the ancient era, at a time when women were not allowed to learn how to write; literacy was, at that time, one way men secured their social position above women. Women would teach each other Nüshu in solidarity with one another and communicate with other female members of the village.

The precise age of Nüshu remains unknown, but it could be as old as the oracle bone script: the pictographic ancestor of the modern-day Chinese characters.[15] Nüshu has a unique feminine delicacy, and it has been called "mosquito-foot writing" because of the thin strokes used for each character. The script is usually written with a fine brush on rice paper. Historically and in the present, women also write it on folded fans for decorative purposes.

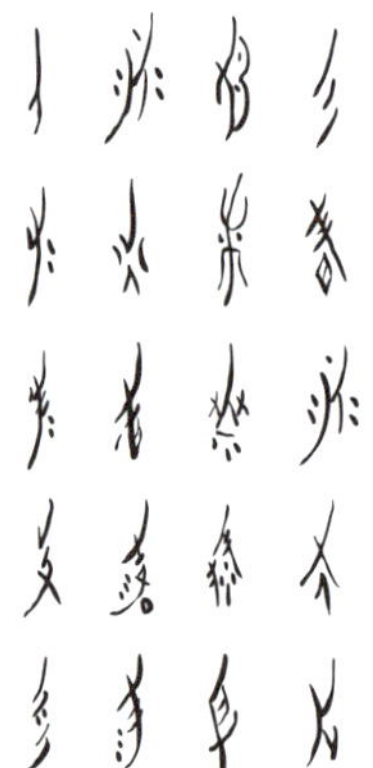

As the study of Chinese characters has become available to more women, interest in Nüshu has declined, but scholars—including Zhou Shuoyi, a man who made tremendous contributions to the study of Nüshu—have protected it over the years.[16] Nowadays, both men and women practice Nüshu, and it is printed without secrecy on merchandise, such as dresses. A tech company has even created smartphones that display Nüshu. Such commercialization has made the script known to more people in China, but its decoding and public display have also completely altered the community it once primarily served.

15. Jing Tsu, *Kingdom of Characters: The Language Revolution That Made China Modern* (Riverhead books, 2023), 173.

16. Andrew Lofthouse, "Nüshu: China's Secret Female-Only Language," *BBC News*, February 25, 2022, https://www.bbc.com/travel/article/20200930-nshu-chinas-secret-female-only-language.

02 | LOGOGRAMS

Most scripts are non-logographic, like alphabets and syllabaries, with each symbol representing a sound without an inherent meaning of its own. In his book **The Stroke: Theory of Writing**, Gerrit Noordzij declares that the history of writing should be addressed as "the evolution of spelling."[1] Such a statement, however, marginalizes the few logographic scripts—writing systems whose symbols represent meaning—that remain in use today.

Each language's standardized character set shapes the language users' relationship to how characters are to be discerned. People who use scripts derived from pictures—contrary to those whose scripts are phonetically based—tend to connect writing to drawing, treating each character box as a compositional frame. Among those cultures, elaborate image-making is celebrated, and the historical artworks they produce tend to compress groups of stories into a single painting or drawing.

"Writing" is an increasingly digital process. It is highly dynamic and lends itself to supplementary forms of communication, such as memes and emojis, which can convey complex ideas and emotions through more visual means. A digital writer in the 2020s can react to a message with a "thumbs-up" or "heart" to express a feeling or confirm receipt. This chapter inspects the soft boundaries between drawing and writing that specific scripts and technological advancements have enabled.

1. Gerrit Noordzij, *The Stroke: Theory of Writing* (Hyphen Press, 2005), 47.

THAI

Thai letters are named after animals and objects. Each letter is always referred to by the same name. As a result, young students tend to connect writing to drawing.

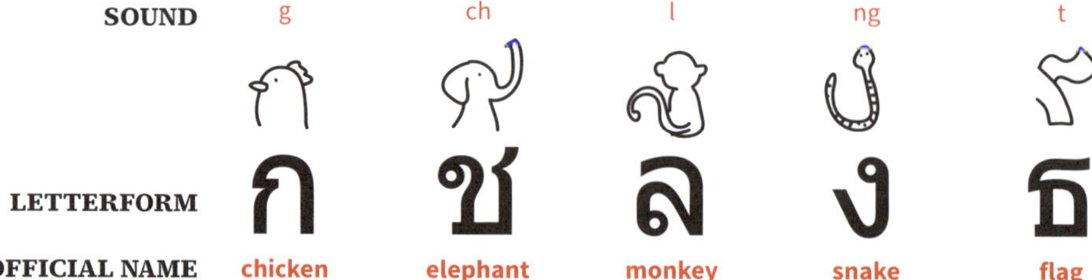

SOUND	g	ch	l	ng	t
LETTERFORM	ก	ช	ล	ง	ธ
OFFICIAL NAME	chicken	elephant	monkey	snake	flag

Tahoma

Providing an illustrative name for each letter makes spelling more uniform. In English, some names of letters sound similar and require extra explanation or clarification (for example, **B** as in **boy** to differentiate from **V** as in **victory**). Another reason for concretely naming each letter in Thai, is that the Thai language contains high consonants, mid consonants, and low consonants. A high **ch** produces a different tone than a low **ch**. A mid **ch** does not exist. Standardized naming makes such tonal distinctions even clearer when it comes to writing.

SOUND	ch(high)	ch(mid)	ch (low)
LETTERFORM	ฉ		ช
OFFICIAL NAME	cymbal	n/a	elephant

Tahoma

The Thai word **chob** (which means "like," pronounced as "chop"), for example, is spelled **elephant, basin, leaf**.

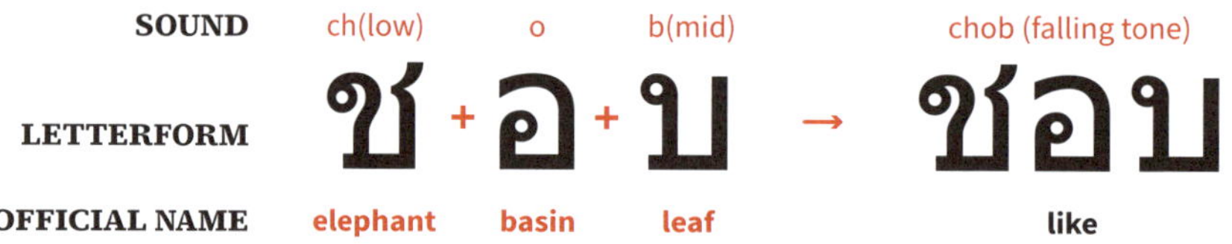

SOUND	ch(low)	o	b(mid)	chob (falling tone)
LETTERFORM	ช + อ + บ →			ชอบ
OFFICIAL NAME	elephant	basin	leaf	like

Tahoma

The Thai script is not strictly a logogram, yet the naming of the letters shows that image-making can be connected to type design.

CHINESE

Dating to the second millennium BCE, the Oracle Bone script is the oldest form of written Chinese. The naming originates in the way characters were carved quite literally into oracle bones, typically turtle shells.

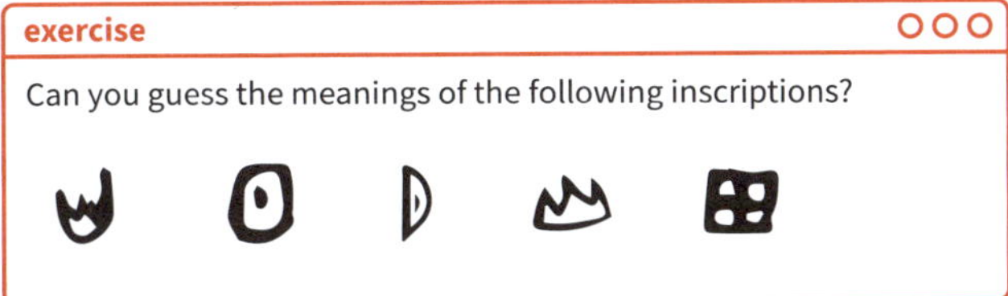

As writing tools and surfaces evolved, Chinese characters diverged from the original images carved into hard surfaces. The increased availability and distribution of brushes and paper enabled a certain delicacy to develop in each character.

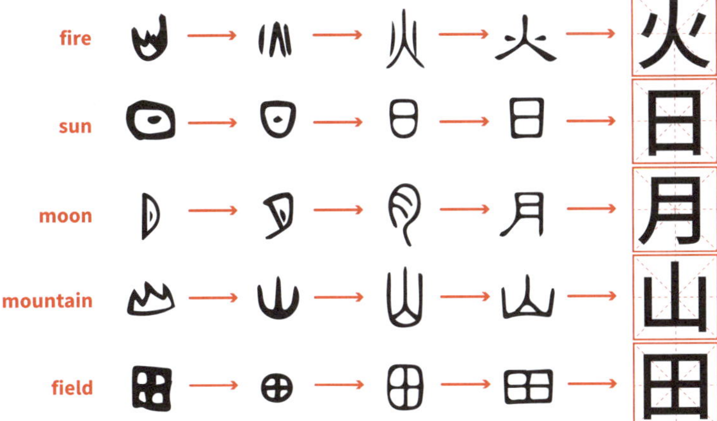

Monolingual Chinese speakers process writing similar to how they process drawing. To facilitate memorization, Chinese language textbooks for both native and nonnative speakers might include the visual evolution of characters in a manner akin to the image above.

To create a more complicated Chinese character, basic characters are combined in a square composition. In the following example, the sun and the moon are united to create the character **ming**, meaning brightness or tomorrow.

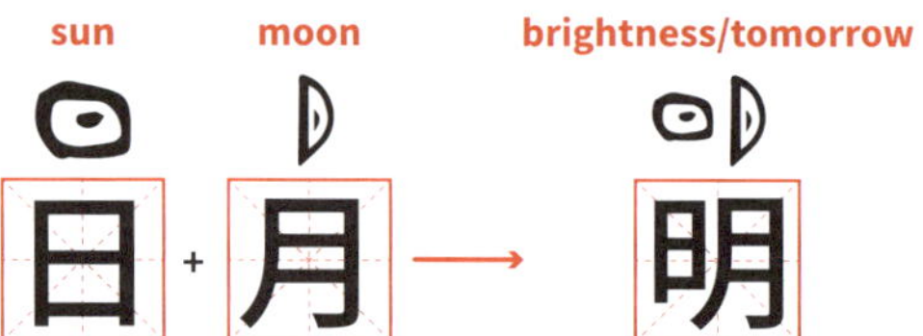

Source Han Sans CN

Jiong is an ancient character that had been abandoned until 2008, when netizens rediscovered it and compared it to a frustrated anime face. It has since enjoyed great popularity both as a written and drawn character.

Source Han Sans CN

Many languages make use of portmanteau—blended words—like the English adjective **hangry**, a combination of **hungry** and **angry**. Chinese speakers also compose new characters in this way. **Bu** means not, and **zheng** means upright. When, for example, the characters **bu** (not) and **zheng** (upright) are combined vertically, they make one unified character, **wai** (tilted).

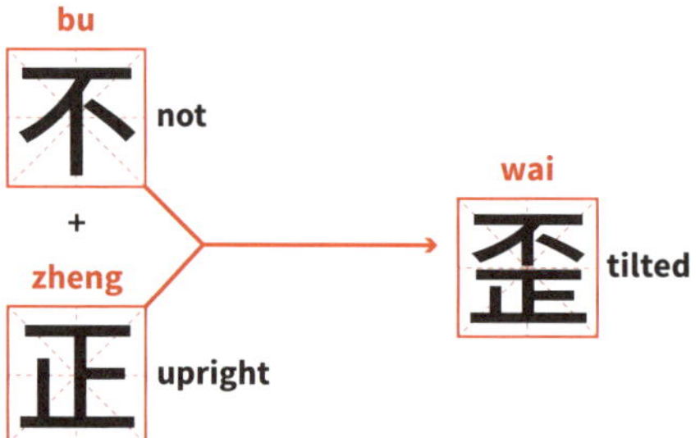

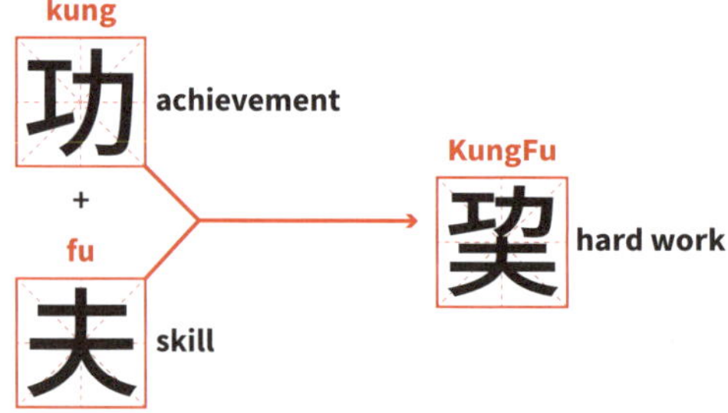

Source Han Sans CN

Most Chinese characters have five to fifteen strokes each, but the character **biang** is a notorious outlier. **Biang** is the sound of pulled noodle dough hitting a tabletop. The character is only used as a proper noun—**Biang Biang Noodle**. The character is so complicated that it cannot be displayed clearly in body text at a small point size.

biang   **biang**   **biang**

8 pt   14 pt   20 pt

Source Han Serif SC

On most websites and apps, it shows up as a tofu (i.e., the glyph that shows up when there is no character available for the displayed font).

⊠面是陕西关中地区传统面食。其名字中的"⊠"字是一个复杂的合体字，常被用更简单的形式替代，如奤奤面或彪彪面。名字来源于制作面条时发出的"biang, biang"声响。陕西八大怪，其中"面条像裤带"就是指这种面。

KaiTi

The average Chinese person also does not remember how to write **biang** because the character is so rarely used. But they can memorize it and reproduce it quickly after only a brief look at it. Years of practice reading and writing Chinese characters enables a reader to instantly dissect the character's composition. This is like how English readers might process a long word, such as **electroencephalogram**. The word may seem daunting to some, but an experienced English reader can divide the word into several other words that they are familiar with. The effect of dissecting this word is comparable to what Chinese readers experience with **biang**, albeit less linearly than in English.

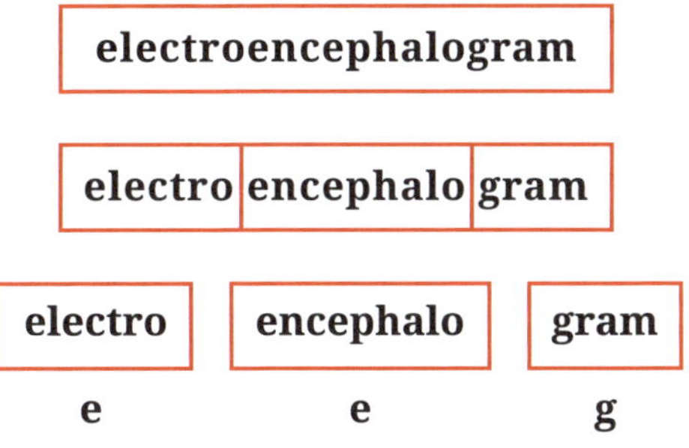

Droid Serif

Chinese characters can be written with either stacking or wrapping composition. A Chinese reader needs to know this to understand the reading direction inside each character. The character composition below is taught to both native and nonnative Chinese readers to facilitate memorization. Recognizing the composition streamlined the process of looking up a character in a dictionary, before computer became widely accessible.

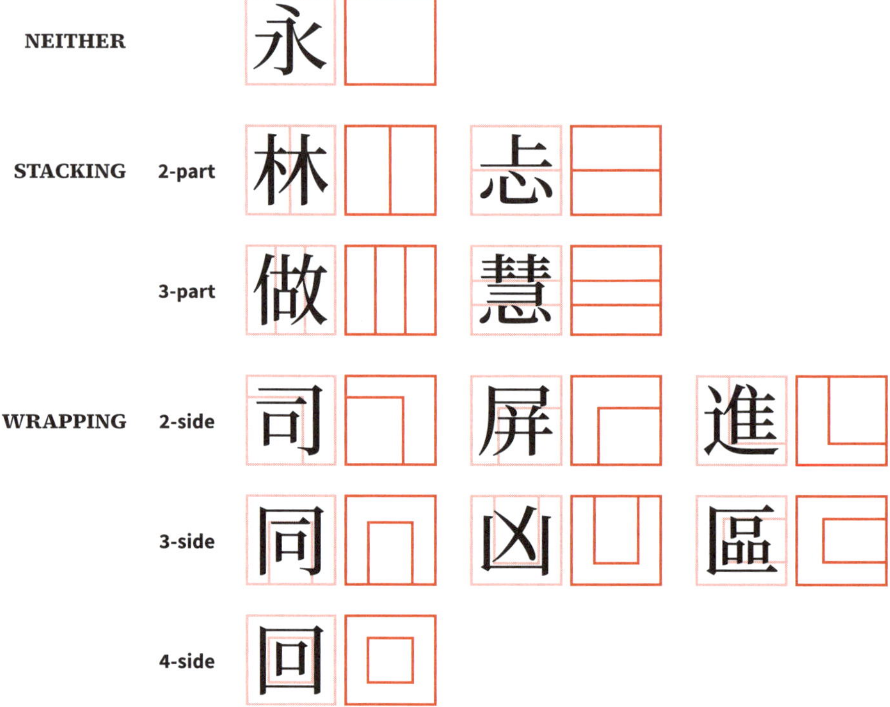

NEITHER

STACKING 2-part

3-part

WRAPPING 2-side

3-side

4-side

Source Han Serif SC

A fluent Chinese reader can quickly break down the composition of any character, regardless of how complicated it appears.

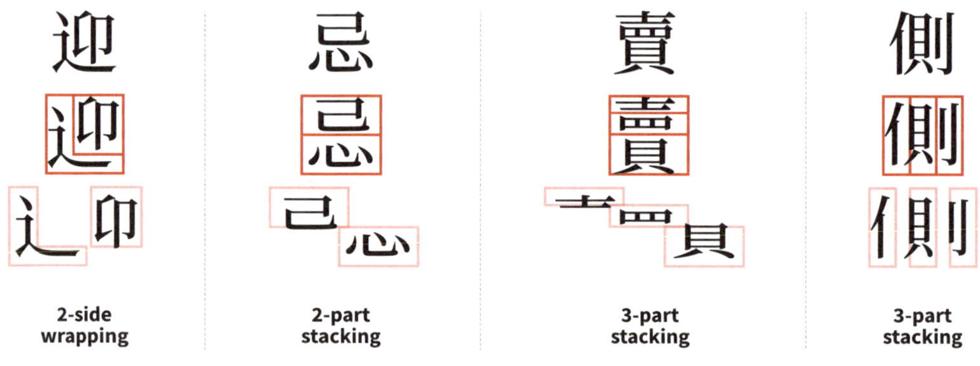

Source Han Serif SC

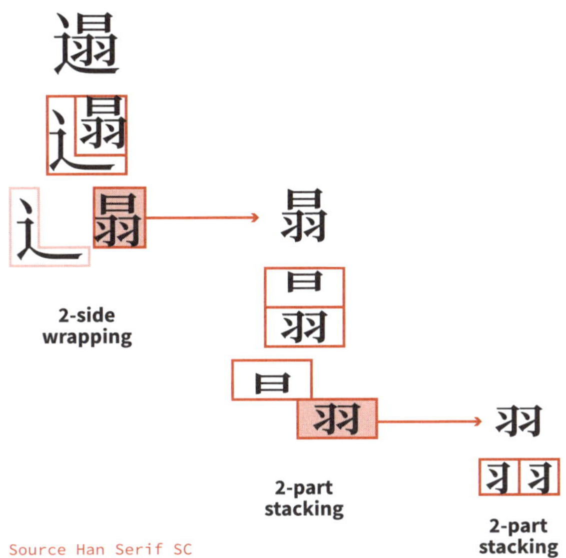

To understand how the **biang** character is written, a fluent reader intuitively breaks it down into smaller components.

CHARACTER ANATOMY

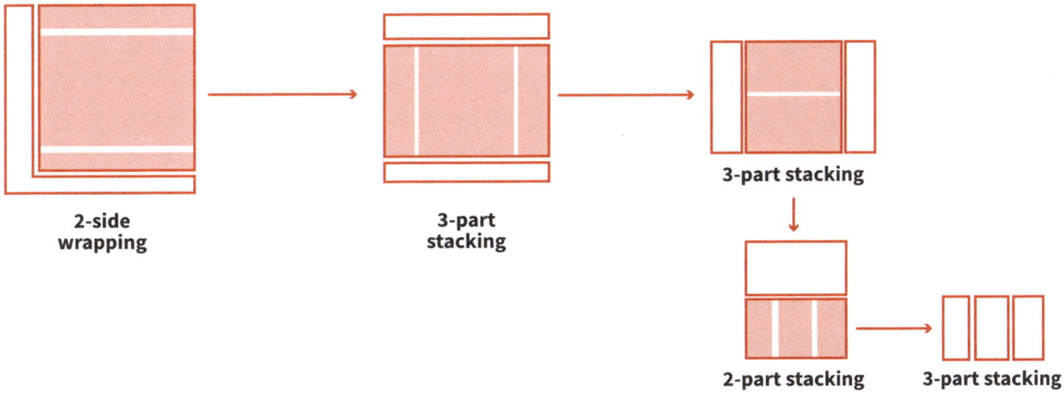

Another notoriously complicated character is **da**. Like **biang**, it looks overwhelming at a glance, but it is structurally three of the same character for "dragon" combined.

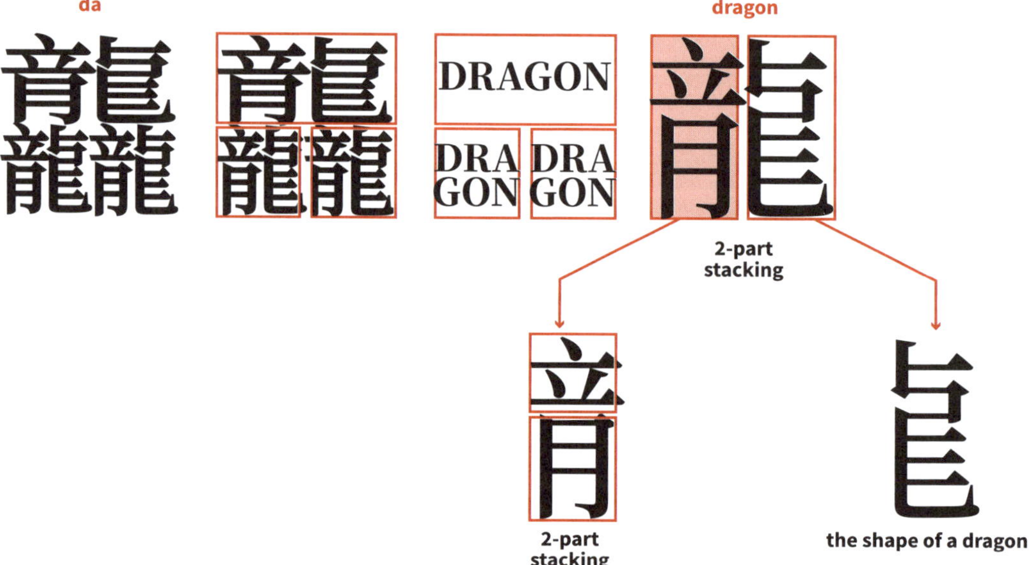

Source Han Serif SC

The intricacies of the characters are deliberate and logical in a way that encourages easy identification. In 1928, two psychologists at the University of Chicago, Loh Seng Tsai and Ethel Abernethy, conducted an experiment to test the difficulty of learning Chinese characters according to the number of strokes in each character.[2] While characters with fewer strokes were found to be easier for learners to reproduce, the number of strokes had no effect on how easily characters were recognized.[3] Below is a set of five Khmer letters and five Chinese characters. Without requiring a person to write all ten from memory, the Chinese characters are simpler to distinguish from one another.

2. Ulug Kuzuoglu, *Codes of Modernity: Chinese Scripts in the Global Information Age* (Columbia University Press, 2024), 129.

3. Kuzuoglu, *Codes of Modernity*, 129.

Siemreap, Source Han Sans CN

Tsai and Abernethy's research proves that complexity does not negatively affect one's ability to learn Chinese characters. What makes Chinese characters intimidating is, instead, the number of them one must be able to recognize—some four thousand—to be literate in this nonphonetic system.

East Asian people's familiarity with complicated compositions extends beyond typography; it reflects everything from the analog artwork produced in the ancient period to the digital forms of the modern era. Compared to the minimalistic designs of popular Western apps, some East Asian ones have been criticized for micro-clusters and information overload.

CLUSTERED

main menu

secondary menu

notification

events

other products

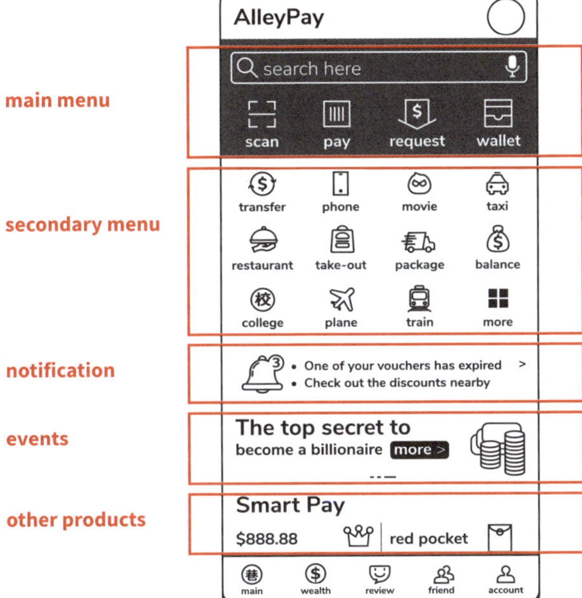

MINIMAL

main menu

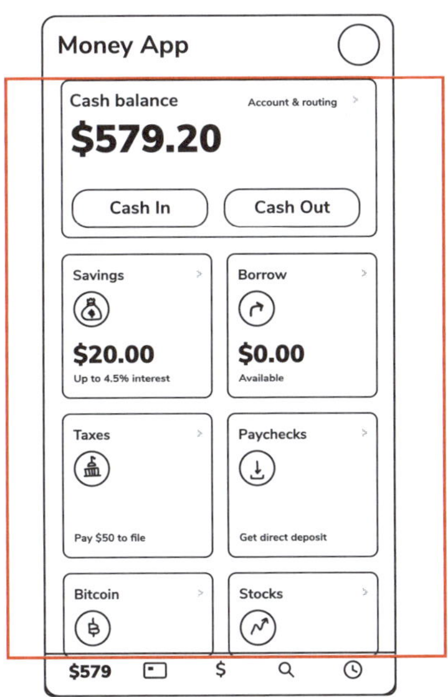

For those users who have grown up with simpler alphabets, less is more.

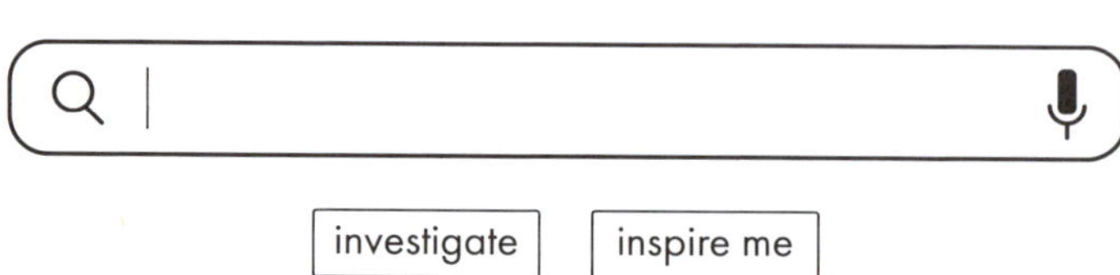

Futura PT

For those who have grown up writing complicated scripts, breaking down groups of information is second nature. Different language users apply different methods of processing information, and micro-clusters do not always lead to confusion.

logo

main categories to explore

郵箱	新聞
詞典	美食
健康	教育
運動	時尚
旅游	財經
購物	電視
電影	電影
體育	天氣
娛樂	政治

biggest news today

焦點　熱點　**重點**　盲點

10 Sherrys writes 10 books in 10 months.

If 10 Sherrys can write 10 books in 10 months, that means each Sherry writes 1 book in 10 months. Now, if you need to write 100 books in 100 months, each Sherry still writes 1 book in 10 months, so you'd still need 10 Sherrys because:
10 Sherrys × 1 book per Sherry per 10 months = 10 books every 10 months.

Over 100 months, they can collectively write 100 books. So the answer is still 10 Sherrys!

secondary category

商業
付款寶
免費廣告
網上商店
流行詞

科學家發現月球內部藏有外星城市，地球將面臨新外交挑戰

全球首例：人類成功移植翅膀實現飛行夢

考古隊在沙漠中找到時光機器，時光旅行不再是夢想

more news

超市蔬菜夜晚會發光，疑似吸收外星能量

tertiary category

社會
網上募款
志工
麥酒市場
油壺基金

貓咪學會說話並要求參與人類政治

Microsoft YaHei, Noto Sans

DONGBA

Modern Chinese characters are no longer considered pictures, but in Yunnan, China, the Naxi minority group still writes in a pictographic script known as **Dongba**. In Dongba, each character is a picture.

Dongba can be written horizontally, from left to right—like in English—with rows stacked downward, or vertically, with columns stacked from right to left, like in Japanese.

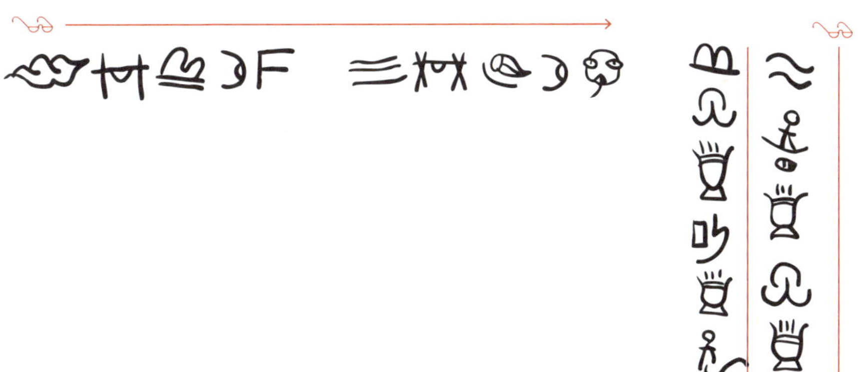

It can also be written nonlinearly, like an illustration.

In mainland China today, people speak standardized Mandarin influenced by the Beijing dialect in the north. In Southern China, though, dialects can be so diverse that villagers even just five kilometers apart may not understand each other. Some Southern dialects resemble the official languages of nearby Southeast Asian countries more than they do Mandarin. Consequently, dialects are passed down through people within the same community and not often learned by "outsiders." Because the Dongba writing correlates to the dialects of the less populous Naxi people, other ethnic groups cannot easily use and preserve the Dongba script.

KAOMOJI

One illustrative typing which has been promoted worldwide is Emoji. Each emoji is a character, displaying slightly differently on each digital application, like how each letter differs in each font. In Japanese, "e" means "picture" and "moji" means "script." Therefore, "e moji" means "picture-like script." Emoji breaks the language barrier for people all over the world. People can make basic communication without any word. In the digital age, an emoji can be considered more friendly than a sentence ending with a period. With the addition of new emojis such as skin color choices, the users are given a bigger vocabulary to express themselves.

Another **moji**—"script" in Japanese—common in East Asia but less often used in the West is **kao moji** (facial script). Kao moji users explore each letter's form without connecting them to their sounds. It treats letterforms as a series of brush strokes rather than as characters with a language-specific meaning. **T**, for instance, can be read as an eye with tears coming down from it; **V**, as a smiling mouth. In this system, **(TvT)** is a teary-eyed face pretending to be happy, **(@_@)** is a dizzy face, and the Greek delta (**Δ**) can be seen as a surprised mouth, as in **(˚Δ˚)b**.

(¯¯o)   ٩(× ×)۶   (つ˘ω˘ς)   凸(￣︿￣)   ௰(￣口￣"௰)

Adobe Arabic, Kozuka Gothic, Source Han Sans SC, Noto Sans Georgian

A kaomoji can be composed using more than one script.

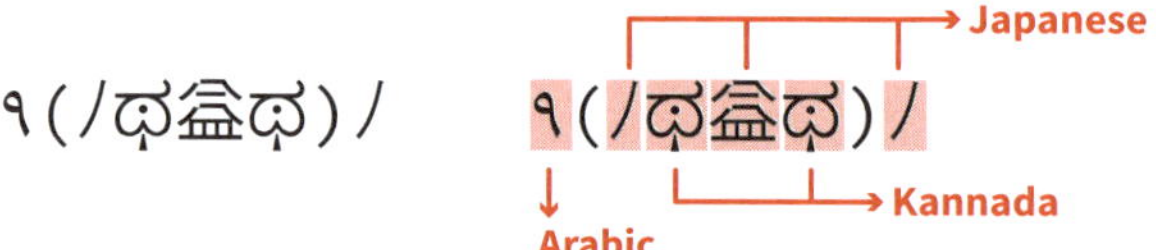

Adobe Arabic, Kozuka Gothic, Nirmala UI

The creators use characters from multiple writing systems without needing to know their native pronunciations or meanings. Users can access kaomoji dictionaries online or download apps that supply kaomoji for different emotions. Compared to emojis, kaomoji takes longer to input, but users do not have to wait until companies release the emoji they need at that moment.

characters on the back cover

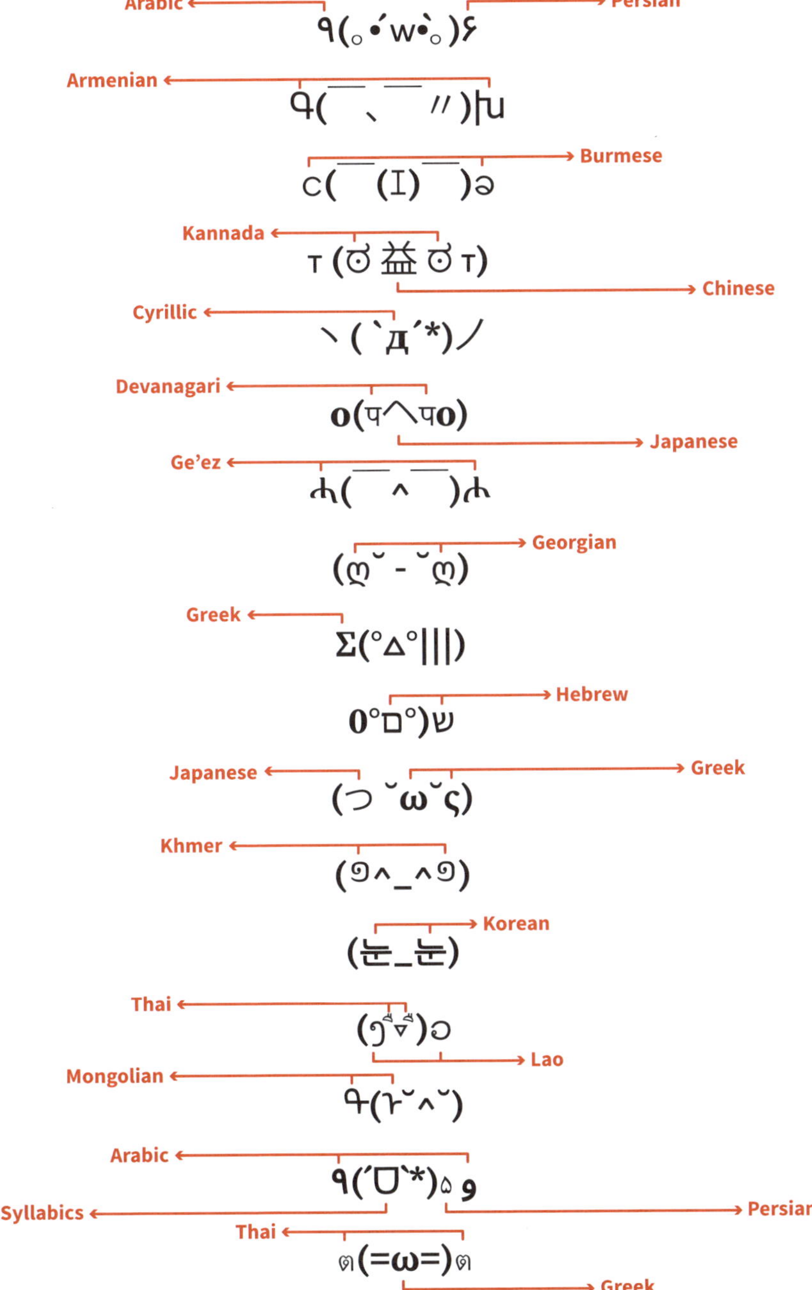

03 DIRECTION

Most contemporary languages are written horizontally, from left to right. Consequently, languages that are written in other directions suffered when being displayed on digital screens until the early 2000s, when technology advanced to resolve this problem. Direction is one of the unique aspects of type design that can be switched fluidly when produced by hand but may be arduous to change in digital formats. Scripts that do not follow the Latin direction therefore require more advanced technology.

People become accustomed to reading directions according to their native languages. When a monolingual English speaker learns Japanese as a vertically set type, the new direction demands a longer processing time. Additionally, many languages are not confined to one, linear direction: Arabic calligraphy can use a curved baseline, and Thai and Devanagari have vowels that stack above or below consonants. The orientation that people learn to read also influences how people look at type generally. Just as people may wear different types of shoes to get to work depending on the specific street conditions they encounter on their way, the direction that people read varies according to the specifications of the scripts they use. This chapter covers all kinds of reading, writing, and typing directions.

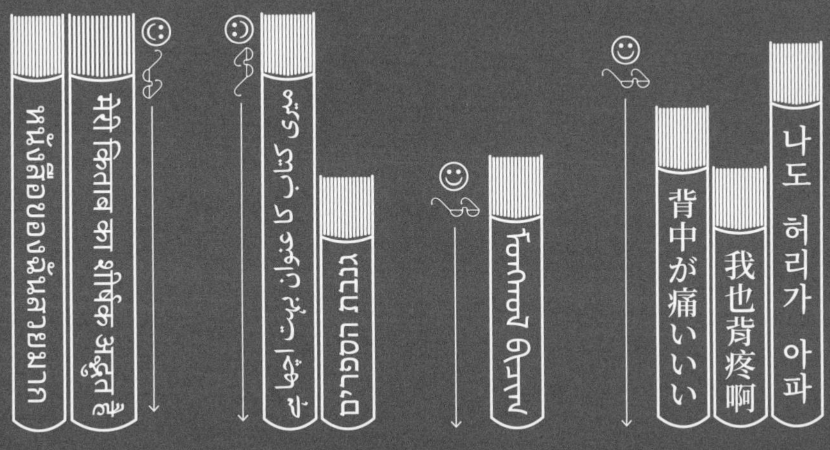

Tiffin Devanagari, Noto Looped Thai,
Nassim Arabic Pro, Noam Text,
Noto Sans Mongolian,
Source Han Serif, Source Han Serif TC, Source Han Serif K

RIGHT TO LEFT

1. Christopher Calderhead and Holly Cohen, *The World Encyclopedia of Calligraphy. The Ultimate Compendium on the Art of Fine Writing: History, Craft, Technique* (Sterling, 2018), 72.

Until 500 BCE, Greek letters were inscribed in alternating horizontal lines that inverted direction, somewhat like an ox plowing the field.[1] The letters changed their direction each time a new line was begun, but this eventually proved inefficient.

2. Hendrik Weber, *Italic: What Gives Typography its Emphasis* (Niggli, 2021), 30.

Between the sixth and early second centuries BCE, people in Southern Europe wrote from right to left.[2] Both the Greek style of alternating directions and the Southern European style of writing from right to left have been lost to history. Modern writing and typing directions can be either horizontal—from left to right or from right to left—or vertical.

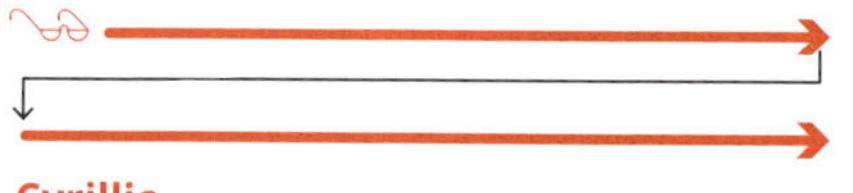

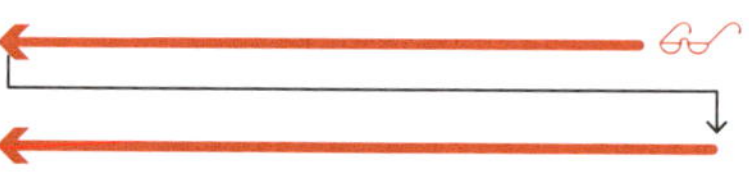

Cyrillic
Английский алфавит базируется на латинском алфавите и включает 26 букв.

Armenian
Անգլերեն այբուբենը հիմնվել է լատիներեն այբուբենի վրա և կազմված է 26 տառից

Georgian
ინგლისური ენა ყველაზე ახლოს ფრიბიულ ენასთანაა.

Greek
Επιπλέον, λειτουργεί ως δεύτερη ή επίσημη γλώσσα σε αρκετές χώρες παγκοσμίως.

Arabic
الأبجدية الحديثة للغة الإنجليزية تعتمد على الأبجدية اللاتينية، والتي تتألف من 26 حرفًا

Hebrew
השפה האנגלית משתייכת למשפחת השפות הגרמאניות ומקורה באנגליה

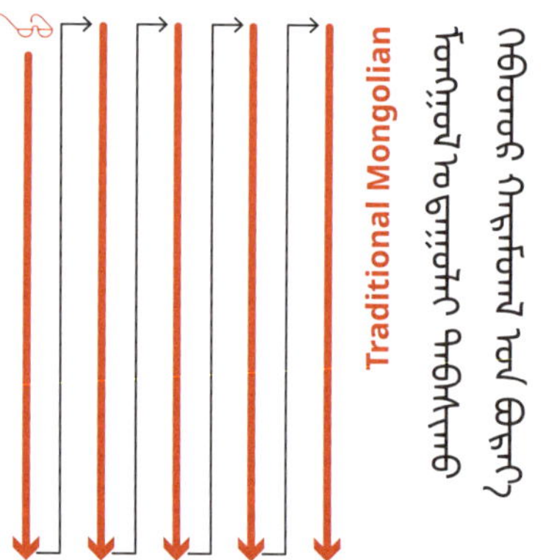

Traditional Mongolian

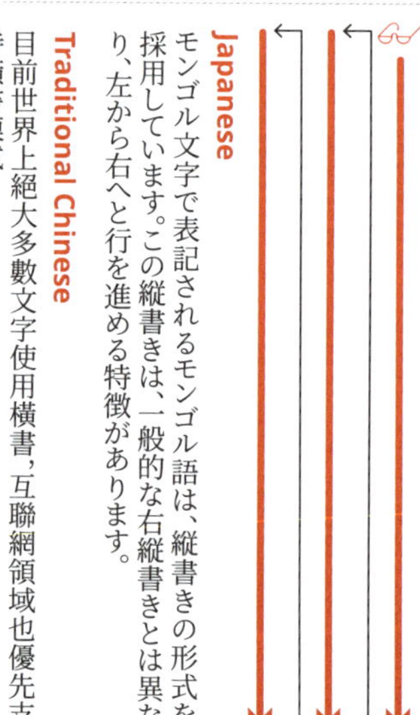

Japanese

モンゴル文字で表記されるモンゴル語は、縦書きの形式を採用しています。この縦書きは、一般的な右縦書きとは異なり、左から右へと行を進める特徴があります。

Traditional Chinese

目前世界上絕大多數文字使用橫書，互聯網領域也優先支持橫書模式

Arabic, Persian, and Urdu are read from right to left. When the text is not justified (i.e., aligned on both margins), the rag (i.e., the irregular edge of an unjustified text block) appears on the left.

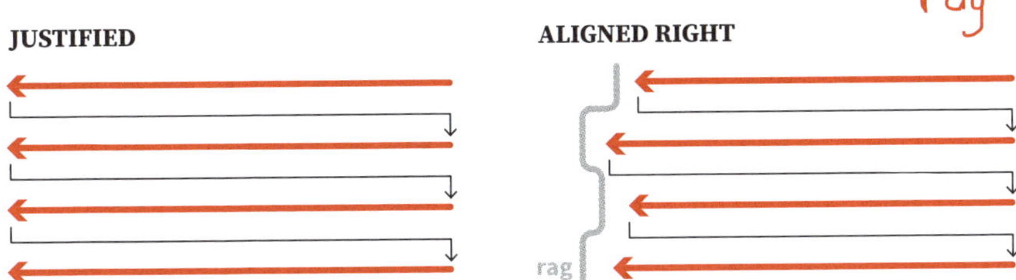

These languages always type from right to left, though most Western websites align text on the left to match Latin styles.

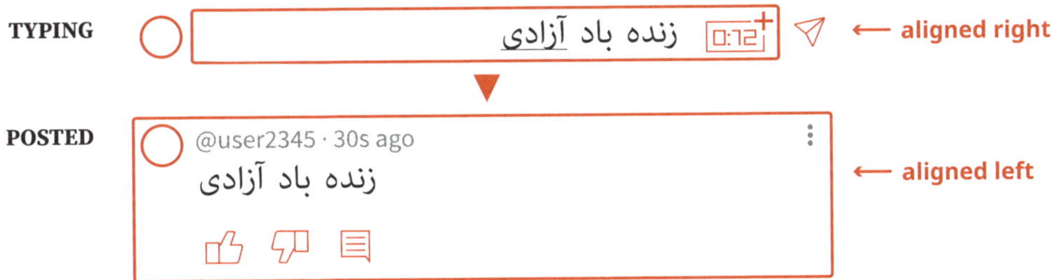

Adobe Arabic

Some applications align the Arabic text on the right; the first sentence, however, is treated differently.

Noto Sans Arabic

3. Titus Nemeth, ed., *Arabic Typography: History and Practice* (Niggli, 2023), 366.

It is more accurate to define Arabic as "bi-directional,"[3] as numerals are conversely written from left to right, like how they are in English texts.

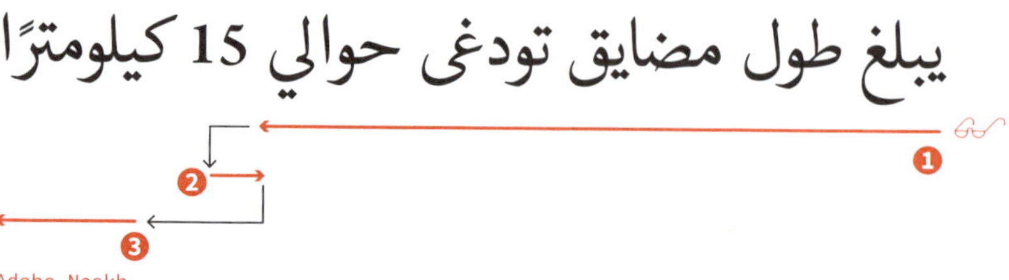

Adobe Naskh

This numeral direction is the same in Hebrew.

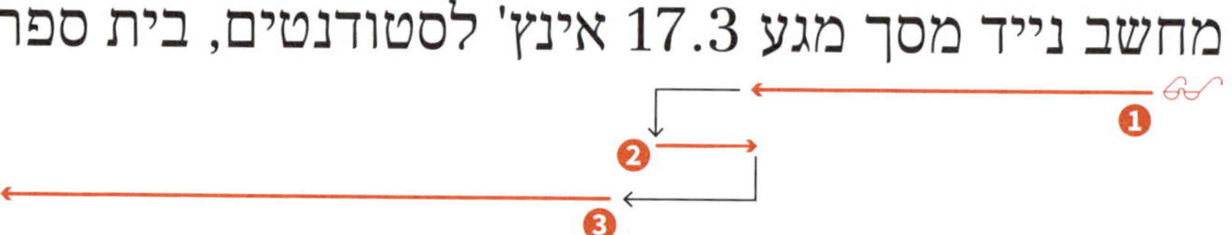

Frank Ruhl Libre

Arabic text may also include some English, which makes it even more bi-directional. Technically, Arabic letters are assigned a strong right-to-left property, and other characters are assigned weak directionality.[4]

4. Titus, *Arabic Typography*, 365.

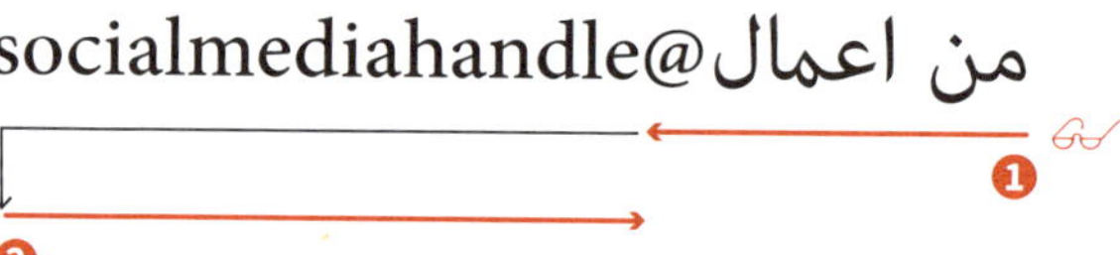

Adobe Arabic

Design software might sequence Arabic and Hebrew letters from left to right, thereby disconnecting them. The technology exists to allow us to type it without knowing its meaning, but it does not display Arabic or Hebrew correctly by default. The option for "Middle Eastern and South Asian Composers" enables users to display text in the correct direction. However, the user must select that option manually in design programs.

Nassim Arabic Pro

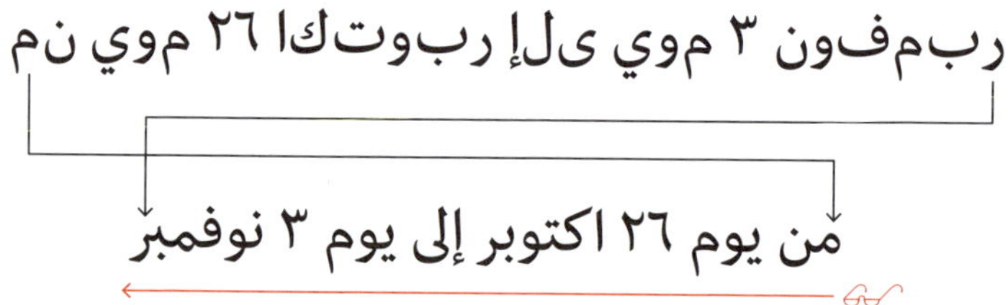

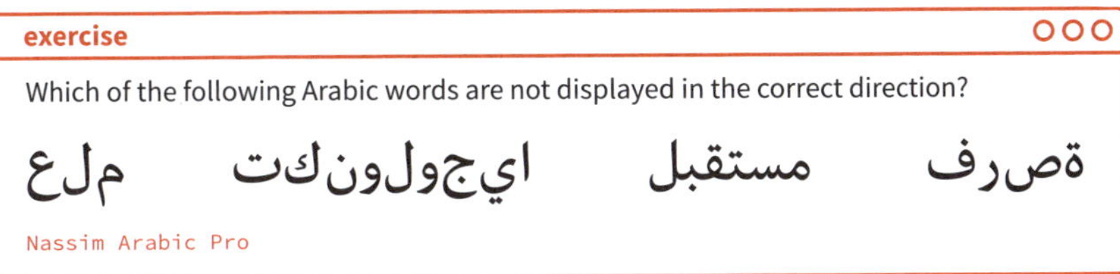

Directional mistakes in Arabic are highly detectable because most letters should connect when typed correctly. If all letters are disconnected, it is easy to notice that something is wrong. Directional errors in Hebrew, a nonconnected script, however, may take nonnative speakers extra time to detect.

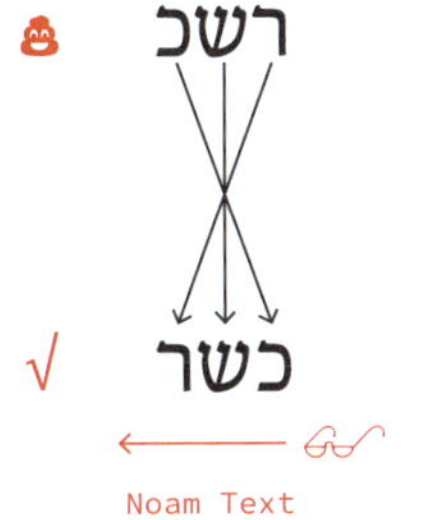

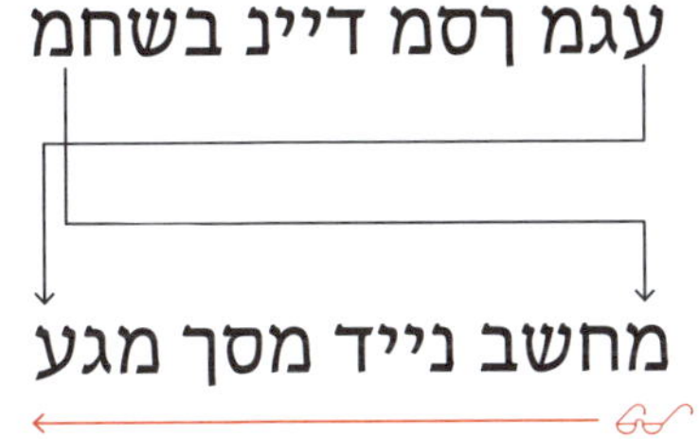

exercise

Which of the following Hebrew words are not displayed in the correct direction?

לאחר   סינוש   המפלגה   בוט

Noam Text

Arabic has faced many challenges in being presented digitally, but technological advances have made displaying it—as well as other scripts in different directions—possible. If Arabic speakers had made the most popular design program but failed to provide customized settings to accommodate Latin, the title of this book might look something like below.

sredrob dnoyeb yhpargopyt

VERTICAL TO HORIZONTAL

In the past, Chinese, Japanese, and Korean were all written and printed vertically and with lines of text progressing from right to left. This direction still dominates print in Japan and Taiwan, but Korean and Simplified Chinese have adopted the same directionality as English.

Chinese characters, which evolved from pictograms, each fit into a square box, like a painting confined to a square canvas. The choice to type Chinese vertically or horizontally can likewise be compared to the curatorial decision to arrange a given set of paintings in two possible configurations.

Source Han Sans CN

5. Ryoko Nishizuka, "Japanese Typography," in *Thinking with Type: A Critical Guide for Designers, Writers, Editors, and Students*, ed. Ellen Lupton (Princeton Architectural Press, 2024), 190.

6. Tsutsumi Kawabe and Christine Flint Sato, "Japanese," in *The World Encyclopedia of Calligraphy: The Ultimate Compendium on the Art of Fine Writing: History, Craft, Technique*, eds. Christopher Calderhead and Holly Cohen (Sterling, 2018), 215.

Kanji (Chinese characters) entered Japan in the first century CE and gained broad usage by the sixth century.[5] In the ninth century, kanji began to be used phonetically to represent syllables in Japanese, however more than one kanji could be used for the same sound. This soon proved to be confusing.[6] Above all, writing in kanji characters was time-consuming.

Consequently, Japanese people developed indigenous phonetic scripts: hiragana and katakana. In each script, there is only one character per sound to avoid confusion. The characters are also simpler than kanji. Hiragana is used for native Japanese words and grammatical functions, while katakana is used for foreign words and onomatopoeia.

HIRAGANA	HIRA	KATAKANA	HIRA KATA
I	(emphasis)	supermarket	at/in pain("bread")

わたしは、スーパーでパン

HIRA KATA	HIRA	HIRA
and milk	(object marker)	bought

とミルクをかいました。

UD Digi Kyokasho

The term **hiragana** is related to **hira** (fluttering), and the script was derived from the cursive form of kanji. The process involved merging strokes, simplifying forms, and rounding off sharp corners. **Katakana** comes from **kata** (partial) and, though it also developed from kanji, is more minimal than hiragana.

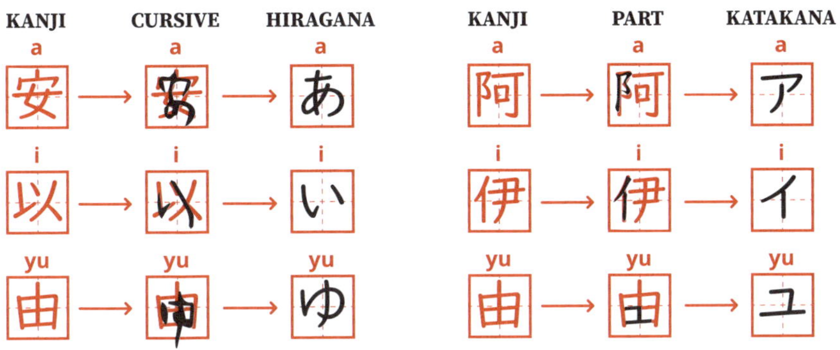

UD Digi Kyokasho

A common method of composing Korean characters is also to arrange the letters in a square or rectangle as in Chinese and Japanese.

210 OmniGothic

ZW MogujasusimgyeolOTF

Chinese, Japanese, and Korean characters are composed in boxes; thus, they can be typed vertically without needing to finetune the space between characters.

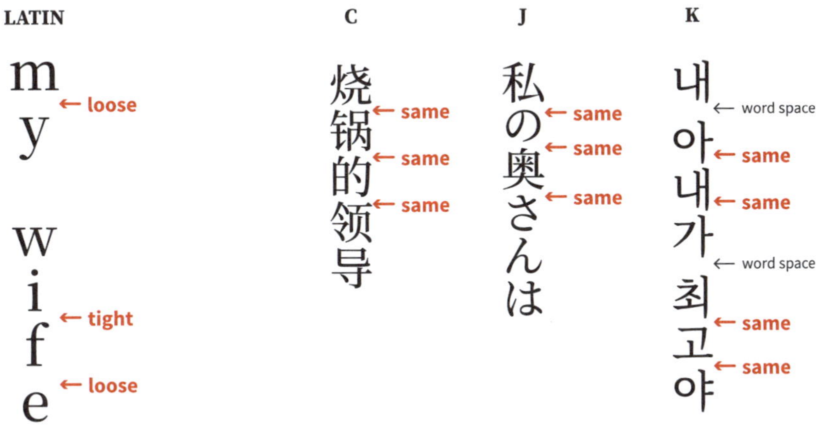

Source Han Serif

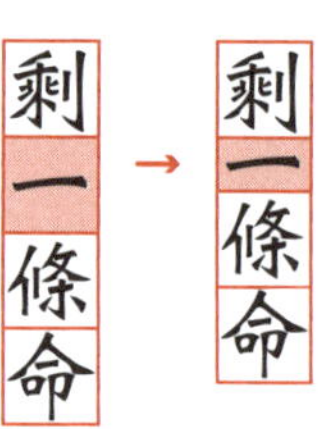

AR WeiBeiB5Std BD

There is, however, one exception in Chinese. The character for the numeral **1** is expressed with only one dash. Therefore, it takes less vertical space than other characters. When typing a text that includes the character for the number **1** vertically, it is therefore better to reduce this character's distance from others.

It is also worth noting that some Korean display typefaces may not assign the same height to each character.

210 Mamablock

In those cases, a similar reduction of the space between characters can benefit the design.

This also applies to vertical types with Latin characters.

210 Mamablock

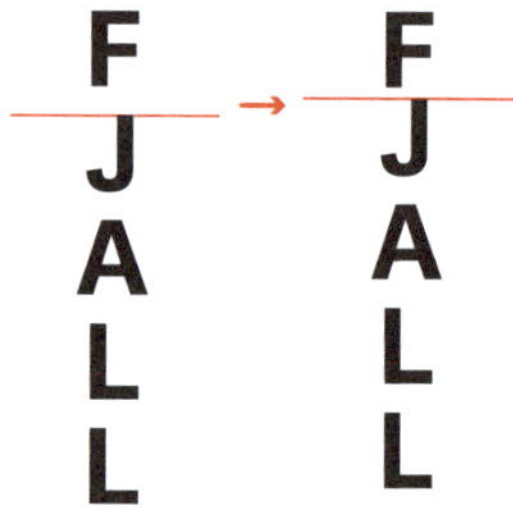

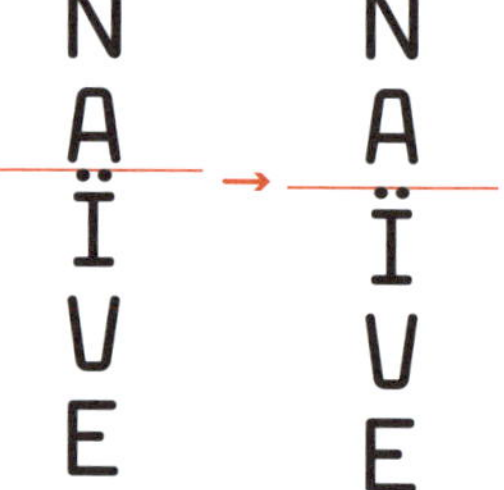

Adelle Sans, Larabiefont

When typing vertically in Japanese and Traditional Chinese, Latin characters are automatically turned ninety degrees to avoid proportional stacking. Designers might type two-digit numbers horizontally while rotating longer numbers vertically.

vertical

速やかに退避する！

energy！非戦闘員は

警報！警報！前方高

BIZ UDMincho

mixed

んと200本。

植えました。な

12才の頃、本を

The same vertical three-digit number typesetting appears on a famous milk package in Japan, which notably prints **100%** in this way.

Most modern Japanese novels and newspapers set text vertically, from right to left. In magazines, where there is often a variety of information and images, text may be set in both directions, even on one page.

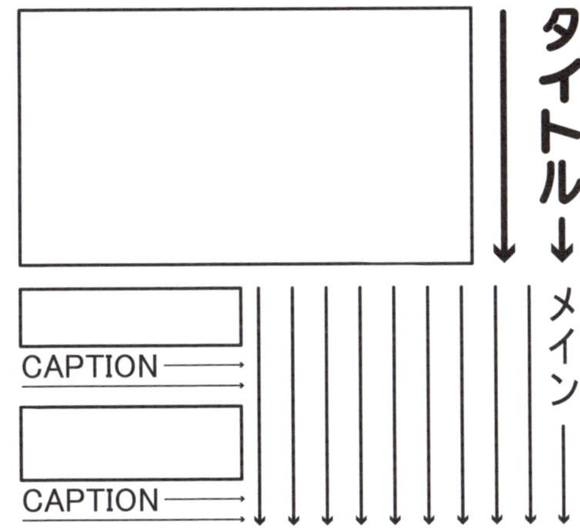

TA_kasanemarugo, MS UI Gothic

Hiragino Kaku Gothic Pro,
Source Han Serif SC

Kan'ei Tsūhō, the Japanese mon coin used during the Edo period, also had words inscribed on it in both directions. Similarly, Chinese characters can be presented in either direction. On signages, a combination of different directions may be used.

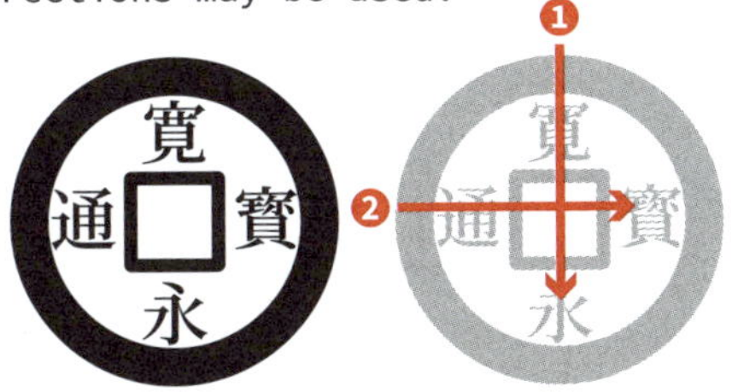

Source Han Serif

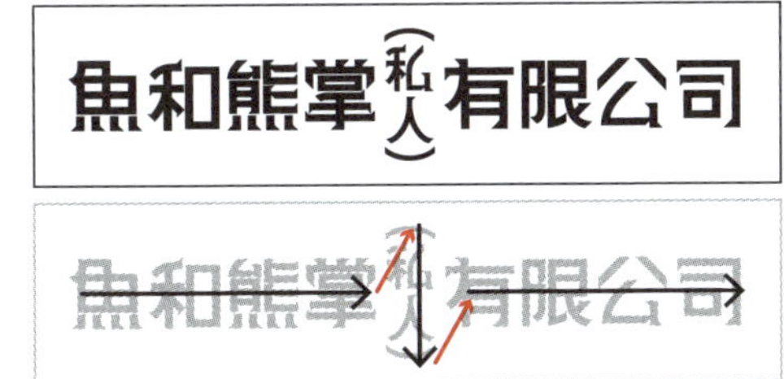

Kinkakuji Normal

Modern Korean is typed horizontally from left to right, like English. Aside from body text, it is easy to spot vertical text on signage.

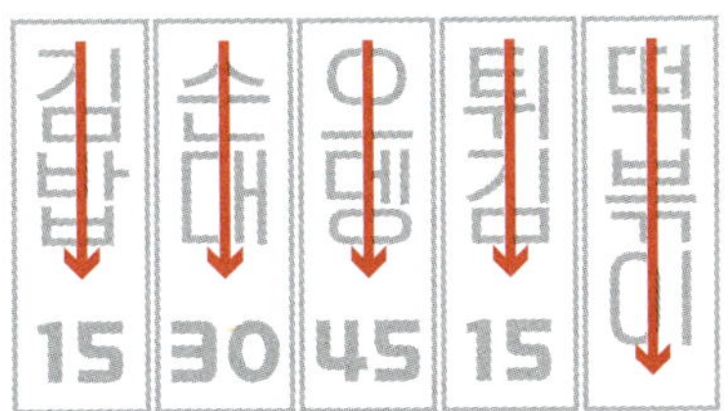

A mixture of vertical and horizontal text is also found on Korean packaging designs.

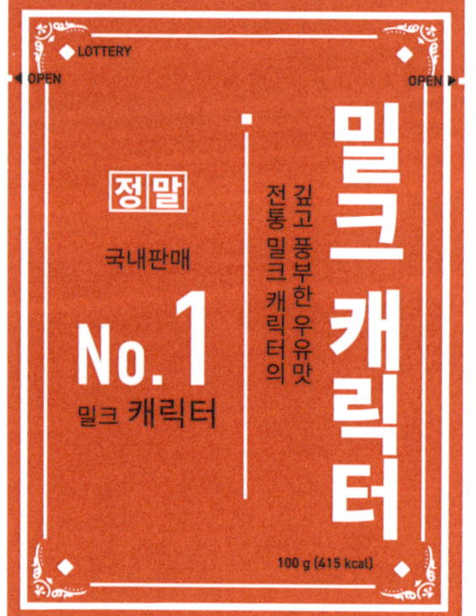

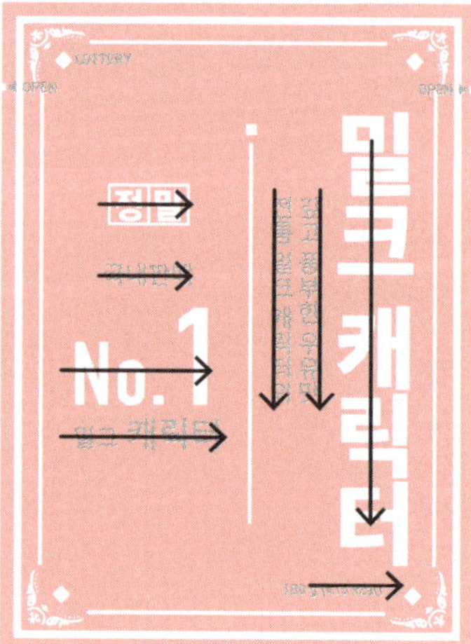

Source Han Sans KR, DIN 2014, DIN Condensed

Some Japanese book covers designed in the 1890s and early 1900s had titles running from right to left. Convention tickets designed between the 1930s and the 1940s in Japan also had text set horizontally, from right to left.

akabara-cinderella

In Taiwan and Japan, some garbage trucks have type printed in different directions on each side of the trucks. One side may read from left to right, the other, from right to left.

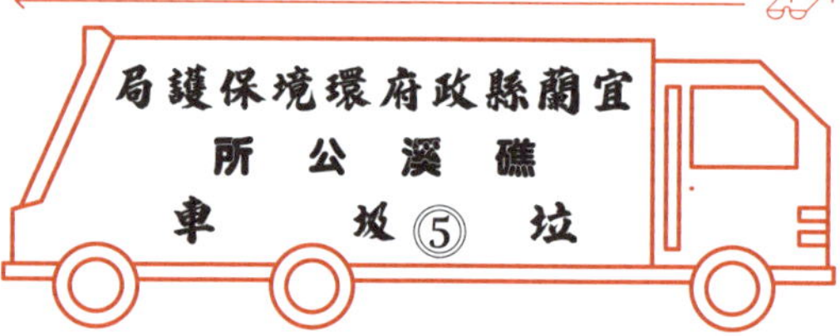

HelloFont ID JuanYong, TA_kasanemarugo, Adriane Text

Chinese-speaking cities that preserve historical landscapes can be an explosion of text directions. In addition to standard reading directions for CJK (Chinese, Japanese, and Korean), Chinese readers depend on context to discern text direction. Each logographic character is like a drawing on a flashcard. After seeing each "drawing," a native reader is able to shuffle and sequence them instantaneously.

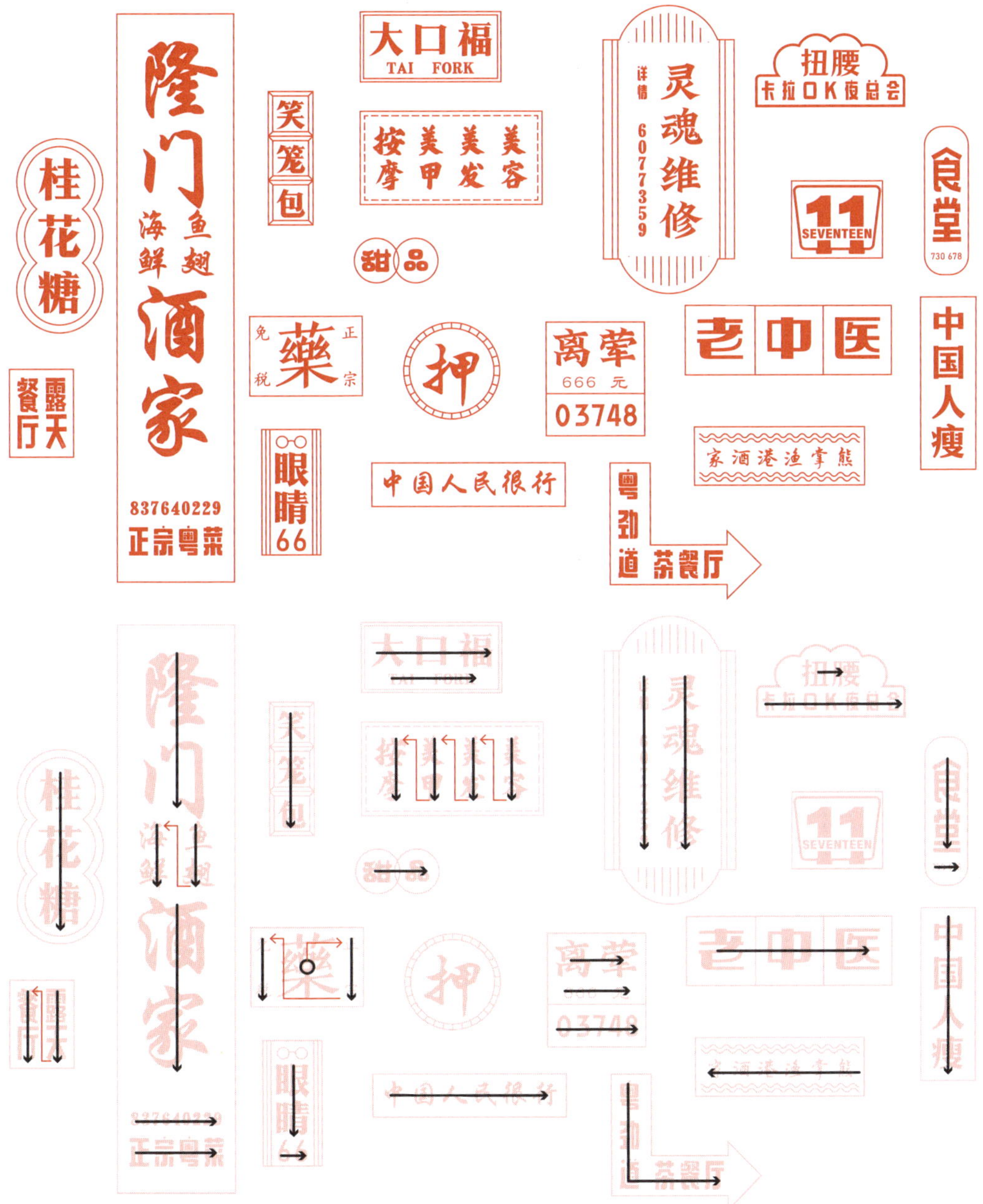

Acumin Variable Concept, Bahnschrift, HelloFont FangHuaTi, Hellofont ID DanMoXingKai, HelloFont ID DaZiBao, HelloFont ID JiangHuTi, HelloFont ID JianSong, HelloFont ID JuanYong, Hellofont ID MeiLingTi, HelloFont ID MingKeBenWanSong, HelloFont ID QingHuaXingKai, Hellofont ID XiaoLiShu, HelloFont ID YongShengCuSong, HelloFont ID YouQiTi

VERTICAL ONLY

Traditional Mongolian can only be written and typed vertically, and on a vertical surface, this default setting works well. Screens, on the other hand, pose several obstacles because most websites and applications are designed for horizontal text. Not surprisingly, these platforms generally do not offer alternative interfaces to the vertical scripts that require them.

In Mongolia, the school system maintains Traditional Mongolian in the curriculum, but the Cyrillic alphabet is widely used in other contexts. In Inner Mongolia—an autonomous region of northern China—people use the Mongolian script exclusively. Comments made in Traditional Mongolian script on social media are rotated ninety degrees to fit the layout designed for the platform's default language, typically English.

Noto Sans Mongolian, Bahnschrift

Users have also become accustomed to a rotated keyboard when typing in Traditional Mongolian.

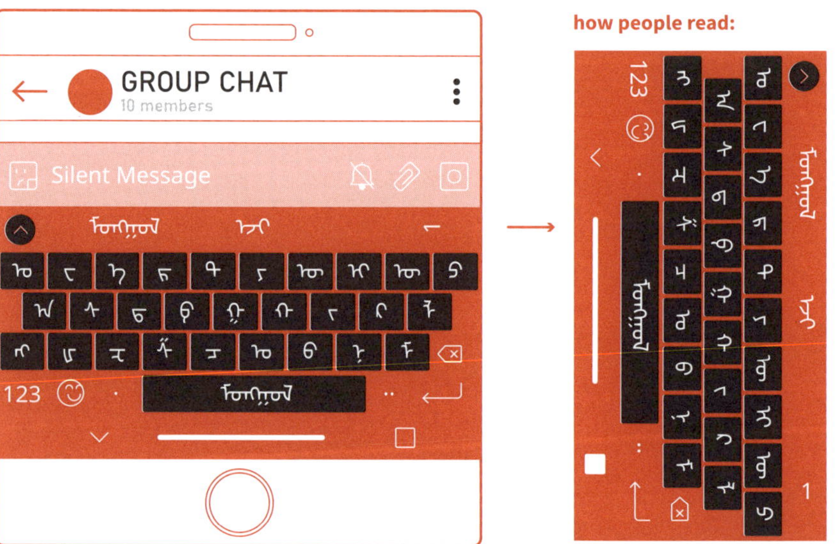

Noto Sans Mongolian, Bahnschrift

Had there been a parallel universe in which the Mongolian people invented social media, would the rest of the world have their scripts set vertically?

PARALLEL UNIVERSE FOR RIGHT-HANDED PEOPLE:

Noto Sans Mongolian, Bahnschrift

If Mongolian was the international language, instead of English, would most of the road signs be vertical, instead of horizontal?

REALITY:

PARALLEL UNIVERSE:

Source Han Sans CN, Mongolian White, DIN 2014

UP, DOWN

Baybayin is a Philippine script used to write in Tagalog. The script gradually surrendered to the Latin script during Spanish colonization, so native Tagalog speakers have a basic reading proficiency in Baybayin, but rarely use it.

LIMITED USAGE

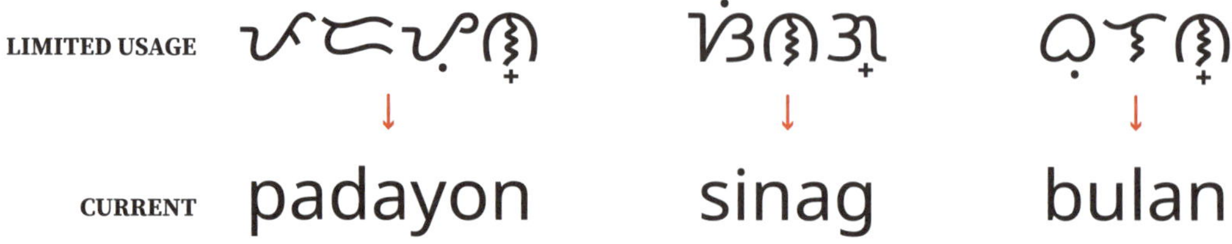

CURRENT

padayon   sinag   bulan

Noto Sans Tagalog Regular

Recently, scholars have been advocating for a richer Baybayin typographic practice. Relatedly, Filipino designers have attempted various styles for digitizing Baybayin according to their ancestors' handwriting. In Baybayin, the vowel changes by adding a dot or plus sign above or below the character.

Noto Sans Tagalog Regular

Thus, the writing and typing is not linear.

Noto Sans Tagalog Regular

If a confident Baybayin user wrote this book, its title might look like the one below.

RIGHT, LEFT, UP, DOWN

An **abugida** is a writing system in which consonant-vowel combinations are represented as single units. Each unit is centered around a consonant with vowels indicated as secondary marks that often resemble diacritics. This differs from an "alphabet" in which vowels and consonants are treated equally. The systems discussed in this section are all abugidas. If an abugida writer had invented moveable type before Gutenberg and spread it around the world, the title of this book might look like the one below.

Abugida languages use the same direction as English but employ a more complex spelling model. Devanagari—the Indic script used in Hindi, Sanskrit, and Nepali—has vowel marks that appear above or below a given letter. Therefore, vertical space is essential for setting the text horizontally.

Noto Serif Devanagari

Burmese, the script used for the official language in Myanmar, also has vowels attached to the consonant, positioned on the right, left, top, or bottom.

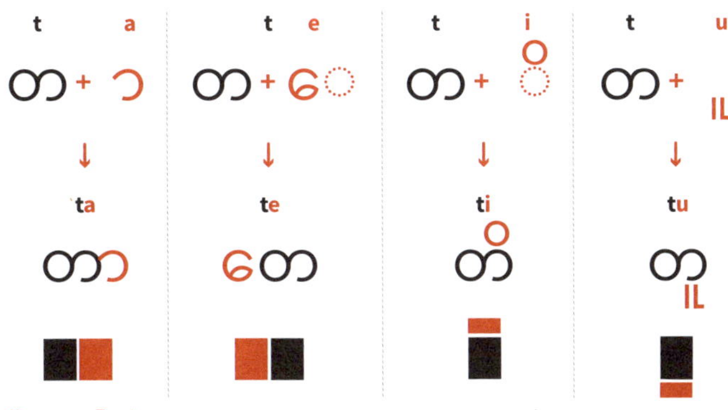

Myanmar Text

More complicated than Devanagari, Burmese sandwiches some vowels between consonants vertically or horizontally. Some consonants can also be inserted into a vowel group, like a Tetris piece.

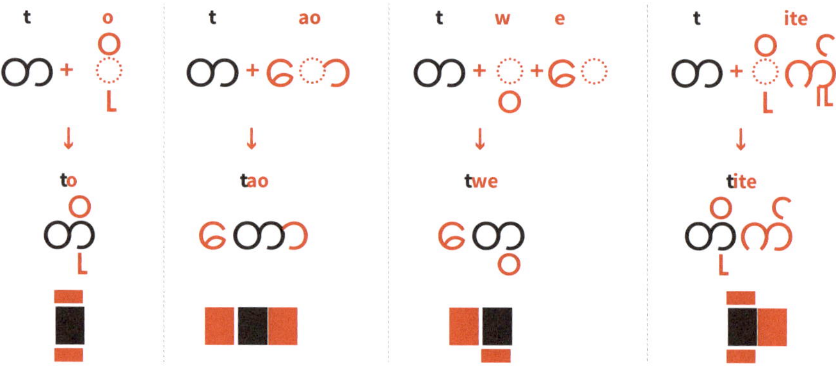

Myanmar Text

Similarly, Thai places vowels in all four directions.

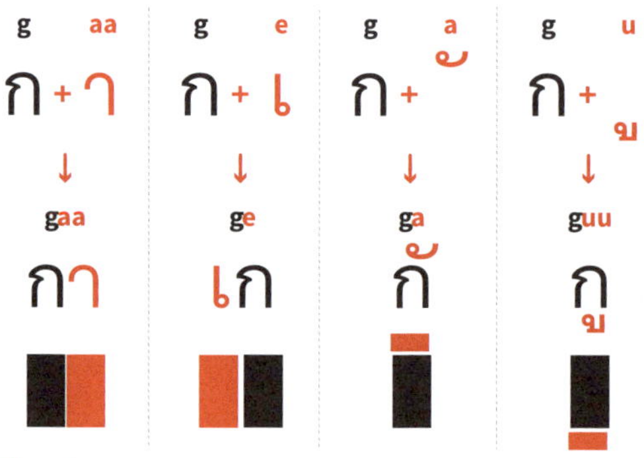

Thongterm

Thai vowels can also, like Burmese ones, wrap around the consonant.

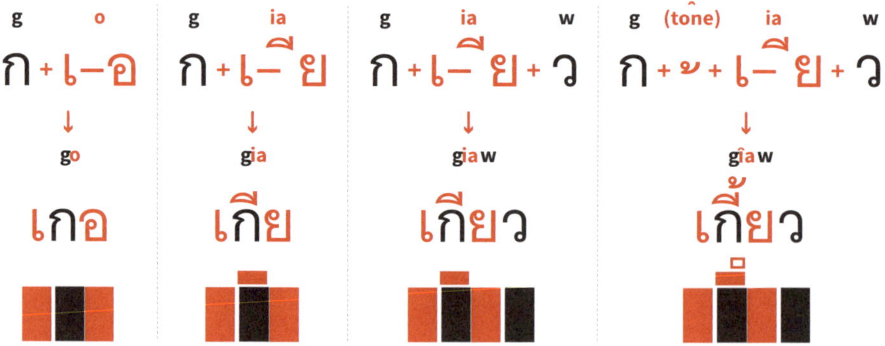

Thongterm

The Thai language has five tones and four tone marks in the script. These marks are not, however, like the tone marks in Simplified Chinese Pinyin, each indicating a specific tone.

	high flat	rising	falling rising	falling	neutral
OFFICIAL CHINESE PINYIN	**mā**	**má**	**mǎ**	**mà**	**ma**
ALTERNATIVE SPELLING	**ma1**	**ma2**	**ma3**	**ma4**	**ma**

Thai tone marks are more complicated, and to know what tone each
mark indicates, readers need to recognize the class—high, middle,
or low—of the consonant.

	่	้	๊	๋
HIGH CONSONANT	low	falling		
MID CONSONANT	low	falling	high	rising
LOW CONSONANT	falling	high		

When combined with the same tone mark, the consonants of the same
sound but different classes produce different tones.

k(high)　　　o　　　ko (falling)

ช + ้ + อ → ข้อ

g(mid)　　　o　　　go (falling)

ก + ้ + อ → ก้อ

k(low)　　　o　　　ko (high)

ค + ้ + อ → ค้อ

Tahoma

Because of this complex system, the direction in which Thai is
read is also complicated.

A WORD

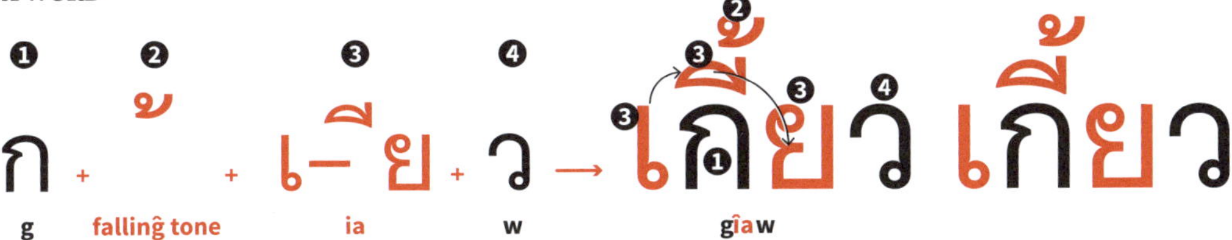

A SENTENCE

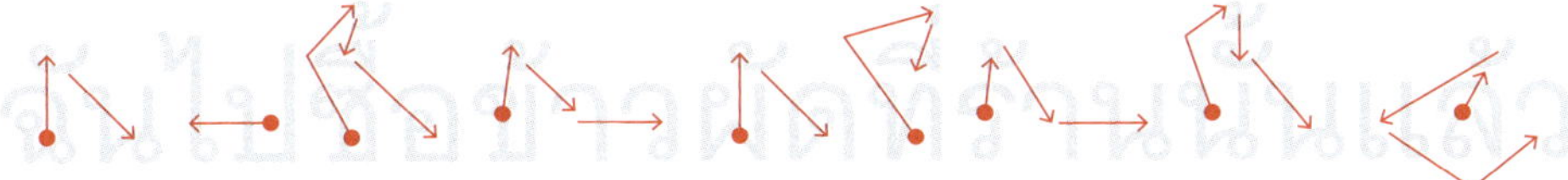

STACKING

In Latin typography classes, professors have been known to call stacking letters vertically a crime. The main reason for this is that most Latin typefaces provide proportional, mixed-width letters. The secondary reason for their aversion to vertical type lies in the varying heights of Latin characters that create an uneven letter space when presented vertically. The most popular approach to creating vertical text in Latin, then, is to type the entire line of text at ninety degrees.

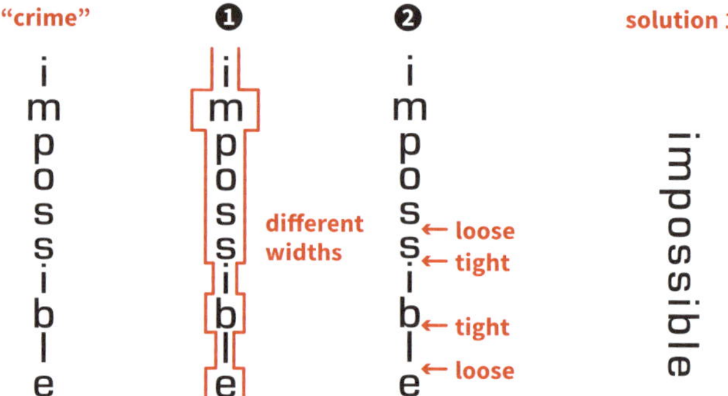

Eurostile

In real life, there are necessarily vertical surfaces for type. Rather than rotating the text, a monospaced typeface offers another solution. When each letter has the same width, as in monospaced type, the first problem resolves itself.

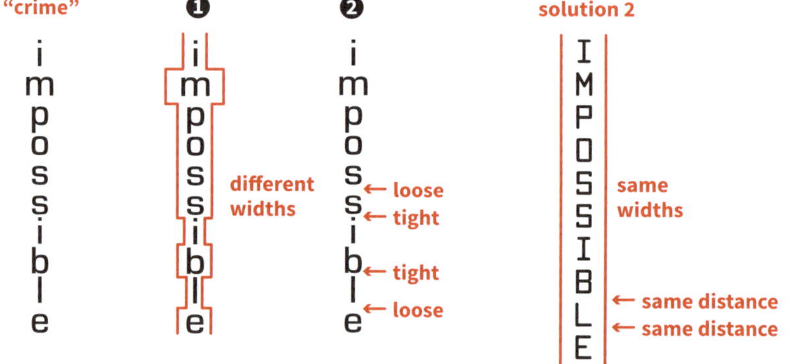

Eurostile, LarabiefontRg-Bold

Devanagari, Burmese, and Thai all have vowels added to consonants in four directions. As a result, it is easier to rotate texts using these scripts by ninety degrees to accommodate vertical surfaces.

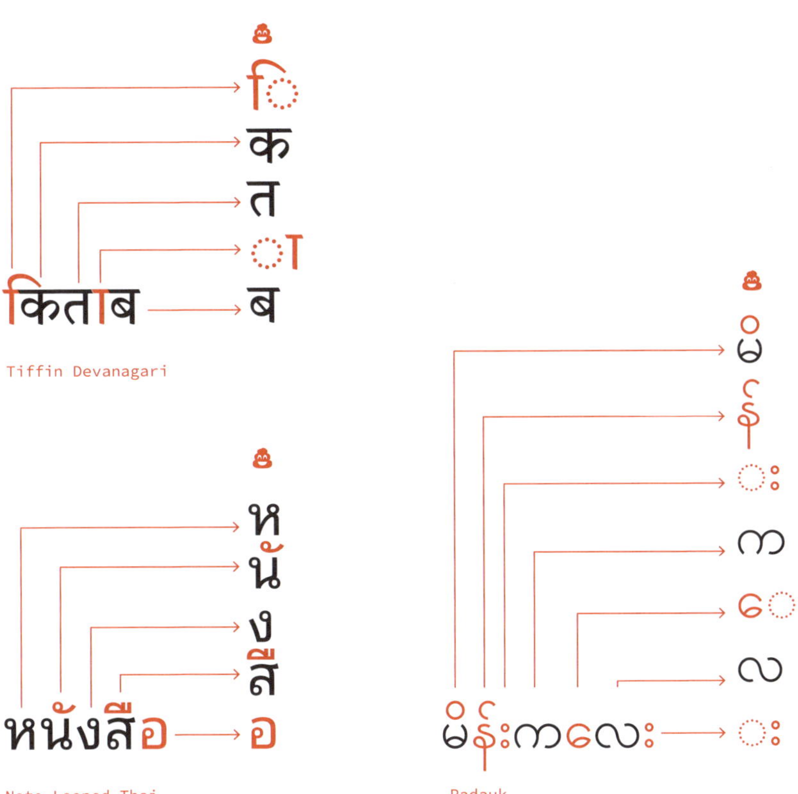

Tiffin Devanagari

Noto Looped Thai

Padauk

In Devanagari, a headline connects the letters in a word, making it almost impossible to stack letters and retain readability. Urdu, Persian, and Arabic texts face similar barriers to stacking because letters in a word are typically connected.

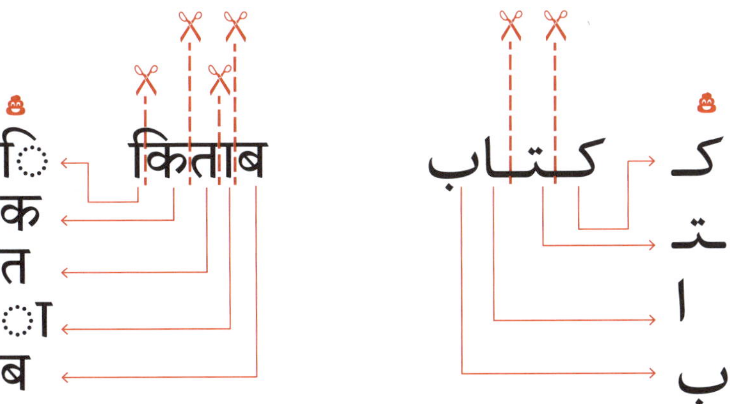

Tiffin Devanagari

Nassim Arabic Pro

Hebrew letters, although not connected, are also rarely stacked vertically. This is possibly due to the varying widths and heights of Hebrew letters. While in Latin this particular challenge is resolved with monospaced typefaces, Hebrew is presented with an additional obstacle—elongating strokes can transform one letter into another.

Noam Text

For the above reasons, vertical stacking should be avoided when using these scripts.

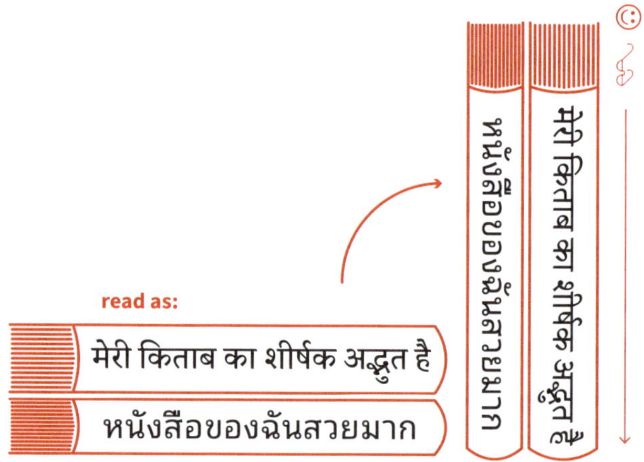

Tiffin Devanagari, Noto Looped Thai, Nassim Arabic Pro, Noam Text

04 LINE SPACING

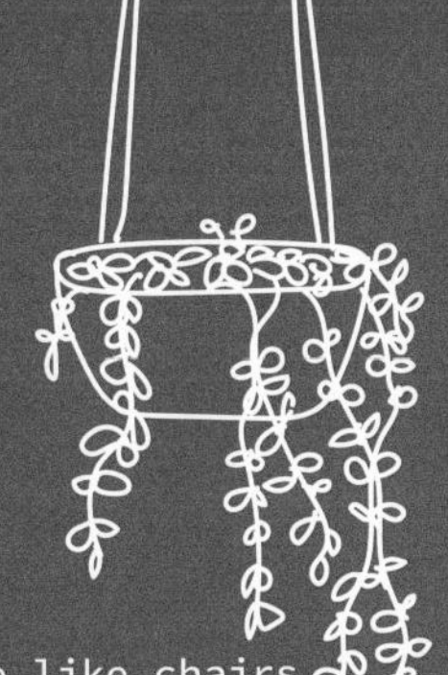

The spaces within and between lines of text are like chairs for letters to sit and work. Latin "chairs" have advanced to ergonomic versions and the letters now sit relatively comfortably. But we need to expand the variety of chairs on the market to adequately accommodate the diverse characteristics and capacities of other alphabets. Some chairs aren't sufficient just because they're comfortable; sometimes they need to swing, spin, and even sing.

In any language, having an appropriate distance between each line of text is essential. Too narrow, and the lines will be too tightly packed to be read easily; too wide, and the eyes will become exhausted as they work to locate the next line. "Good spacing" differs per script. Because Latin languages dominate the modern world, scripts with extremely tall or deep elements tend to be unintentionally trimmed in digital environments.

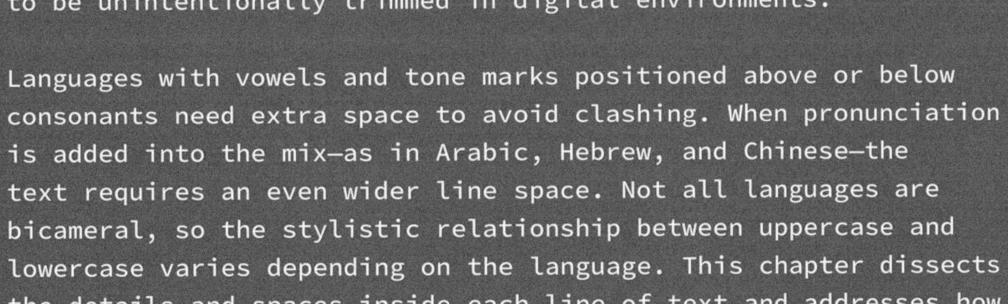

Languages with vowels and tone marks positioned above or below consonants need extra space to avoid clashing. When pronunciation is added into the mix—as in Arabic, Hebrew, and Chinese—the text requires an even wider line space. Not all languages are bicameral, so the stylistic relationship between uppercase and lowercase varies depending on the language. This chapter dissects the details and spaces inside each line of text and addresses how these elements affect legibility.

LEADING AND BASELINE

The space between each line of text is called **leading** (rhymes with "letting"), because in hand typesetting, lead strips are inserted between types. In ancient China and Korea, moveable types were also made of porcelain, copper, and other materials in addition to lead. When typing in Adobe programs, the default leading is 120 percent—if the font size is 10 pt, the space is 12 pt.

10 pt font

Leading plays a crucial role in determining
readability and overall aesthetics of the text.   12pt
Proper leading ensures that lines of text are
adequately spaced, allowing readers to...   —— baseline

Adobe Garamond Pro

Some books refer to leading as "vertical spacing," but this is only accurate for horizontally typed scripts. For vertically typed scripts, such as Traditional Mongolian, Japanese, and Traditional Chinese, "horizontal spacing" is more appropriate.

10 pt font

20pt

行間（ラインスペーシング）は、日本語のタイポグラフィにおいて非常に重要な要素です。行間の調整は、文章全体の可読性や視覚的な印象に大きく影響します。適切な行間が設定されていると、文章が読みやすくなり、目の負担を軽減することができます。特に日本語は縦書きと横書きの両方が使われるため、それぞれに適した行間を選ぶ必要があります。縦書きでは、文字が上下に並ぶため、狭すぎる行間は文字が詰まりすぎて読みにくくなります。一方、横書きの場合は、行間が広すぎると文章の流れが途切れるように感じられることがあります。そのため、使用するフォントや文章の内容、デザインの目的に応じて柔軟に調整することが求められます。適切な行間設定は、視覚的なバランスだけでなく、読者が文章を快適に読むための鍵となるのです。

BIZ UDMincho

BASELINE DIRECTION

In calligraphic Arabic, Persian, and Urdu typefaces, the direction of the text is not linear. Letters can be stacked vertically, and this requires more vertical space between each line.

letters	LINEAR	STACKING			
بي	بي	بي	بي	بي	بي
جـ ج	جح	جح	جح	جح	جح
ا خ ـ ـ ج	لخحج	لخحج	لخحج	لخحج	لخحج

Noto Sans Arabic, Adobe Naskh, Layaan, Amiri, Gulzar

Depending on the manuscript style (which influences the type design), baselines of Arabic letters may slant in different directions. Here, letter proportions are more important than maintaining a flat baseline.

هل طلبنا منك أن تشربهم؟

هل طلبنا منك أن تشربهم؟

هل طلبنا منك أن تشربهم؟

Adobe Arabic, Layaan, Gulzar

HANGLINE

Every script can be placed on a baseline, just as every succulent can be potted in a planter. But some scripts require more space below the baseline, just like some planters need extra space around them to allow plants to hang over the edge.

In Devanagari, the headline is a visible and iconic typographic element. Headlines connect letters within a word, with few exceptions.

सोच पर ध्यान देते हैं कि नहीं — headline / baseline

Adobe Devanagari

The headline also exists in Tibetan, but is part of the letter and does not connect letters in a word.

Uchen

In Hebrew, only one letter—**lamed**—has an ascender, and only five letters—**khaf**, **nun**, **fei**, **tzadi**, and **qof**—have descenders.

INDIVIDUAL LETTERS

qof tzadi pe nun lamed

אבגדהוזחטיכרל'מםנןסעפףצץקרשת

IN A SENTENCE

pe lamed qof lamed qof

הנס ברינקר, או מחליקיים של כסף

Frank Ruhl Libre

Latin letters sit on the baseline, whereas Hebrew letters hang from the "mem-height line."[1]

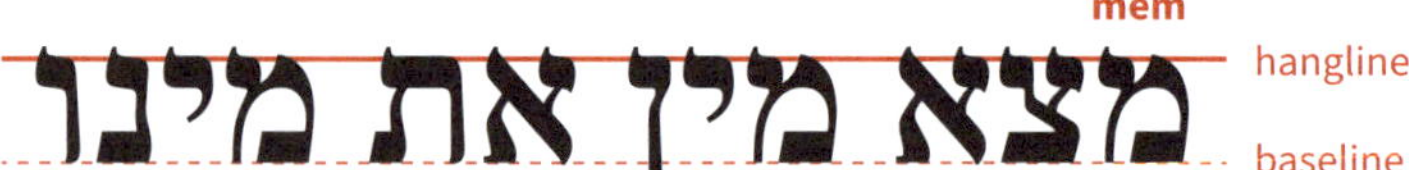

מצא מין את מינו — hangline / baseline

Frank Ruhl Libre

1. Christopher Calderhead and Holly Cohen, *The World Encyclopedia of Calligraphy. The Ultimate Compendium on the Art of Fine Writing: History, Craft, Technique* (Sterling, 2018), 91.

2. Jeongming Kwon, "Hangul,"
in *Bi-scriptual Typography
and Graphic Design with
Multiple Script Systems:
Arabic, Cyrillic, Greek,
Hangeul, Hanzi, Hebrew,
Devanagari, Kanji/Hiragana/
Katakana*, ed. Ben Wittner,
Sascha Thoma, Timm Hartmann
(Niggli, 2019), 169.

3. Kwon, "Hangul," 170.

In Korean, there are two methods of finishing a character set: "combined Hangeul" and "completed Hangeul."[2] The former is faster because each letter is designed once for one position in the character. The second method considers how each letter fits inside the square unit with other letters to balance space, making it much more laborious. A font provides at least 2,350 characters in the combined method or 11,172 in the completed method.[3]

Dongle

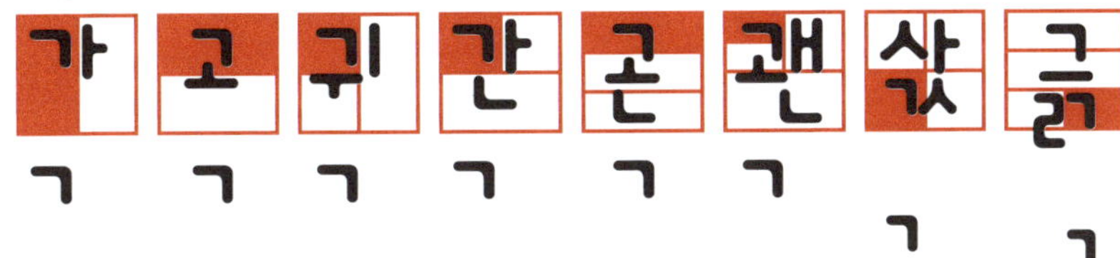

210 OmniGothic

Most Korean typefaces use the squared style (second one above), but the de-squared style is popular for display types (used at large sizes for titles and headings, rather than for long body text). The de-squared style, inspired by the first method, creates a beautiful rhythm along the bottom of the text.

SQUARED

DE-SQUARED

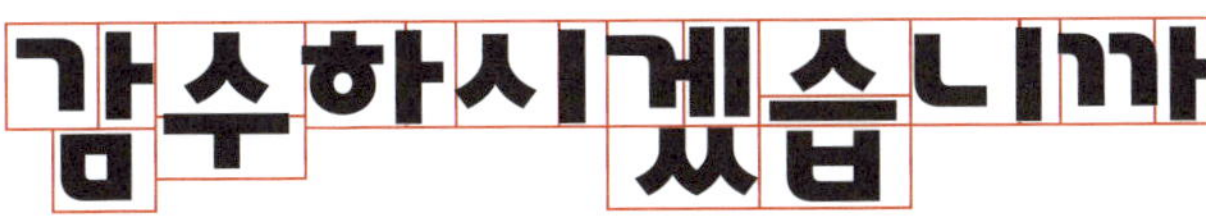

Source Han Sans KR, 210 Mamablock

WIDE-LINE SPACING

Whether double-spaced or single-spaced, Latin text is displayed properly. But Burmese might have its top cut off on some websites if the designer does not apply a wider line spacing than they would for Latin.

Noto Sans Myanmar

Burmese text might also be cut off at the bottom.

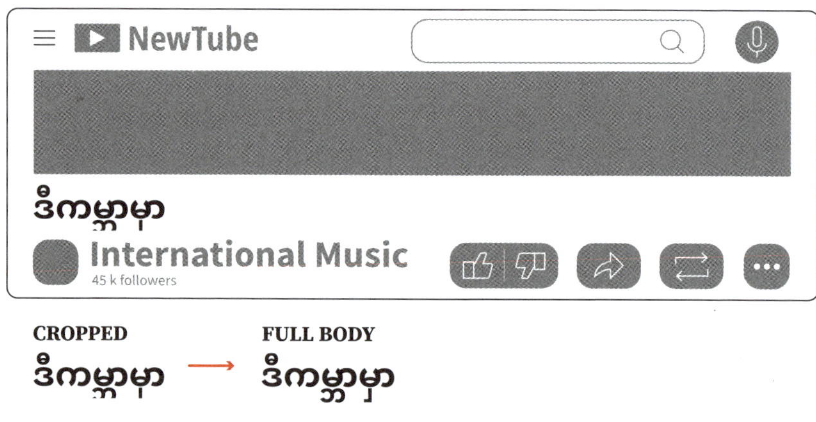

Noto Sans Myanmar

In Burmese, most letters sit in the center. However, its ascenders and descenders that extend above and below the main body are taller than those found in Latin. When these script features are ignored, unintentional cropping occurs.

Padauk

Similar to Burmese, Devanagari has taller ascenders and descenders that need to be considered. They might also be cut off on some websites, like Burmese.

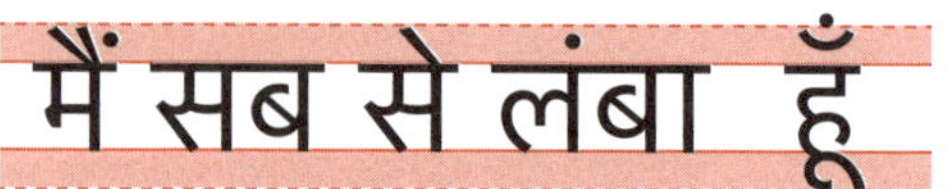

Kohinoor Devanagari

Thai needs more space above and below the (vertical) center than Devanagari does because of Thai's stacking of consonants, vowels, and tone marks. When a vowel and a tone mark are both present, the tone mark is stacked above the vowel.

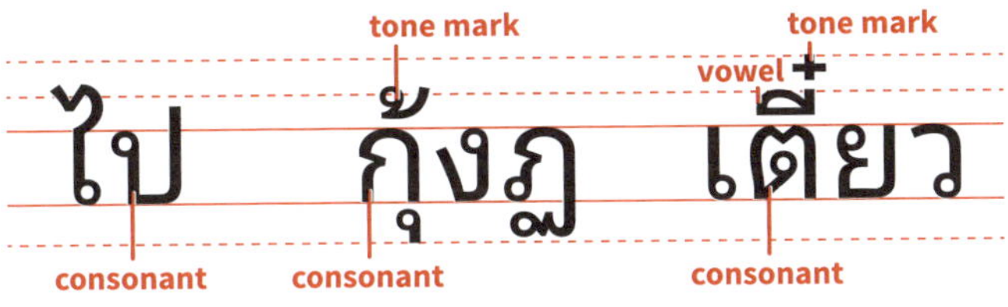

Noto Looped Thai

Because of the positioning of the vowels and tone marks, Thai requires a much broader line spacing than Latin to avoid clashing.

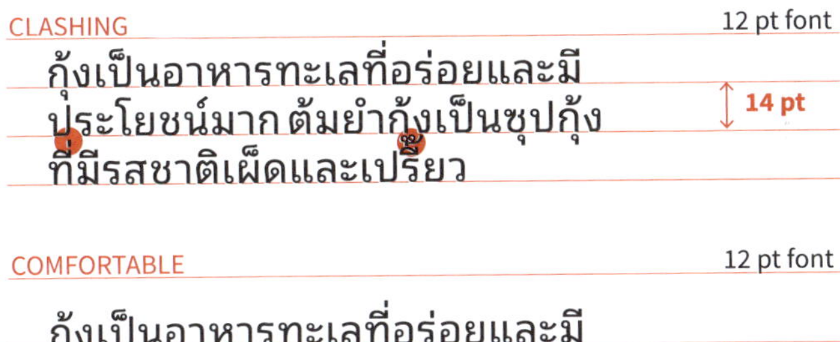

COMFORTABLE
12 pt font
20 pt

Noto Looped Thai

Some Thai typefaces use even taller ascenders and descenders—along with swashes—as a stylistic choice.

Charmonman

When using these typefaces, the line space should be even wider.

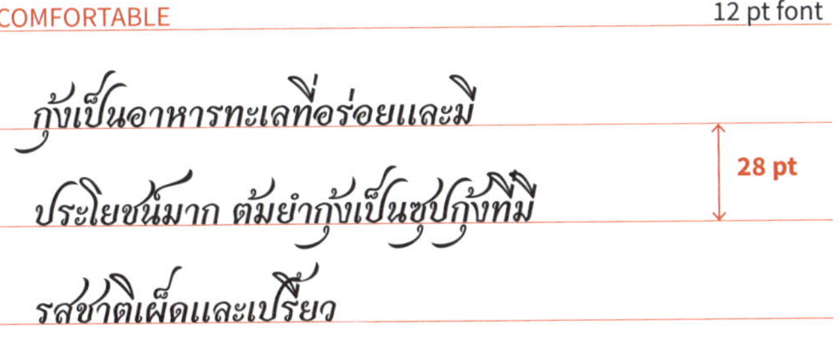

Charmonman

In Thai, designers choose extra-tall ascenders and descenders. In Javanese—one of Indonesia's traditional scripts developed on the island of Java and used to write the Javanese language—tall descenders are baked into the script's genes. Without enough vertical space, the descending elements become illegible.

Noto Sans Javanese

Chinese characters have many strokes, so the line space should be wider than for Latin, at least 150 percent to 200 percent of the font size for a long text. The rationale for this differs from that of Thai. Chinese characters do not risk clashing with one another because each is contained in a square, but the complicated structures of them require more space for readers to move their eyes at the end of each line to find the beginning of the next.

EXHAUSTING   10 pt font

如果沒有足夠的行距,我們容易產生視覺
疲勞。歐美的文字一般采用1.2-1.5 倍行   12 pt
距,而中文一般取1.5 倍行距为宜。文字量
大的讀物則會采用1.65-1.7 倍行距。

COMFORTABLE   10 pt font

如果沒有足夠的行距,我們容易產生視覺
疲勞。歐美的文字一般采用1.2-1.5 倍行   15 pt
距,而中文一般取1.5 倍行距为宜。文字量
大的讀物則會采用1.65-1.7 倍行距。

COMFORTABLE   10 pt font

如果沒有足夠的行距,我們容易產生視覺
疲勞。歐美的文字一般采用1.2-1.5 倍行   20 pt
距,而中文一般取1.5 倍行距为宜。文字量
大的讀物則會采用1.65-1.7 倍行距。

Source Han Sans CN

The Khitan people were nomads residing in modern-day Mongolia, Northeast China, and Russia. Their now-extinct language used two independent scripts for written communication: Khitan small script and Khitan large script. Researchers over the past three decades have successfully deciphered a large portion of these two scripts. Khitan large script resembles Chinese characters in terms of character structure and writing direction, while Khitan small script includes characters that occupy different spaces than Chinese characters do. There are seven types of composition within a Khitan small script character.

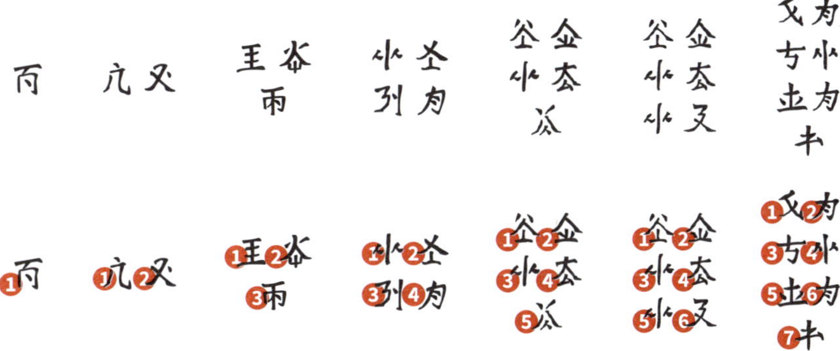

Like Chinese, Khitan can be read horizontally from left to right and vertically from right to left. In either typesetting, the line space should be wide enough to accommodate Khitan small script characters of more than four parts. The example sentence set horizontally and vertically ends with a Khitan character of six parts.

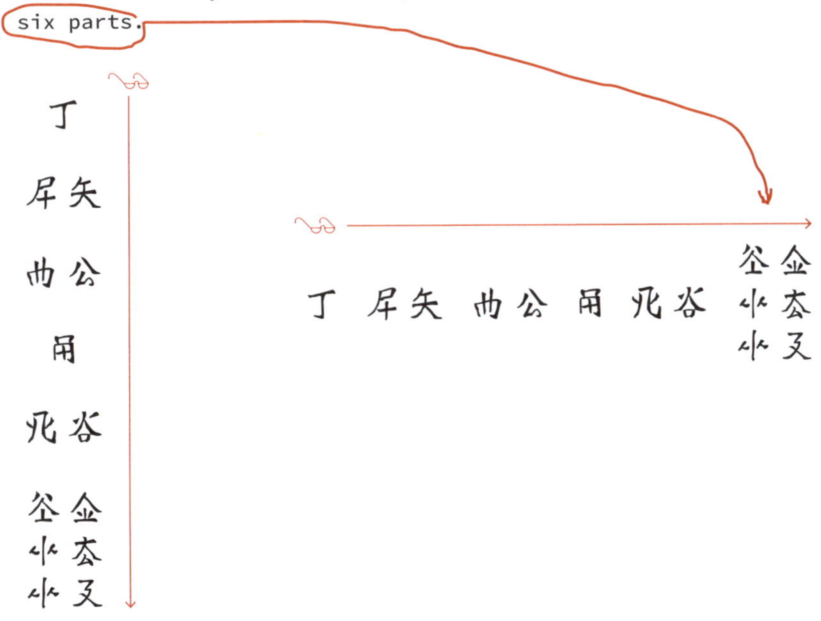

PRONUNCIATION

An **abjad** is a writing system that represents only consonants and that requires readers to infer vowel sounds. This differs from alphabet systems, which include letters for both consonants and vowels. For this reason, abjads are also called "consonantal" scripts. In consonantal scripts such as Arabic and Hebrew, people first learn how to read with the aid of vowel marks. After gaining a basic reading proficiency, they read without these vowel marks.

Adobe Naskh, Arek Armenian, Noam Text

Like the abbreviations **BTW** (by the way) and **LMK** (let me know) in English, Korean speakers can also shorten words to just consonants when texting. As in English, such abbreviations have not been adopted in formal writing.

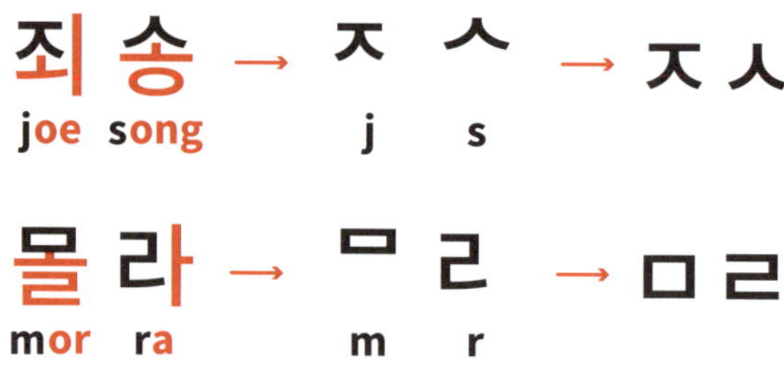

Source Han Sans KR

When vowels are included in Hebrew and Arabic, there should be more space between each line to avoid clashing.

WITH VOWELS

כָּל יוֹם הוּא הִזְדַּמְנוּת לִלְמֹד מַשֶּׁהוּ חָדָשׁ וּלְהַרְאוֹת כַּמָּה אַתֶּם מֻכְשָׁרִים! תַּאֲמִינוּ בְּעַצְמְכֶם, כִּי אַתֶּם חֲזָקִים וּמְסֻגָּלִים לְהַשִּׂיג הַכֹּל

Noam Text

WITHOUT VOWELS

כל יום הוא הזדמנות ללמוד משהו חדש ולהראות כמה אתם מוכשרים! תאמינו בעצמכם, כי אתם חזקים ומסוגלים להשיג הכל

WITH VOWELS

السَّلَامُ هُوَ رِسَالَةُ الْإِنْسَانِيَّةِ وَغَايَتُهَا. إِنَّ تَحْقِيقَ السَّلَامِ يَحْتَاجُ إِلَى التَّفَاهُمِ وَالتَّعَاوُنِ بَيْنَ الشُّعُوبِ. يَجِبُ أَنْ نَعْمَلَ جَمِيعًا لِإِزَالَةِ الْكَرَاهِيةِ وَالْعُنْفِ، وَنَزْرَعَ مَكَانَهُمَا الْمَحَبَّةَ وَالِاحْتِرَامَ. السَّلَامُ يُعَبِّرُ عَنْ أَمَلٍ كَبِيرٍ لِمُسْتَقْبَلٍ أَفْضَلٍ لِلْبَشَرِيَّةِ

WITHOUT VOWELS

السلام هو رسالة الإنسانية وغايتها. إن تحقيق السلام يحتاج إلى التفاهم والتعاون بين الشعوب. يجب أن نعمل جميعًا لإزالة الكراهية والعنف، ونزرع مكانهما المحبة والاحترام. السلام يعبر عن أمل كبير لمستقبل أفضل للبشرية

Amiri

Something similar also occurs in Chinese, although Chinese is not a phonetic writing system. In children's books, pronunciation text is placed next to characters. **Pinyin** is the romanization system in mainland China; more of its history will be discussed in chapter 7. **Zhuyin** or **Bopomofo** is the transliteration system in Taiwan, and Zhuyin has its own script. With either Pinyin or Zhuyin, the spacing should be much wider than it is without the pronunciation text.

PINYIN

zuì bù qǐ yǎn de rén wǎng wǎng

最 不 起 眼 的 人 ，往 往

néng zuò zuì liǎo bù qǐ de shì

能 做 最 了 不 起 的 事

ZHUYIN

最 不 起 眼 的 人 ， 往 往

能 做 最 了 不 起 的 事

Portada Text ARA var, Source Han Serif, Source Han Serif TC

OVERSHOOT

One important principle to remember when designing with text is that what is mathematically the same may not be visually the same. In the following example, the triangles and circles appear shorter than the squares, despite all the shapes being of the same height.

Some exaggeration is needed to make these shapes appear to be the same size.

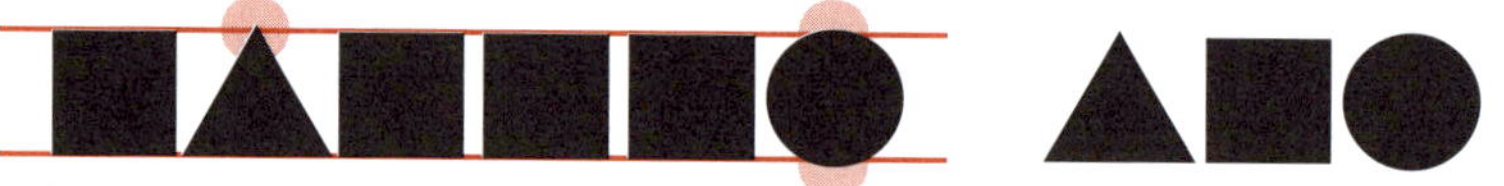

In typography, the part of the letterforms that goes above or below the guidelines to achieve the optical effect of having the same height as other characters is called "overshoot."

Magpie

In "serif" Hebrew typefaces, the bottom of the Hebrew letter **ayin**, for example, usually extends below the baseline.

Frank Ruhl Libre

Narkissim

In Devanagari, there are likewise letters whose lower forms extend below the baseline to achieve visual balance, such as **ha** and **da**.

Noto Serif Devanagari

Kohinoor Devanagari

LEVEL CHANGES

Within each Arabic letter, the teeth—unique typographic elements in connected scripts like Arabic and Mongolian—can change levels, adding more stylistic flow to the script.

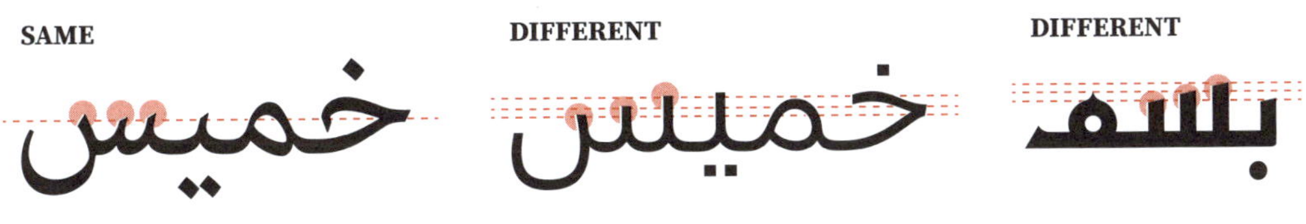

SAME   **DIFFERENT**   **DIFFERENT**

Adobe Arabic, Segoe UI, Reem Kufi

In other scripts, dots are more common than teeth but can likewise be adjusted for stylistic effect. Within the same font, the level of the dots may also change according to the following letter. Below is an example of how the two dots for **y** can vary in the middle of a word.

Adobe Arabic

SIMILAR

بين فيلم ليس   ـيـ ـيـ

Adobe Naskh

DIFFERENT

بين فيلم ليس   ـيـ ـيـ

Below is the same word typed in different typefaces. The height relationship between the two dots in the middle letter y and three dots in the final letter ch changes in each.

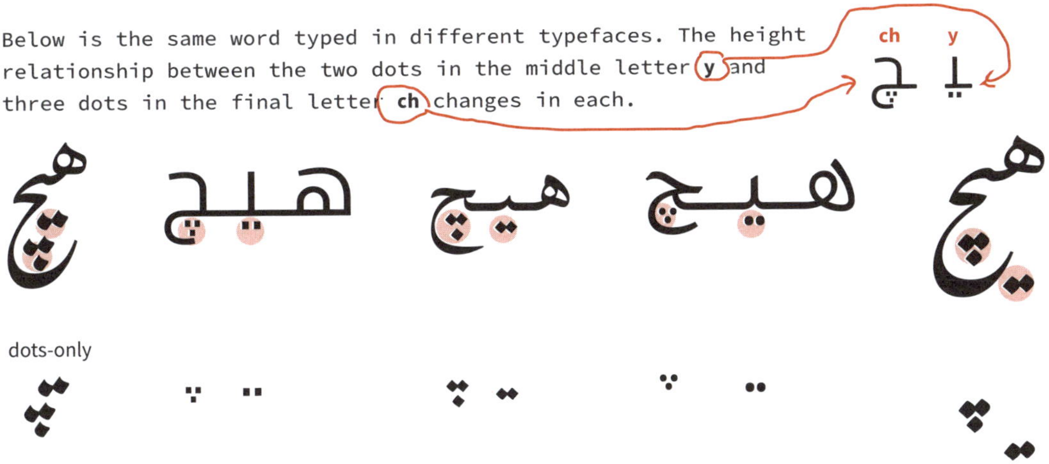

هيج   هيـج   هـيـج   هيج   هيج

dots-only

Gulzar, Cairo, Adobe Naskh, Cordale Arbc, Noto Nastaliq Urdu

The position of the dots is more flexible in calligraphy, as can be seen in the work of contemporary artists Parviz Tanavoli and Maryam Taghavi. Tanavoli, an Iranian sculptor and educator, has made large-scale, stainless-steel sculptures without these dots, while Tehran-born and Chicago-based artist Taghavi has created a wooden sculpture with all the dots at the bottom in addition to her other works that celebrate the dots.

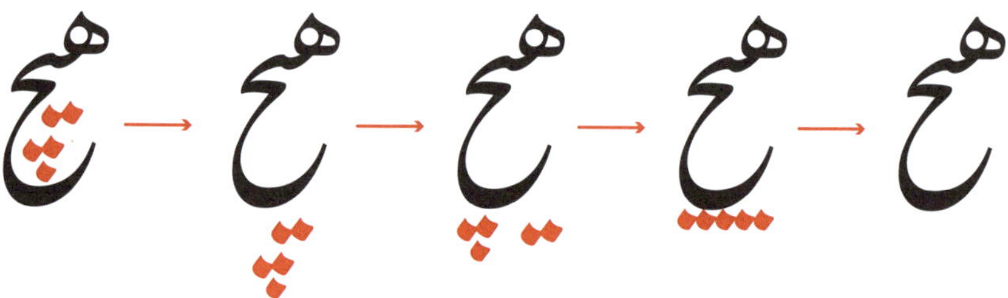

Gulzar

While Arabic dots indicate different letters, the Japanese language has the double, quote-like dots called "dakuten." They turn voiceless sounds, like **k**, into voiced ones, like **g**.

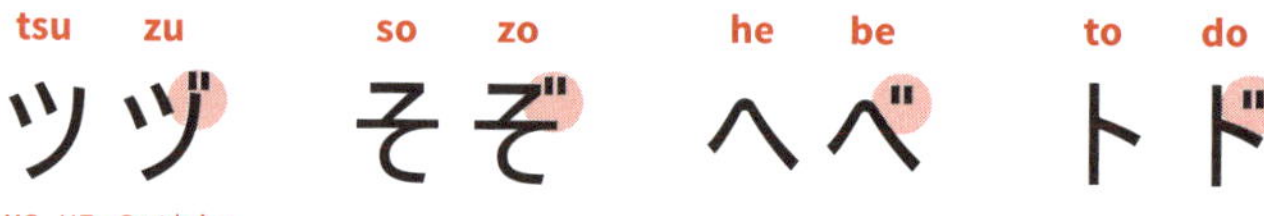

MS UI Gothic

The position of the dots changes according to the kana's form.

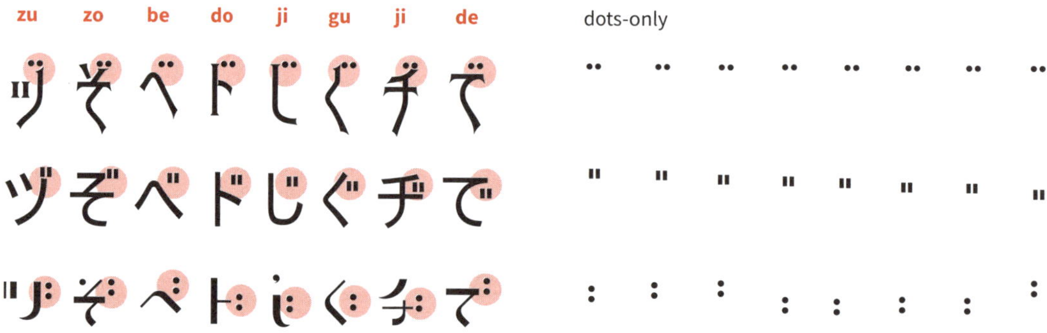

akabara-cinderella, MS UI Gothic, AB-andante

The circle-like dot called "handakuten" turns voiceless sounds, like **ha**, into semi-voiced ones, like **pa.** Their vertical position also varies based on the kana's form.

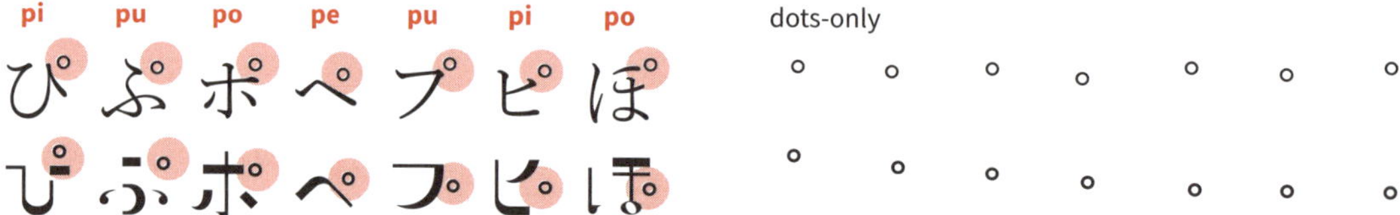

Yu Mincho, AB-andante

X-HEIGHT AND COUNTER SPACE

In Latin typography, "x-height" refers to the height of the lowercase *x*, which is also the height of letters **a, c, e, m, n, o, s, u, v, w, x,** and **z.**

x-height line
x-height

Acumin Pro

The bigger the x-height, the more legible the Latin text is at a smaller scale, because short letters like **a, n, e, o, s,** and **v** are easier to recognize.[4]

4. Karen Cheng, *Designing Type* (Yale University Press, 2020), 38.

20 pt font

tall x-height

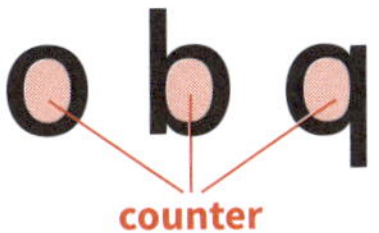

short x-height

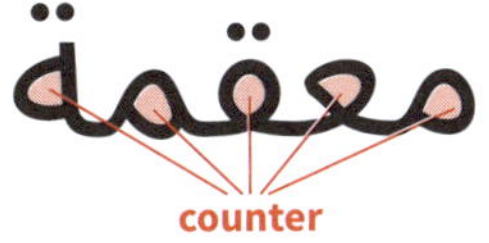

6 pt font

Hand gloves are a key tool in combating COVID-19, acting as a barrier against potential surface transmission. They provide added protection when handling objects or surfaces in public settings.

Hand gloves are a key tool in combating COVID-19, acting as a barrier against potential surface transmission. They provide added protection when handling objects or surfaces in public settings.

Acumin Pro, Gill Sans MT

The space that is entirely or partially closed by forms inside a letter is called a "counter."

o b q   معقمة

counter   counter

Acumin Pro, Noto Sans Arabic

In Arabic, when counter sizes are similar, it is hard to differentiate letters. Diversifying counter sizes increases legibility.[5] Unlike Latin, increasing the x-height of letters altogether does not make an Arabic font more readable.

5. Titus Nemeth, ed., *Arabic Typography: History and Practice* (Niggli, 2023), 370.

similar

معقمة

معقمة

معقمة

معقمة

معقمة

divergent

Noto Sans Arabic, Athelas ARA var, Adobe Arabic, Nassim Arabic Pro, Amiri

Chinese characters each fit into a square box. We can compare the size of the inner counter space in Chinese to the counter in Arabic illustrated on the previous page.

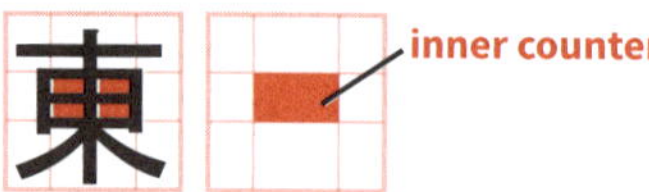

MS UI Gothic

The smaller the innner counter, the more legible the characters. As with Arabic, shape distinctiveness in Chinese is more important to readability than x-height when it comes to small body text.

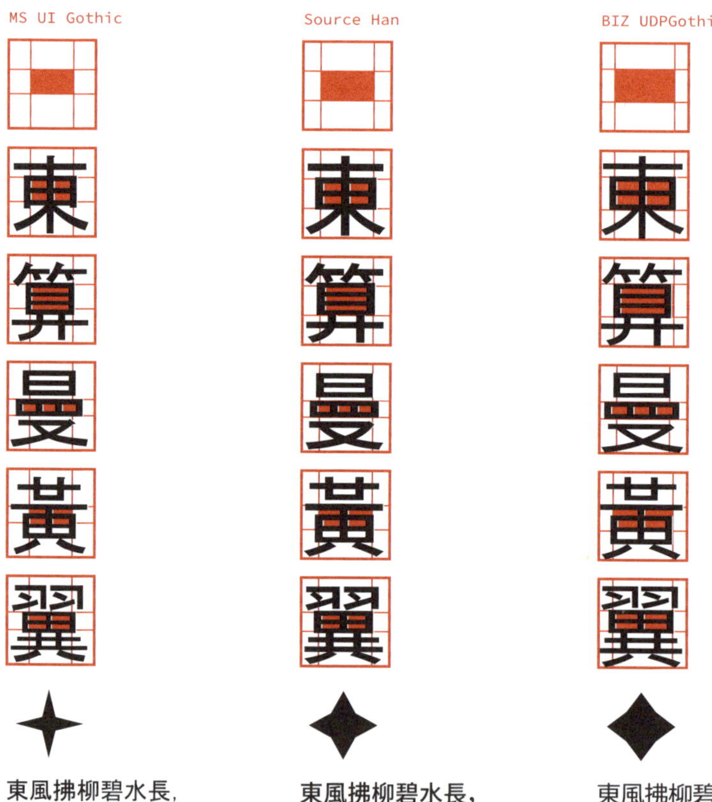

MONOCASE / UNICASE

The scripts mentioned above—except Latin—are considered monocase scripts because they do not have uppercase and lowercase forms. Hugh J. Schonfield, a British Bible scholar, proposed a lowercase for Hebrew while redesigning the "uppercase" letters in the original writing system with a Latinized vertical emphasis.[6] His design was never adopted widely.

6. Luc Devroye, "The Schoenfieldian Script Page," accessed November 23, 2024, https://luc.devroye.org/fonts-43554.html.

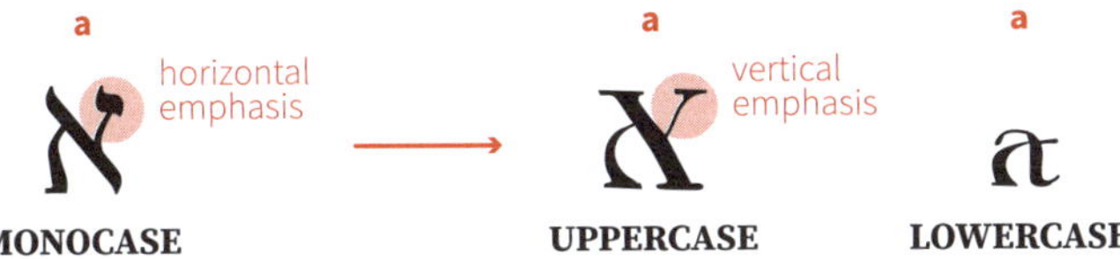

Frank Ruhl Libre, author's sketch

In contrast, the unifying of Latin uppercase and lowercase was once envisioned by members of the famed German design school, Bauhaus. Herbert Bayer argued that a single-case Latin alphabet would be easier to learn, cheaper to print, and faster to set because oral language does not distinguish case.[7] In 1926-29, German typographer Jan Tschihold created a Universal type that combined elements of uppercase and lowercase. In Universal type, the letter **N**, for instance, retains its angular feature, while letter **A** preserves the roundness of a lowercase **a**.[8] Monocase Latin remains more of a design experiment than a standard practice.

7. Ellen Lupton and J. Abbott Miller, *The ABC's of Triangle Square Circle: The Bauhaus and Design Theory* (Princeton Architectural Press, 2019), 47.

8. Lupton and Miller, *Triangle Square Circle*, 47.

Georgian is another script that has only one case. Some typefaces offer an "uppercase" by bringing all letters above the baseline to unify height. This kind of "uppercasing" can be found, for example, on road signs or in titles.

Noto Serif Georgian, Loos Compressed   Loos Compressed

In "lowercase" Georgian, the **t'** goes above the x-height line but is usually shorter than the other letters that have ascenders.

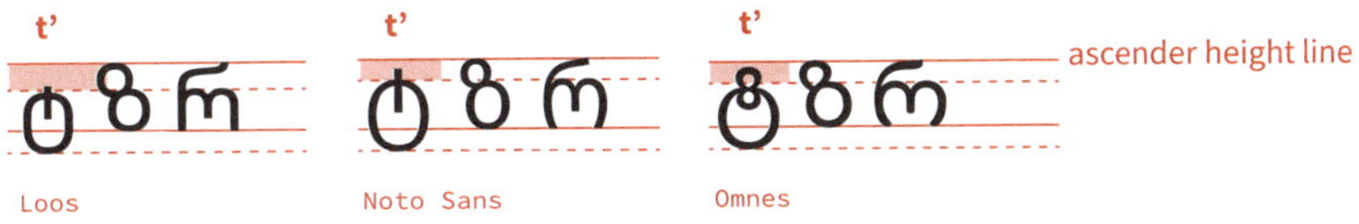

Loos   Noto Sans   Omnes

UPPERCASE AND LOWERCASE

The original Greek and ancient Latin were written only in capital letters.[9] Likewise, the earliest form of Cyrillic only had one case. Around 780 CE, Charlemagne commissioned a more user-friendly script for Latin, part of which included minuscule (lowercase).[10]

Among bicameral scripts, some differentiate uppercase and lowercase in shapes more than other scripts. Cyrillic has this for only four letters (illustrated on the next page), while Greek and Latin have more.

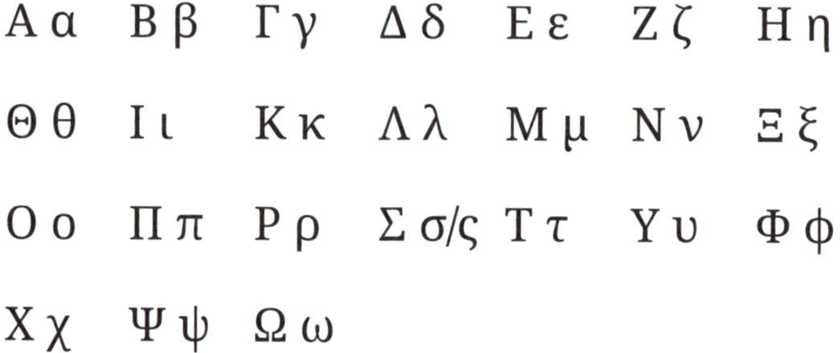

Α α Β β Γ γ Δ δ Ε ε Ζ ζ Η η

Θ θ Ι ι Κ κ Λ λ Μ μ Ν ν Ξ ξ

Ο ο Π π Ρ ρ Σ σ/ς Τ τ Υ υ Φ φ

Χ χ Ψ ψ Ω ω

Droid Serif

A lowercase **chi** is not like a Latin **x**. It has a descender, and the intersection of the two strokes is near the baseline.

Droid Serif

Sigma has two lowercase forms. The first is used when sigma appears at the beginning or in the middle of a word. The second form is used when it appears at the end of a word.

UPPERCASE	ΣΠΙΤΙ	ΓΙΟΣ	ΣΤΡΑΤΟΣ	ΣΩΣΤΟΣ
LOWERCASE	σπίτι	γιος	στρατός	σωστός

Droid Serif

exercise ○○○

Based on the information above, can you write the missing letters in the following Greek words?

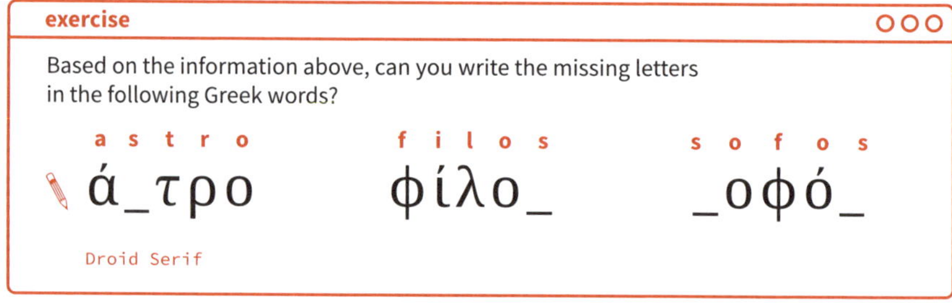

Droid Serif

11. Lara Captan and Kristyan Sarkis, "Cyrillic," in *Bi-Scriptual Typography and Graphic Design with Multiple Script Systems: Arabic, Cyrillic, Greek, Hangeul, Hanzi, Hebrew, Devanagari, Kanji/Hiragana/Katakana* (Niggli, 2019), 67

12. Calderhead and Cohen, *World Encyclopedia of Calligraphy*, 76.

13. Captan and Sarkis, "Cyrillic," 69.

From the ninth to the fourteenth century, the Cyrillic alphabet derived from the Greek uncial (no majuscule or minuscule).[11] From 1708 to 1710, to make the writing appear more Latin than Greek, Peter the Great, then tsar of Russia, began reforming the alphabet, alongside his other efforts to bring Russia culturally closer to Europe. The number of characters was reduced from forty-five to thirty-eight—notably, letters like **omega (ω)** and **psi (ψ)** were removed. He also systemized capital and lowercase letters, although most lowercase forms were derived directly from their capital counterparts.[12] The outliers are highlighted below. After the Russian Revolution in 1917, another reform solidified the modern Cyrillic alphabet with **s** and **i** removed.[13]

А а   Б б   В в   Г г   Д д   Е е

Ё ё   Ж ж   З з   И и   Й й

К к   Л л   М м   Н н   О о   П п

Р р   С с   Т т   У у   Ф ф

Х х   Ц ц   Ч ч   Ш ш   Щ щ   Ъ ъ

Ы ы   Ь ь   Э э   Ю ю   Я я

Source Serif Variable

In Cyrillic, some letters go below the baseline but not as far as the descender line.

Source Serif Variable

To design lowercase Cyrillic, one cannot simply shrink the size of the uppercase, because a lowercase letter is not a proportionally smaller capital letter.

48PT LOWERCASE

Ж Я Ю Д

38 PT CAPITAL ABOVE 48PT LOWERCASE

Ж Я Ю Д

Droid Serif

SUMMARY

uppercase

BICAMERAL

cap-height line

baseline

lowercase

"uppercase"

baseline

tall ascenders

MONOCASED

deep descenders

hangline

MONOCASED

MONOCASED

inner counter

MONOCASED

baseline

curved/slanted baseline

Aktiv Grotesk, Arek Armenian, Noto Sans Georgian, Padauk, Leelawadee, Laila,
210 Mamablock, Frank Ruhl Libre, UD Digi Kyokasho, Amiri, Noto Nastaliq Urdu

WORD SPACE AND CHARACTER SPACE

Word spaces, or the lack of thereof, are rarely discussed in typography, perhaps because people often take them for granted, despite how they greatly ease the reading experience. Typographically, interletter spacing influences the overall texture of a text block; the structure of a character guides the methodology of spacing.

In connected scripts, we need to count in the connections where letters overlap. The elements that fit inside a glyph box also contribute to the diversity of the character's width. In square character systems, like in Chinese, the box that contains the character controls the spacing. In addition to spacing, there are other unique typographic elements that can further activate the negative space around characters, such as the dakuten (dots placed above consonants) in Japanese script. It is like building houses that may have exotic chimneys but also share gardens with neighbors; the characters may share small and large communal spaces without losing their identifiability.

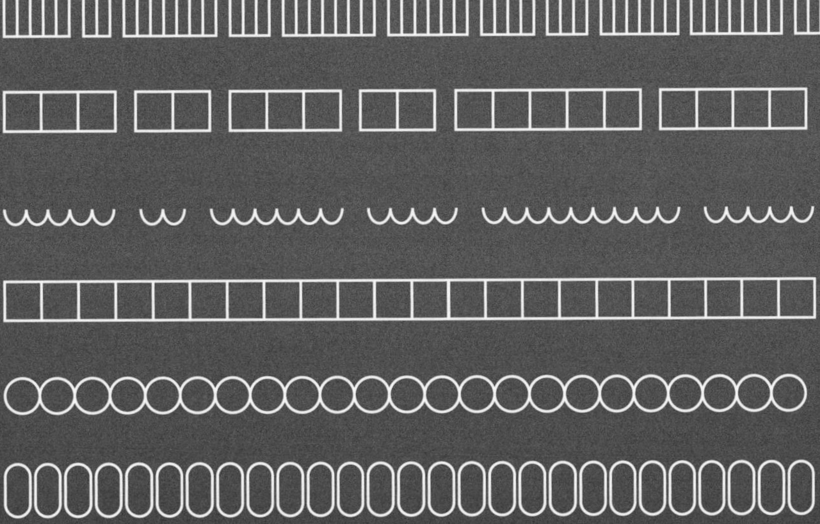

WORD SPACE

1. Onur F. Yazıcıgil, *Pergamon: A Greek Script Typeface Design* (YEM Yayınları, 2023), 61.

2. Clair Cock-Starkey, *Hyphens & Hashtags: The Stories Behind the Symbols on our Keyboards* (Bodleian Library, 2021), 8.

In the ancient Roman world, there was no word spacing.[1]

BUFFALOBUFFALOBUFFALOBUFFALOBUFFALOBUFFALOBUFFALOBUFFALO

Nassim Arabic Pro

In 780 CE, along with the creation of lowercase came word spacing.[2] Modern Latin script readers are more accustomed to spaces between words, except in hyperlinks.

Buffalo buffalo Buffalo buffalo buffalo buffalo Buffalo buffalo

Nassim Arabic Pro

In Japanese, there are no spaces between words. When there are homonyms and homophones in a row, readers utilize lexical skills to internally insert breaks between words.

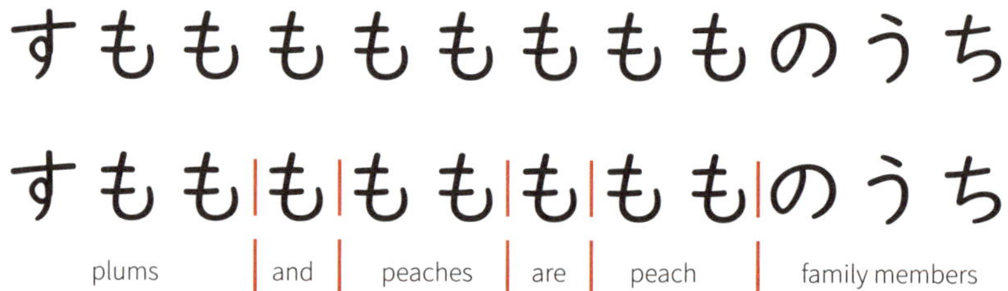

UD Digi Kyokasho

Similarly, there are no word spaces in Chinese.

KaiTi

Neither is blank space used to separate words in Thai. It is used to separate sentences.

หมอนลอยน้ำมาว่ายน้ำไปถอยหมอน

หมอนลอยน้ำมาว่ายน้ำไปถอยหมอน

Adobe Thai

Nor in Burmese.

အပြန်အလှန်လေးစားမှုကိုဖော်ဆောင်စေတယ်။

Padauk

In Korean, there are spaces between words, according to orthographical rules. The word space is narrower than the character width, by approximately 30 percent.

서울특별시 특허허가과 허가과장 허 과장.

■ SPACE~2 MM   ■ CHARACTER~6 MM

Source Han Sans KR

Canadian Aboriginal Syllabics letters are used to write Indigenous languages, including Cree, Inuktitut, and Ojibwe in Canada and the United States. In this writing system, vowels change through rotation.

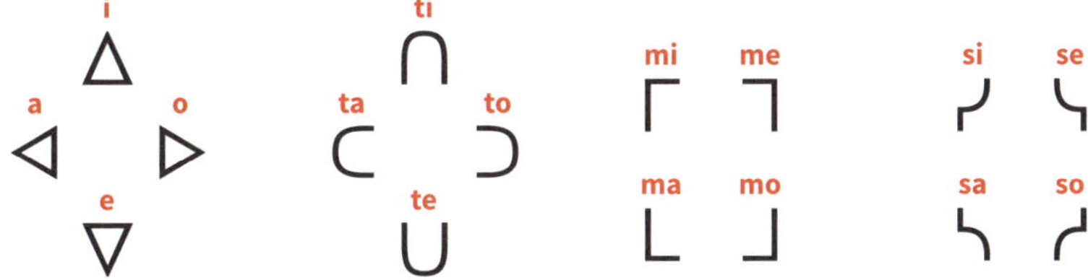

Noto Sans Canadian Aboriginal

Due to this feature of the script, the letters have larger open counters than do Latin letters, necessitating wider word space for readability.[3]

3. Kevin King, "Syllabics Typographic Guidelines and Local Typographic Preferences," *Typoteque*, January 24, 2022, https://www.typotheque.com/articles/syllabics-typographic-guidelines.

EXHAUSTING

ᐃᐪᐃᖃᐅᖅᑐᖅ ᖃᓚᐅᐦᕐᖅᐸᐃᑎᑕᑦ ᐃᒡᕐᓐᓕᐸᑎᑕᑦ ᑎᑎᕐᐅᕆᖃᐅᕐᕈᑦ ᒐᖅᕐᒐᖅᐸᖅᑕᑦ ᐃᒡᖃᑎᒐᕐᓐᑐᕐ.

COMFORTABLE

ᐃᐪᐃᖃᐅᖅᑐᖅ ᖃᓚᐅᐦᕐᖅᐸᐃᑎᑕᑦ ᐃᒡᕐᓐᓕᐸᑎᑕᑦ ᑎᑎᕐᐅᕆᖃᐅᕐᕈᑦ ᒐᖅᕐᒐᖅᐸᖅᑕᑦ ᐃᒡᖃᑎᒐᕐᓐᑐᕐ.

Noto Sans Canadian Aboriginal

LETTER SPACE

Arabic and Persian use word spaces. In a word, there can also be spaces between two letters that do not connect. Therefore, many words are not rendered in a continuous line, so the letters that only connect on the right of a word reserve a tiny space (indicated by the coffee cups below) on the left.

Athelas ARA var

The letter spaces are narrower than word spaces.

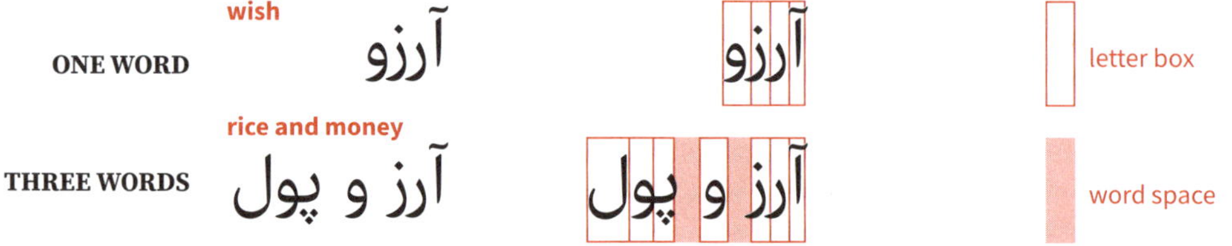

Athelas ARA var

letter space | word space

In the example below, the first word consists of only isolated letters. The second row, however, has three words; the space between the isolated letters is smaller than the space between each word.

ONE WORD · wish · آرزو · آرزو · letter box

THREE WORDS · rice and money · آرز و پول · آرز و پول · word space

Athelas ARA var

In most sentences, both letter spaces and word spaces coexist.

letter box

word space

letter space

Athelas ARA var

OVERLAP

Arabic and Mongolian letters overlap to connect letters seamlessly within a word.

Mongolian Baiti

Nassim Arabic Pro

In Devanagari, the letters of each word also connect at the headline, where they overlap.

Adobe Devanagari

In Latin, tracking (i.e., the space between each letter) is increased to make a word appear longer. In Arabic, the connection between two letters is extended. This is called **kashida** (stretched, in Persian) or **tatweel** (long, in Arabic).

TRACKING: 000	kashida	tatweel
TRACKING: 300	k a s h i d a	t a t w e e l
REGULAR	كَشيدة	تَطْوِيل
STRETCHED	كَشـــيدة	تَطْوِيــــل

Nassim Arabic Pro

Kashida/tatweel is a standard tool employed to adjust the length of a line of text in Arabic and Persian. Hyphenation, a common tool for adjusting the lengths of a line in Latin, is not used in Arabic. Below is an image in which kashida/tatweel is used to maintain an equal length for each line. It is best to elongate only one connection per word;[4] otherwise, the passage can become difficult to read.

4. Titus Nemeth, ed., *Arabic Typography: History and Practice* (Niggli, 2023), 374.

هل تســــــعى
للوصــــــول لأعلى
مشاهــــــدات
للمــــــدرسة

Nassim Arabic Pro

MONOSPACED: CHINESE CHARACTER SPACING

In the seventh century CE, the Chinese adopted woodblock printing. An entire text passage would be carved, in reverse into a wooden block—one block per page—that would then be inked and pressed onto paper, revealing the correctly oriented passage. In the early fifteenth century, European monastic copyists also began engraving whole pages on woodblocks.[5]

5. Syhan Argur, "The Gutenberg Bible," in *ABC of Typography*, ed. David Rault (SelfMadeHero, 2019), 43.

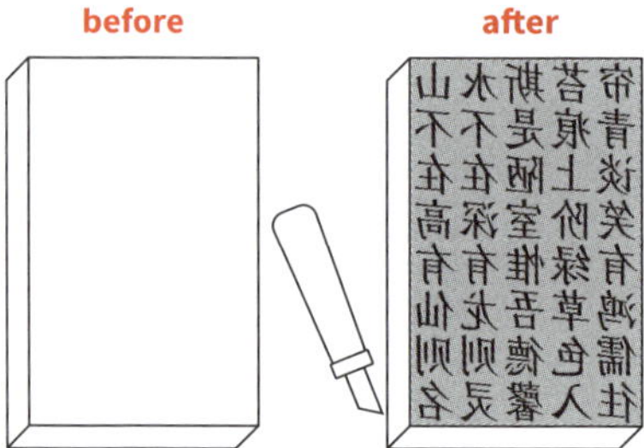

HelloFont ID MingKeBenWanSong

In the eleventh century, Bi Sheng invented the Chinese moveable type to save time and wood. Each Chinese character was carved onto a small woodblock—imagine a collection of small stamps all being pressed at once. Printers would arrange the wooden characters inside a frame to print a full page. After printing, the characters could be reused for another page. This process pre-dated Gutenberg's moveable type of the 1450s.

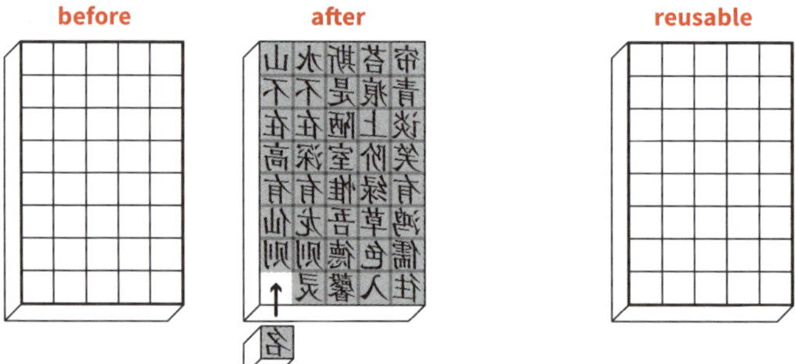

HelloFont ID MingKeBenWanSong

Since there were thousands of Chinese characters, printers needed a large space to store Chinese types; they also needed to learn the system that sorted and sequenced the type to print efficiently. Otherwise, one could have easily spent a full day unable to find all the characters needed for one page. These factors made Chinese moveable type less favorable than full text woodblock printing.

Another factor was the complexity of the characters— the detailed forms of each character were easily damaged. For centuries, printers have tested various materials to prolong the longevity of individual character types without great success.

Had the types been placed next to each other tightly, how would they have set the space between each character? The secret is in the character's body, which does not go all the way to the edge of the physical type. The space it takes remains inside the surface frame.

BODY FRAME

SURFACE FRAME

KaiTi

The smaller the surface frame, the wider the character spacing.

NARROW

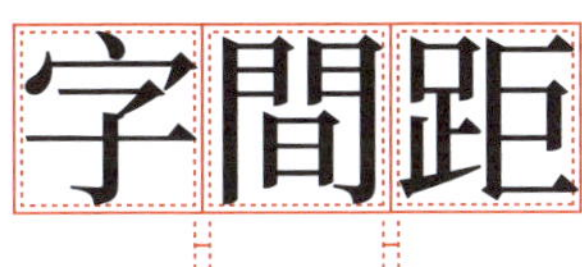

过小的字间距可能导致文字显得拥挤，从而降低文本的美观性和易读性。在不同的语言和字体中，字间距的设定也有所不同。例如，在中文排版中，由于汉字本身是方块字，字间距通常会较小，以保持视觉上的紧凑感；而在英文或其他西文排版中，字间距需要与字体设计和

MEDIUM

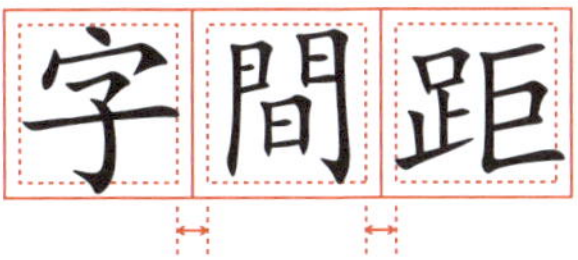

过小的字间距可能导致文字显得拥挤，从而降低文本的美观性和易读性。在不同的语言和字体中，字间距的设定也有所不同。例如，在中文排版中，由于汉字本身是方块字，字间距通常会较小，以保持视觉上的紧凑感；而在英文或其他西文排版中，字间距需要与字体设计

WIDE

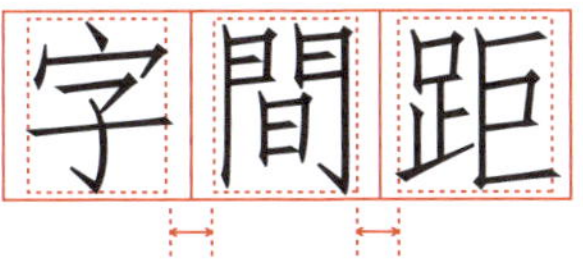

过小的字间距可能导致文字显得拥挤，从而降低文本的美观性和易读性。在不同的语言和字体中，字间距的设定也有所不同。例如，在中文排版中，由于汉字本身是方块字，字间距通常会较小，以保持视觉上的紧凑感；而在英文或其他西文排版中，字间距需要与字体设计

Source Han Serif SC, KaiTi, FangSong

JAPANESE CHARACTER SPACE

Like the Chinese type, Japanese kanji controls character space with the size of the surface frame.

VIRTUAL BODY

SURFACE FRAME

UD Digi Kyokasho

Many hiragana and katakana glyphs are narrower than kanji ones.

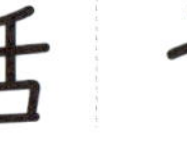
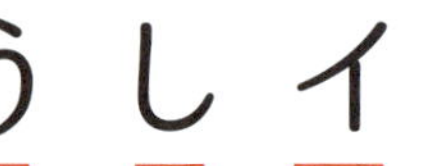

UD Digi Kyokasho

There are two methods of spacing Japanese characters. **Tsume kumi** uses the characters' individual sidebearing (i.e., the space before and after a character).

TSUME KUMI

side bearing/tsume

UD Digi Kyokasho

Beta gumi, on the other hand, is a different character spacing method that uses the same virtual body to space all characters, regardless of their width.

BETA GUMI

TSUME KUMI

UD Digi Kyokasho

---

exercise   ○○○

Which one below is beta gummi?

文字のしごと スペースの仕事

文字のしごと スペースの仕事

UD Digi Kyokasho

In Japanese, there are two common conditions in which a kana (hiragana and katakana) must be printed smaller than a kanji is.

今日はちょっと寒くて、急にコートを着たくなっちゃったんだ。でも、急いで出かけたから、忘れちゃって、結局寒いまま歩いちゃった。駅に着いたら、友達が待ってて、「やっぱり寒いよね！」って言われて、二人で笑っちゃった。そのあと、カフェに行って、ホットミルクを飲んでほっとしたよ。

Yu Mincho

First, reducing the size of a kana (usually 78%) means linking its sound to the kana that precedes it.

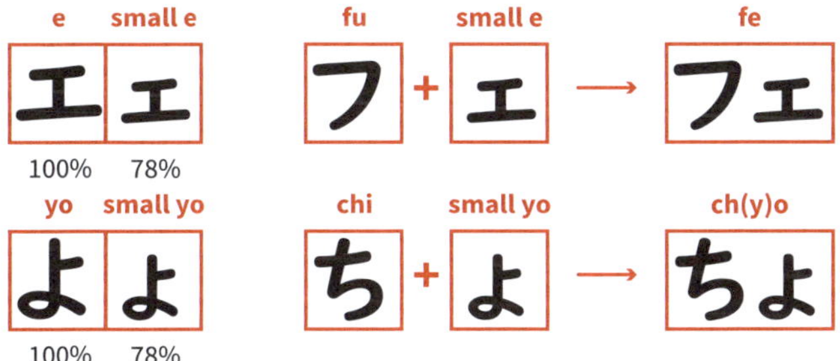

Second, a small **tsu** refers to doubling the consonant after **tsu**.

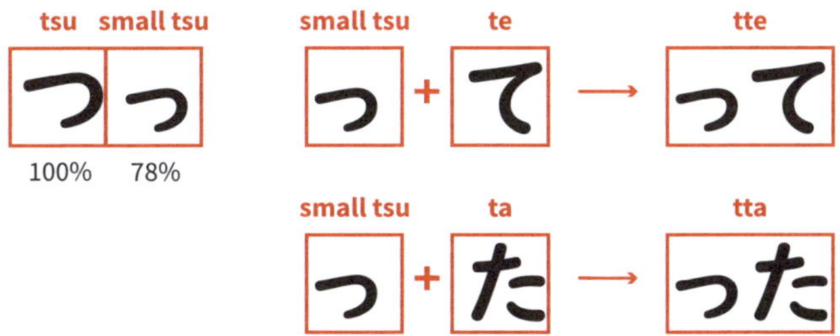

UD Digi Kyokasho

Another element that needs attention in spacing is the dots placed on the top right of a consonant.

Yu Mincho

In some typefaces, the top right of the kana is trimmed off to leave space for the dots.

In others, the dot is connected to the kana.

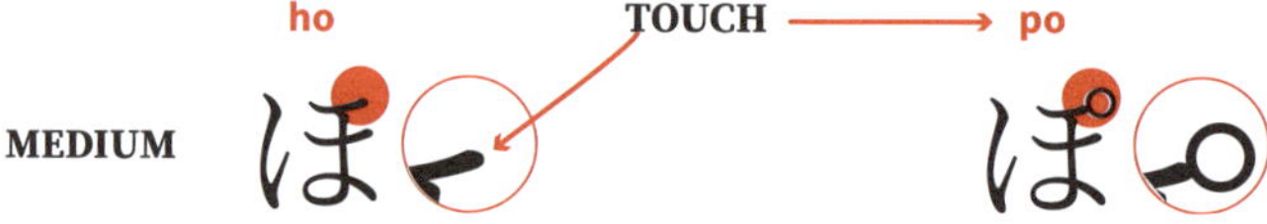

In others, they are not connected.

The space between the kana and dots contributes to a typeface's personality.

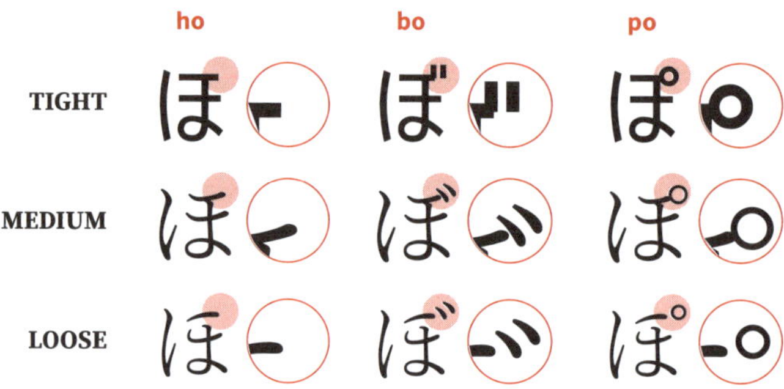

MS UI Gothic, Source Han Serif, Yu Mincho

In display type, designers can also play with the space between the consonants and dots. In the example below, a small tsu is placed under the dot.

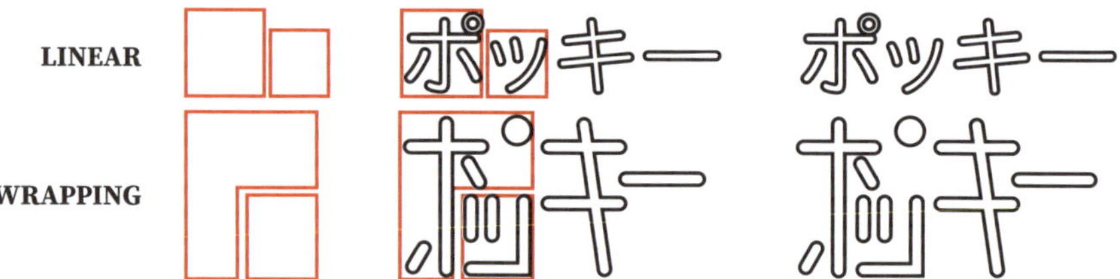

Heisei Maru Gothic Std

6. Erik Spiekermann, *Stop Stealing Sheep & Find Out How Type Works* (The Other Collection, 2022), 141.

7. Fred Smeijers, *Counterpunch: Making Type in the Sixteenth Century, Designing Typefaces Now* (Hyphen Press, 1996), 35.

WIDE CHARACTER SPACE IN CHINESE, JAPANESE, AND KOREAN (CJK)

If Latin letters are set too far apart, they become seemingly unrelated signs;[6] readers will tend to forget what they have read when given too much time to get to the next letter.[7]

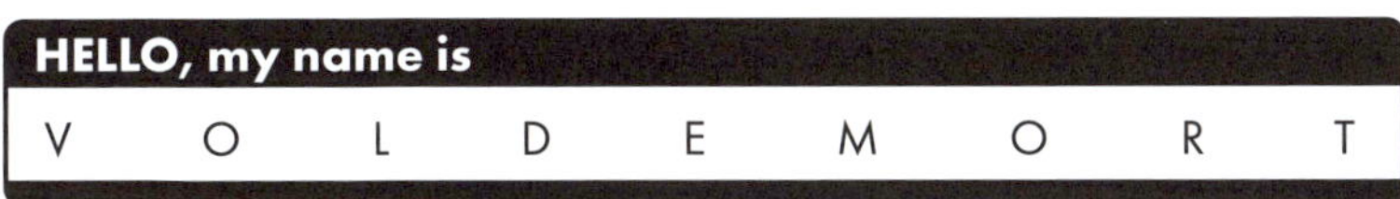

Futura PT

Incorrectly increasing letter spacing in Devanagari results in a broken headline, which should be avoided.

√ सुप्रकटविभागान्तर्गत

💩 सुप्र कट वि भा गा न्तर्ग त

Noto Sans Devanagari

Incorrectly breaking the letter connection in Arabic is likewise inappropriate.

√ فسيكفيكههم

💩 مهكيفكيسف

Anaqa VF

In Latin, individual letters do not possess internal meaning, so each letter only represents a sound and letters need to be connected and sequenced to produce meaningful words. CJK characters include a lot of information such that readers do not need to connect all characters to understand each character's meaning because of their dense connotations. Extremely wide CJK character spacing, therefore, does not hinder readability. Comparatively, individual letters in a phonetic alphabet like Latin cannot express meaning.

Source Han Sans KR, Hiragino Kaku Gothic ProN, Source Han Sans CN

Wide character spacing is common on CJK nameplates or on reserved signs in restaurants.

Source Han Serif K

RixJangs_Pro, NextExit Variable

It is also found frequently on menu boards. In the example below, justification applies to vertical text.

Malgun Gothic, Bahnschrift

In CJK, justification is common in film credits. Below is an example in Korean. The first name consists only of two characters, while all the others are made up of three characters. When the column is justified, there is a wider space between the characters of this first name than those of the ones below it.

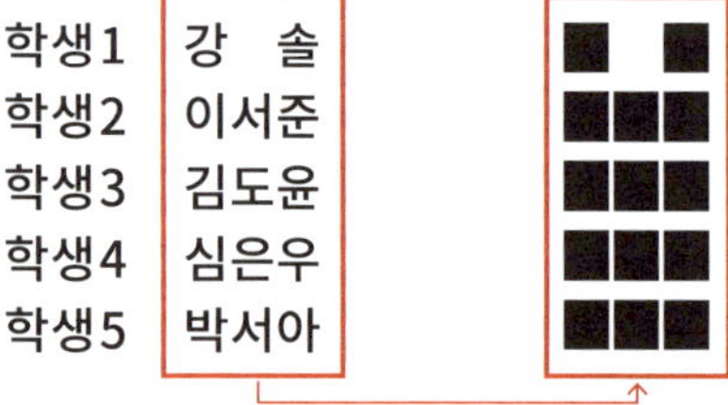

Source Han Sans KR

Below is an example of the back matter of a Chinese book. The titles of each staff member (first column on the left) are justified, so there is a larger character space for those titles with fewer characters.

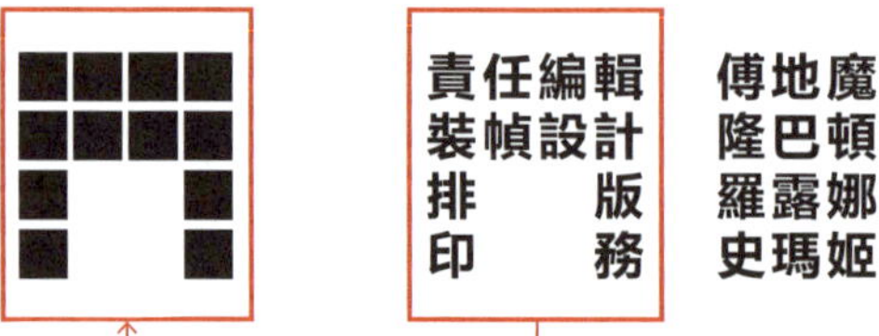

Microsoft YaHei UI

In Chinese, it is more common to see two-character names than in Korean. Below is an example of justified names in Chinese.

武术指导

宋江　卢俊义　吴用　公孙胜　关胜　林冲　秦明　呼延灼

花荣　柴进　李应　朱仝　鲁智深　武松　董平　张清

杨志　徐宁　索超　戴宗　刘唐　李逵　史进　穆弘

雷横　李俊　阮小二　张横　阮小五　张顺　阮小七　杨雄

HelloFont ID MingKeBenWanSong

Gestalt proximity in visual perception refers to the principle that objects that are closer together will be perceived as a group.

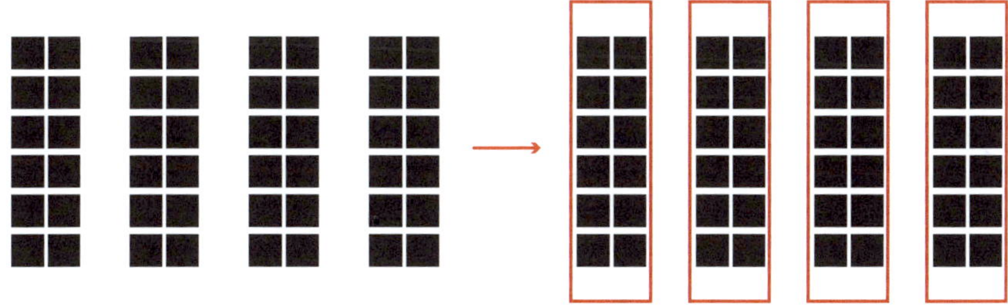

In the above justified list of Chinese names, this principle of proximity helps us to group the columns.

group 1

宋江　卢俊义　吴用　公孙胜　关胜　林冲　秦明　呼延灼

group 2

花荣　柴进　李应　朱仝　鲁智深　武松　董平　张清

group 3

杨志　徐宁　索超　戴宗　刘唐　李逵　史进　穆弘

group 4

雷横　李俊　阮小二　张横　阮小五　张顺　阮小七　杨雄

HelloFont ID MingKeBenWanSong

However, inside each column, the principle is subject to
a language-specific context. What works in Latin does not
apply in Chinese.

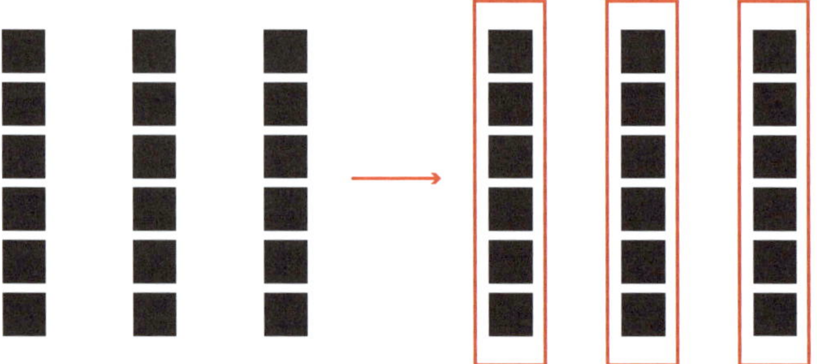

Chinese readers instinctively group characters with the same name
together despite the wider character spacing.

group 1   **Latin**

HelloFont ID MingKeBenWanSong, LarabiefontRg

The Gestalt principle still works in the context of CJK names,
while the readers group the characters differently from how they
would group the Latin letters.

group 1

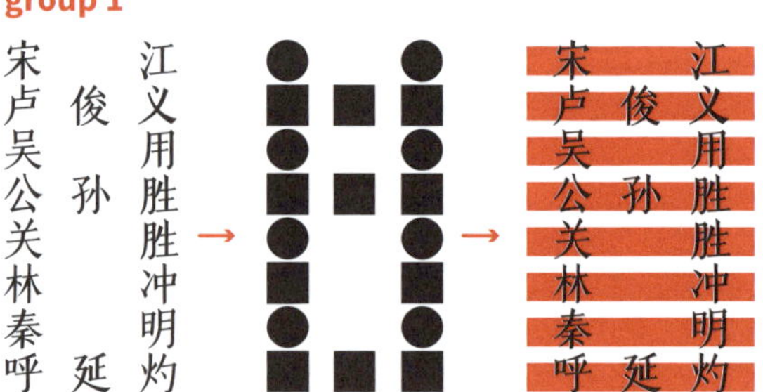

HelloFont ID MingKeBenWanSong

Orthography also influences character spacing conventions. The lengths of Japanese names vary more than in Chinese and Korean.

皇一
水瀬祈
高橋理恵
早見沙保里
勘解由小路三鈴

Below are two names that are each three characters long. The first has a one-character family name, and the second has a two-character family name. In credit lists, separating the family name and the given name is more important than spreading out the characters evenly to distinguish between the two easily.

星 新一 ⟶ 星　　新一
長塚 節 ⟶ 長塚　　節

*The character space is exaggerated to show the spacing convention.

Below are some different combinations.

*The character space is exaggerated to show the spacing convention.

Below are a variety of character spaces when justifying names in the credit lists.

Cast

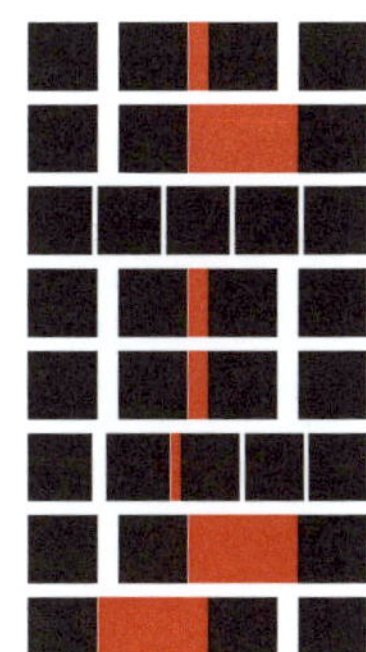

大 島 怜 羅
西 尾　　証
伊藤七留美
立 石 茂 淑
北 島 絢 那
小山内実翔
平 林　　享
境　　夏 月

SUMMARY

no word space 

  character space

wide character space does not
interfere with readability

no word space ยักษ์ใหญ่ไล่ยักษ์เล็ก

word space 우울할 때는 단맛이 최고야

word space अकेलापन सबसे बड़ा दुश्मन है   ● connection

word space طريق نجاحه

stretchable connection

طريق نجاحه

طريق نجاحه

word space THE TRACKING IS 0

THE TRACKING IS 100   letter space

Hiragino Kaku Gothic ProN, Forma DJR Thai Text,
Source Han Sans KR, Poppins, Co Headline Arbc, DINosaur

The word **punctuation** did not refer to our modern system of pauses until the 1660s.[1] In fact, what we now know as punctuation evolved in different languages over several centuries. Unlike the universal wayfinding icons found on signs at international airports, punctuation and numerals can be challenging for those in some parts of the world to decipher. Varying in shape, numerals occupy different spaces and positions in relation to characters depending on the script being used. They therefore embody the richness and diversity of human histories as much as other characters do. The present-day reliance on US/European technology and the demand for an international economy, has prompted the rest of the world to adopt Hindu Arabic numerals and Latin punctuation.

Even though a complete, non-Latin typeface will include native script-appropriate numerals, Hindu Arabic numerals tend to dominate commercial contexts like signage and price tags. This is an example of script preservation enabled by technological development that has not led to wide readoption. Cultural and historical practices of reading, writing, and thinking surrender to habits and convenience. This chapter questions the communication engineering that has been heavily influenced by Western preferences and considers the proliferation of Southeast Asian numerals.

1. Clair Cock-Starkey, *Hyphens & Hashtags: The Stories Behind the Symbols on Our Keyboards* (Bodleian Library, 2021), 7.

PUNCTUATION: ADOPTION

Many parts of the world did not use punctuation until the 1900s due to printing costs and a lack of standardization.

In early Sinhala (a language primarily used in Sri Lanka) writings, there was only one punctuation mark. It looked like the Latin diacritic **tilde** (~) and was used as a period so that they could use the limited supply of palm leaves they wrote on more sparingly.[2]

In Bengali text, Latin punctuation debuted in the late eighteenth century, when Western missionaries encouraged the establishment of type foundries for religious and political reasons.[3]

Punctuation was not widely used in Persian until the 1800s.[4] Most Persian manuscripts did not contain punctuation until the 1840s, when a flower-like symbol was used as a period.[5]

For centuries, Chinese ancestors read books without any punctuation marks. During the Qin Dynasty (217-207 BCE), punctuation was marked manually using a different color after printing, usually red, but no marks were standardized until the 1920s.

2. S. Leelaratne, "Sinhala and Palm Leaf Writing," in *The World Encyclopedia of Calligraphy: The Ultimate Compendium on the Art of Fine Writing: History, Craft, Technique*, eds. Christopher Calderhead and Holly Cohen (Sterling, 2018), 149-50.

3. Fiona Ross, "An Approach to Non-Latin Type Design," in *Language Culture Type: International Type Design in the Age of Unicode*, ed. John Berry (AtypI Graphics, 2002), 65-66.

4. Titus Nemeth, ed., *Arabic Typography: History and Practice* (Niggli, 2023), 361.

5. Borna Izadpanah, "Persian and Arabic Printing in Qajar Iran," in *Arabic Typography: History and Practice, ed. Titus Nemeth* (Salenstein: Niggli, 2023), 137.

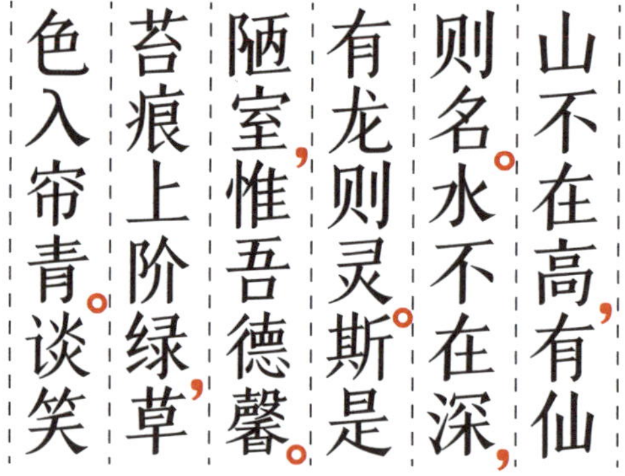

HelloFont ID MingKeBenWanSong

While other scripts, despite their dissimilarities with Latin, adopted Latin punctuation with modification, Thai uses minimal marks other than tone marks. Thai sentences do not commonly end with a period. Neither does Thai use commas, colons or dashes. Because there is no word spacing in Thai, sentences can be separated by blank spaces.

คิดถึงภูเขาสีเขียวที่เต็มไปด้วยต้นไม้ใหญ่ ดอกไม้เล็ก ๆ ก็กำลังผลิใบ ออกดอกออกผล ป่าในหน้าฝนเป็นช่วงที่อากาศดี มีโอกาศพบเจอทะเลหมอกสวย ๆ เรียกได้ว่าเป็น เวลาของเหล่านักเดินป่า ที่จะออกไปเดินศึกษาธรรมชาติ

Adobe Devanagari

PUNCTUATION: SHAPE

In Cyrillic, quotation marks differ from those used in English.
The basic quotes are the same as those used in French, Italian,
Spanish, and Norwegian; the secondary quotes are the same as
those used in Latvian.

“He said this”   “He said ‘this’”

«Он сказал это»   «Он сказал: „это“»

EB Garamond

Many marks were directly taken from Latin. Despite the similar
shapes, marks borrowed from Latin may differ in usage across
different scripts. In Greek, the question mark resembles the
English semicolon.

Τι; Δεν καταλαβαίνω.

What? I don't understand.

EB Garamond

In Devanagari, a vertical line is used to end a sentence, like a
period in Latin.

ठीक है धन्यवाद।

Adobe Devanagari

In Burmese, however, one vertical line is used for a small break.
The full stop of a sentence is marked by two vertical lines.

အထူးသဖြင့် လက်ဖက်ထမင်း၊ မုန့်ဟင်းခါး၊
အုန်းနို့ဟင်းလျာတို့မှာ မြန်မာနိုင်ငံ၏ အမှတ်တရ
အစားအစာများဖြစ်သည်॥

Padauk

In Arabic and Hebrew, both written right to left, the punctuation
marks are placed on the left, following the reading direction. In
Arabic, the shapes are mirrored vertically from how they would be
used in a Latin text written from left to right; in Hebrew, they
are not changed.

أهلا! هل أنت مشغول؟   היי! אתה עסוק?

Amiri, Narkissim

PUNCTUATION: SPACE

In Armenian, a few punctuation marks are placed over accented syllables, instead of on the right side.

Ողջույն! Նա ամուսնացած է:

Arek Armenian

In English, each punctuation mark takes up a different width depending on its shape.

Adobe Garamond

Huh?Yes!Comma,please."Period"

Adelle Sans

Huh?Yes!Comma,please."Period"

The best example of spacing can be seen in the differences between a hyphen, en-dash, and em-dash in US English. Each serves a different grammatical purpose, and each takes a different width.

Her type-inspired exhibition is on view
May 2–15—but she has not given me
the address.

Georgia

Most punctuation marks in Latin are not considered to have the same vertical mass as letters. Instead, they are pushed outside the margins of an aligned text to eliminate "holes" on the vertical edge. This is called "hanging punctuation."

"The quotation mark isn't pushed
outside the margin."

"The quotation mark is pushed
outside the margin."

Georgia

In justified Latin text, hanging punctuation is set along the right edge.

Why did the period break up with the comma? The period realized it needed more certainty in life. The comma was always pausing, never ready to commit to a full stop. Tired of the indecision,

Why did the period break up with the comma? The period realized it needed more certainty in life. The comma was always pausing, never ready to commit to a full stop. Tired of the indecision,

Some designers consider the width of the punctuation when center aligning text; others do not.

“PLEASE STAY ON THE PATH, OR YOU WILL BE EATEN BY OUR PLANTS AND OUR ANIMALS.”

“PLEASE STAY ON THE PATH, OR YOU WILL BE EATEN BY OUR PLANTS AND OUR ANIMALS.”

Tifinagh is a script used to write the Berber languages spoken by indigenous communities in North Africa and the Middle East. The above punctuation spacing judgment does not work well in Tifinagh: the letter **a** is a small circle shorter than any other letter. In scripts similar to Latin, only punctuation marks are ever this small.

a   **period**

ⵣⵀⵀⵓ ⵝⵥⵔⵔ | ⴱⵥⵔⴱⵥⵔ ⵙ ⵊⵔⵥⵥⵗ ⵏₒⵜ ⵜⵥⵥⵔₒ | ⵜⵉⴱₒⵤⵜ ⵜₒⵔⵊⴱⵥⵙⵜ. ₒⵙⵔⵔⵙ ‖ⵙ ⵓⵀⵀⵥⵔ | ⵀₒⵔⵊ ₒ‖ ⵊⵔ ⵣⵗⵔⵥ ⵓⵊⵔ ⵔₒ ⵔₒⵇⵇₒ ⵣⵔⵗⵔₒⵙ‖ ⵗⵥⵔⵔ.

In Chinese, a punctuation mark occupies the same amount of space that a character does. In Simplified Chinese, the mark is usually placed at the bottom left of "box," while in Traditional Chinese, it is usually positioned in the center.

SIMPLIFIED CHINESE

标点符号有句号，逗号，问号，感叹号等。

TRADITIONAL CHINESE

標點符號有句號，逗號，問號，感嘆號等。

KaiTi, Adobe Ming Std L

When considering the reading experience, Chinese characters are dense in strokes, and there is no word space. Grammatically, one character can include enough information to function as a full word, further contributing to the script's density. The space around punctuation marks gives readers room to breathe, and native readers are used to the negative space around punctuation marks. Below is a famous example of a densely written essay in which the space around the punctuation eases the reading experience.

石室詩士施氏，嗜獅，誓食十獅。氏時時適市視獅。十時，適十獅適市。是時，適施氏適市。氏視是十獅，恃矢勢，使是十獅逝世。氏拾是十獅屍，適石室。石室濕，氏使侍拭石室。石室拭，氏始試食是十獅。食時，始識是十獅屍，實十石獅屍。試釋是事。

Adobe Ming Std L

In rare situations where there are three or four punctuation marks in a row, it is better to reduce the spacing among them.

听说标点在中文里的住房条件要比在西文里的要好？”（《世梨说新语》字间距章节讨论了标点符号占用的空间）

听说标点在中文里的住房条件要比在西文里的要好？”（《世梨说新语》字间距章节讨论了标点符号占用的空间）

KaiTi

PUNCTUATION: ROTATION

Like Chinese, Japanese punctuation also takes up the same amount of space as a character. In horizontally typed Japanese, common marks like the comma and period appear at the bottom left, as in Simplified Chinese.

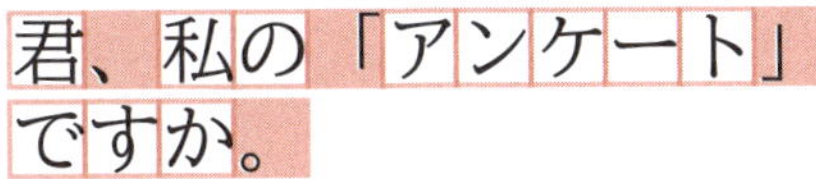

BIZ UDMincho

When typed vertically, marks are placed at the top right. In vertical text, some marks are rotated ninety degrees.

Rotating marks like this can also make Latin punctuation look better in vertical typesetting.

Adelle Sans

BIZ UDMincho

In Japanese katakana, the dash is neither a hyphen nor an en-dash. Instead, it is used to extend the vowel sound that precedes it. In vertical text, it is rotated vertically.

アンケート ルール モール
a n ke e to   ru u ru   mo o ru

BIZ UDMincho

Hyphenation is a standard tool in Latin that changes the number of letters in a line. Outside the Western world, Indian social reformer Ishwar Chandra Vidyasagar supported using hyphens to justify Bengali text.[6] Hyphens are not used in Japanese, Korean, or Chinese, because square characters cannot be broken into halves. Justification in CJK can be achieved by narrowing the sidebearing of punctuation marks.

[6]. Fiona Ross, "Non-Latin Type Design," in Berry, *Language Culture Type*, 69.

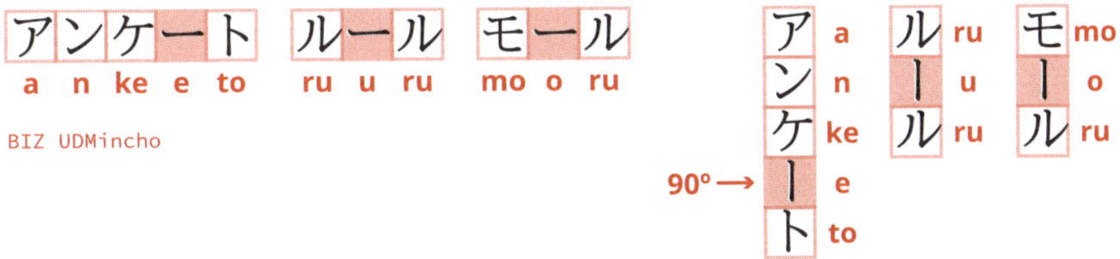

在漢文記載的一面記錄爲金章宗泰和六年

又名《泰和題名殘石》, 1206年農曆2月2日

Source Han Serif SC

NUMERALS: SHAPES

7. Vladimir Yefimov, "Civil Type," in Berry, *Language Culture Type*, 128.

8. Yefimov, "Civil Type," 129.

Cyrillic numerals used to be denoted by adding **titlos**, an extended diacritic symbol, to letters, but they made reading mathematical work cumbersome.[7] Hindu Arabic numerals were introduced during Peter's reform of the Cyrillic letters from 1708 to 1710.[8]

The use of Arabic numerals in Latin originated in India, where they were introduced to Europeans by Arabic speakers in the tenth century. These are known as Hindu Arabic numerals; numerals that resemble Arabic letters are called Eastern Arabic numerals.

HINDU ARABIC NUMERAL

0 1 2 3 4 5 6 7 8 9

EASTERN ARABIC NUMERAL

٠ ١ ٢ ٣ ٤ ٥ ٦ ٧ ٨ ٩

Adobe Garamond Pro, Nassim Arabic Pro

Many Arabic-speaking countries use both sets of numerals, which go from left to right despite text being written right to left.

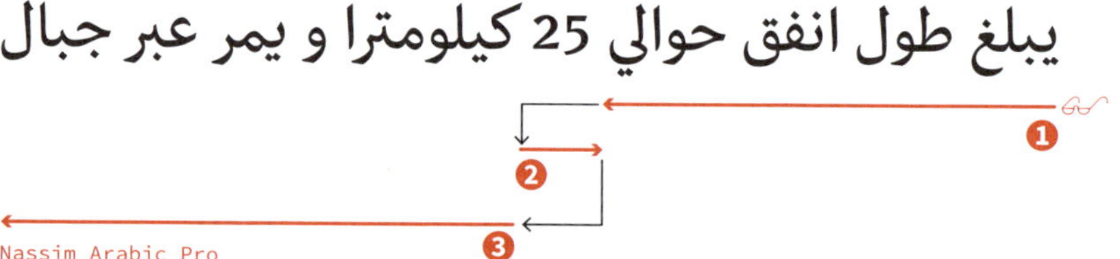

A string of numbers is read from left to right in sections.

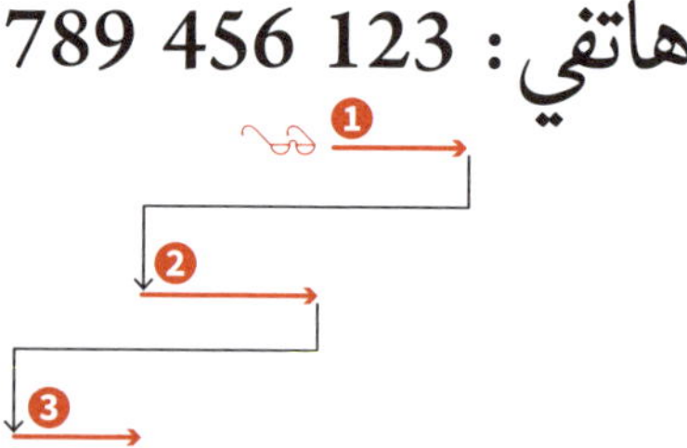

Eastern Arabic numerals are also read from left to right.

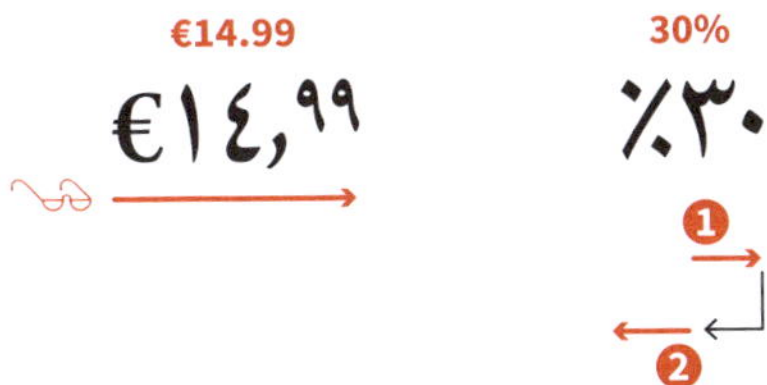

Adobe Naskh

exercise ○○○

Based on the information on the previous page, can you write down the
Hindu Arabic Numerals for the Eastern Arabic Numbers?

EASTERN ARABIC NUMERAL	١٧	٢٠	٩٤	٣٦	٨٥
HINDU ARABIC NUMERAL	____	____	____	____	____

In Persian, the numerals **4**, **5**, and **6** are different from their
Arabic forms. Iranian people are proficient in all three numeric
systems (Hindu Arabic, Arabic, and Persian). A complete Arabic
typeface usually includes all three sets of numerals, just as
Latin typefaces often include Greek and Cyrillic letters.

Georgia, Nassim Arabic Pro

In Latin languages, we also read other styles of numbers, such as
Roman numerals.

I II III IV V VI VII VIII IX X

i ii iii iv v vi vii viii ix x

Times New Roman

In some languages using Cyrillic, Roman numerals are used to
refer to centuries.

III століття
3rd century

XV век
15th century

XIX стагоддзе
19th century

Georgia

In India, diverse writing systems coexist. Gujarati script is used for the Gujarati and Kutchi languages. Bengali script is used for the Bengali language and is one of the official scripts of India. Bengali has historically been used for Sanskrit. Kannada is used for the Kannada language, which is spoken in Southern India. Like Arabic, these scripts also have their own numeral systems.

Adobe Devanagari, Nirmala UI

In other Asian countries, the diverse writing systems also preserve their own numerals. The shapes of them blend better with their native letters than Hindu Arabic numerals.

exercise ○○○

Based on the "1" in Thai, can you circle the "1" in
Lao, Khmer, Burmese, and Tibetan?

Forma DJR Thai Micro, Leelawadee UI, Khmer, Padauk, Uchen

Some numerals are more similar across these scripts than others.

Forma DJR Thai Micro, Leelawadee UI, Khmer, Padauk, Uchen

If the Thai speakers had invented calculators and spread them worldwide, our calculators might have been in Thai numerals.

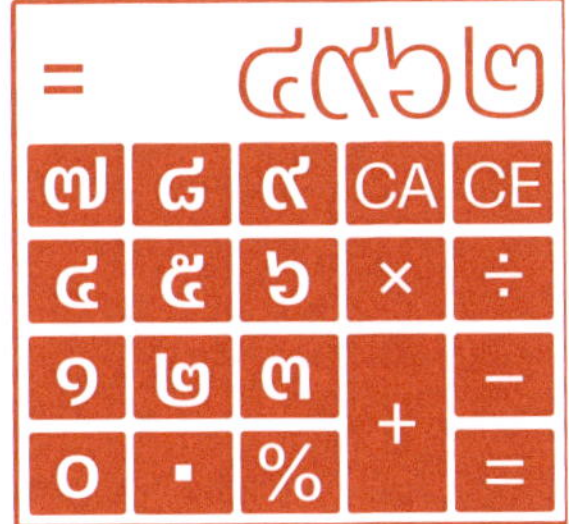

Forma DJR Thai

The popular card games might have used Thai numerals instead of Hindu Arabic numerals.

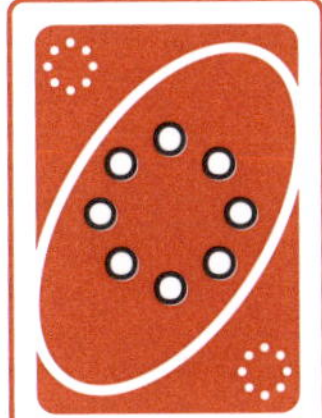

Forma DJR Thai

NUMERALS: CASING AND POSITION

Until the eighteenth century, it was common to see non-lining numerals, because they blend better with lowercase letters. Lining numerals may look like uppercase letters due to their unanimous height.

NON-LINING

0 1 2 3 4 5 6 7 8 9 digits

LINING

0 1 2 3 4 5 6 7 8 9 DIGITS

Constantia, Adobe Garamond Pro

In Arabic, because some letters also go below the baseline, some type designers choose to sink the numerals slightly. This makes numerals less obtrusively tall in a given line.

Nassim Arabic Pro

رقمي المفضل هو ٩٤

Adobe Naskh

رقمي المفضل هو ٩٤

Although Chinese is a monocased script—it does not have uppercase and lowercase characters—there are upper- and lowercase numerals. Today, Hindu Arabic numerals are used out of convenience and can easily be spotted on price tags and road signs. Lowercase Chinese numerals are used for days, months, and the naming of historical events. The lowercase **1** is represented by a single dash, **2** by two dashes, and **3** by three dashes. Uppercase Chinese numerals are used for amounts on checks and banknotes. The complexity of the uppercase makes it harder to alter the amounts. Zhu Yuanzhang, the Hongwu Emperor of Ming, mandated uppercase in official documents to prevent fraud in the fourteenth century.

0	1	2	3	4	5	6	7	8	9	10	20	100	1000
LOWERCASE													
〇	一	二	三	四	五	六	七	八	九	十	廿	百	千
UPPERCASE													
零	壹	贰	叁	肆	伍	陆	柒	捌	玖	拾	念	佰	仟

Source Han Sans CN

KERNING AND LIGATURE

A designer's skill in adjusting the space between two letters demonstrates their mastery of typography, especially in Latin typography. In connected scripts like Arabic and Traditional Mongolian, the amount of overlap also contributes to spacing. In scripts where letters are combined both vertically and horizontally, like in Thai, the vertical spacing also demands attention. In some situations, the combination of two letters yields a new shape entirely, like in Devanagari. These new shapes are essential components of space adjustment.

Each script's letter spacing depends on the method used to construct a word. Disconnected letters use kerning, the process of adjusting the space between letters. In addition to kerning, connected letters join with each other to form a new glyph. This process is like building a miniature house: when joining pieces of wood, the amount of glue (kerning) should be coherent; when using modeling clay, small chunks morph into a new block (glyph).

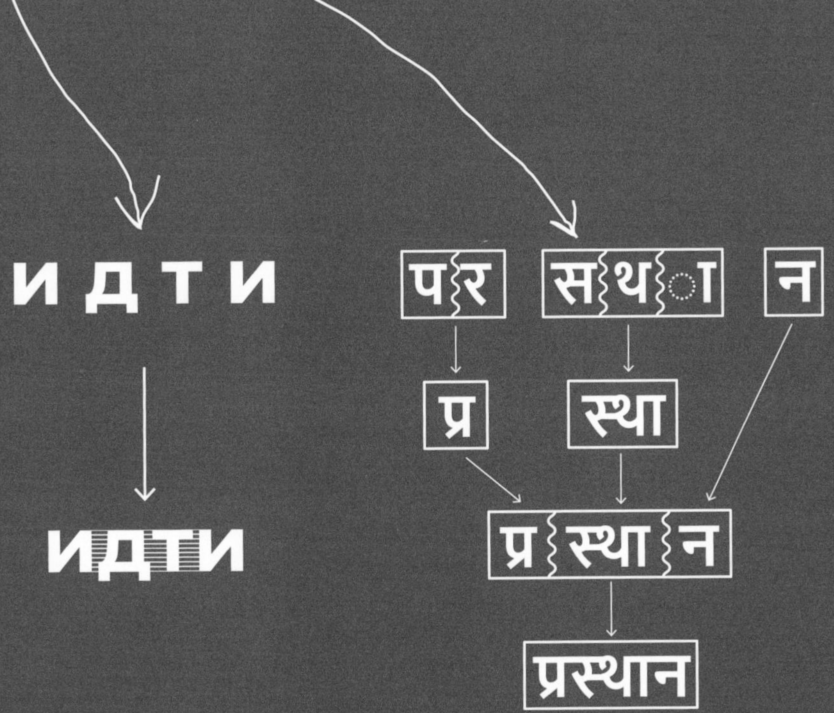

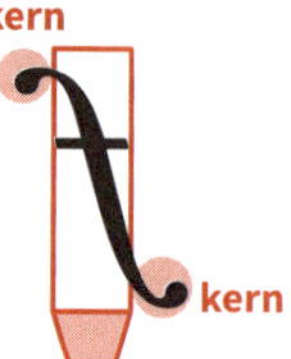

KERNING

In the days of setting metal type, a kern was a physical part of the letter that hung outside the body. Nowadays, **kerning** refers to the process of adjusting the space between two letters.

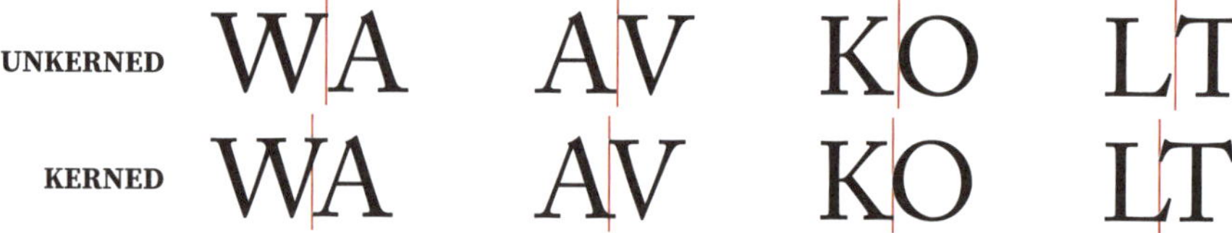

UNKERNED WA AV KO LT

KERNED WA AV KO LT

Adobe Caslon Pro

Different scripts require different kerning pairs. Below are a few kerning examples in Georgian.

KERNED ზაზუნა კაკაოს შემა

Calibri

The Arabic **r** and **w** usually need to be closer to the next letter to create an even texture.

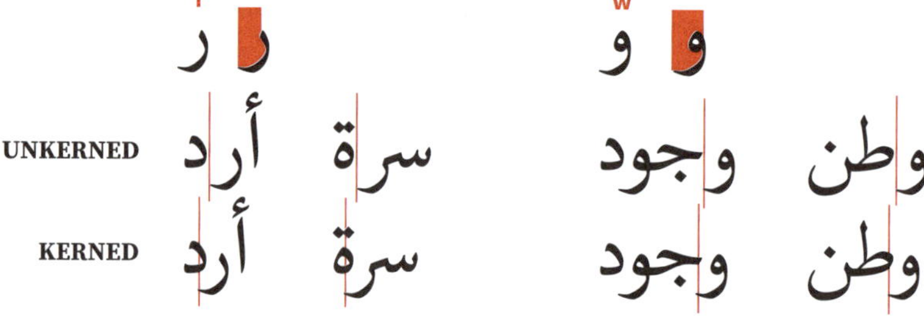

UNKERNED

KERNED

Adobe Naskh

Burmese has a vowel **a** that is taller than all the consonants, so to achieve a consistent texture, we slide it closer to the consonant that precedes it.

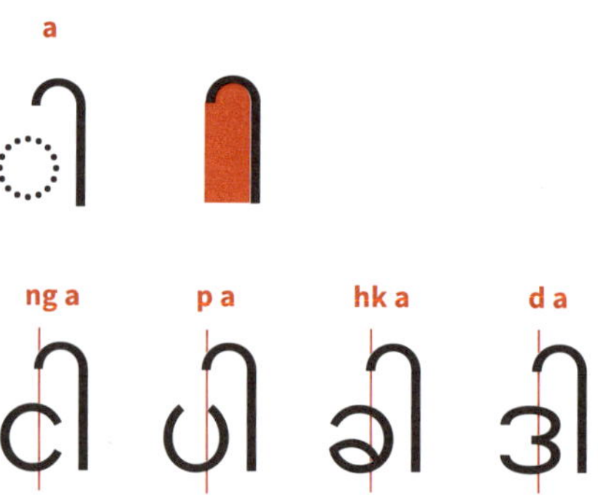

Myanmar Text

Ge'ez is the script used for the Amharic language spoken in Ethiopia. In Ge'ez, consonants start with the **ä** sound; the vowel changes through systematic distortion.

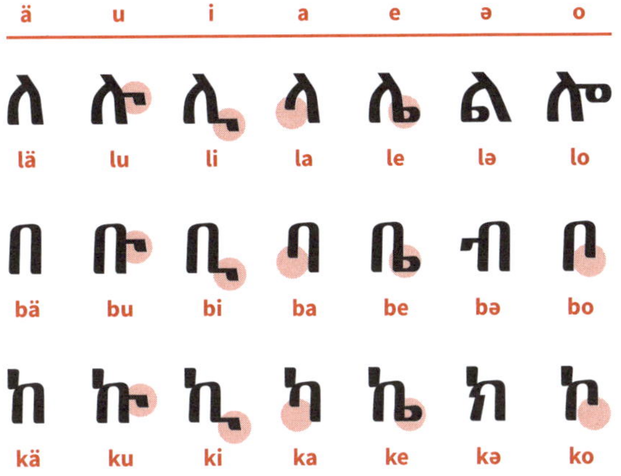

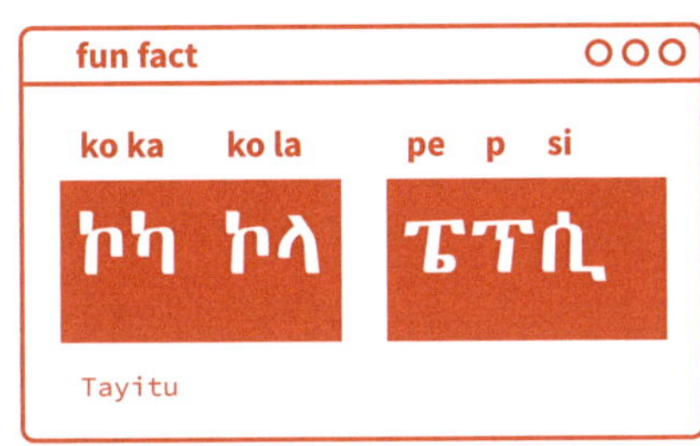

Tayitu

Due to the dynamic stroke variation in each letter, the space between each letter in Amharic varies more than it does in Latin.

Noto Sans Ethiopic

The design of the letter also affects spacing. In some Armenian typefaces, we find letters with extra extended feet at the descender level, which should not push the following letters.

Trebuchet MS, Arek Armenian

In Cyrillic, the shape of the **d** varies greatly across typefaces. Be sure to examine how curved the left side downstroke is before deciding on the kerning.

more curved

less curved

Baskerville Display PT, Montserrat

LIGATURE

In Latin typography, when two letters have elements clashing, a glyph with two letters combined is designed to avoid the awkward overlap; this is known as a ligature.

CLASHING

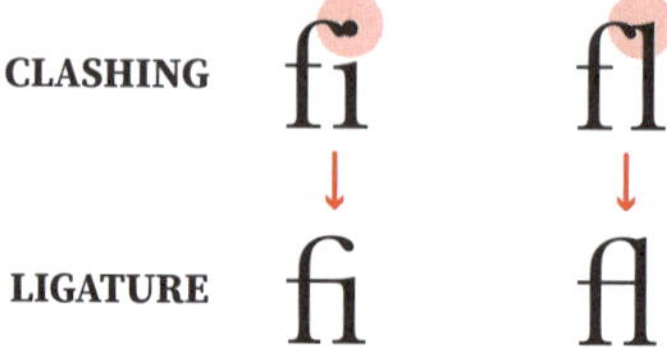

LIGATURE

Baskerville URW

Ligatures exist in both serif and sans-serif typefaces.

Adobe Caslon Pro   Adelle Sans

The ampersand (&) is also a ligature of the letters **e** and **t**, even though in many typefaces this may not be the most apparent.

Museo Sans   Catamaran   Baskerville URW

Italic, lowercase Greek also demonstrates how ligatures can eliminate clashing.

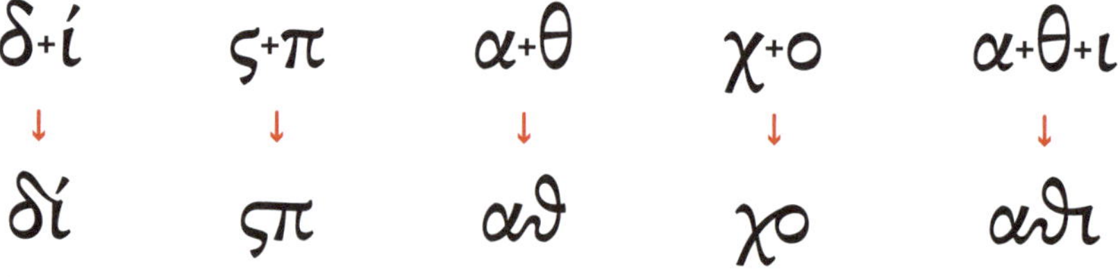

Change

Armenian typefaces also offer elegant ligatures.

TWO LETTERS

LIGATURE

LIGATURE

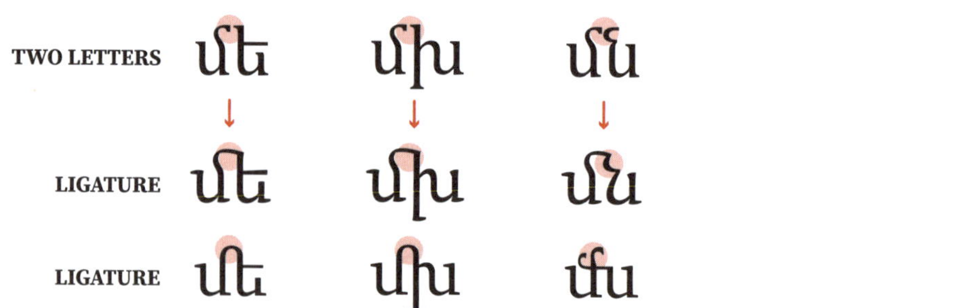

Cambria, Arek Armenian, Sylfaen

CONNECTED SCRIPTS

In Latin, ligatures are usually optional, but in Arabic, they are essential. Arabic letters that connect are identified by the number of teeth and dots present.

	final	middle	initial	
s	يمس	مسه	سمع	2 teeth, 0 dot
n	عمن	منص	نعم	1 tooth, 1 dot above the tooth
b	سبب	مبس	بمص	1 tooth, 1 dot below the tooth
t	بيت	يتص	تسع	1 tooth, 2 dots above the tooth
y	تري	ميه	يست	1 tooth, 2 dots below the tooth
m	بتم	يمر	متج	1 eye
ay	تسع	تعب	عنب	1 knot

Nassim Arabic Pro

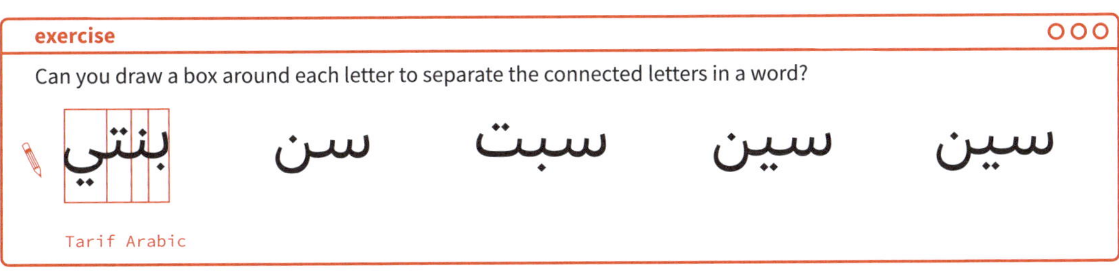

exercise ○○○

Can you draw a box around each letter to separate the connected letters in a word?

بنتي سن سبت سين سين

Tarif Arabic

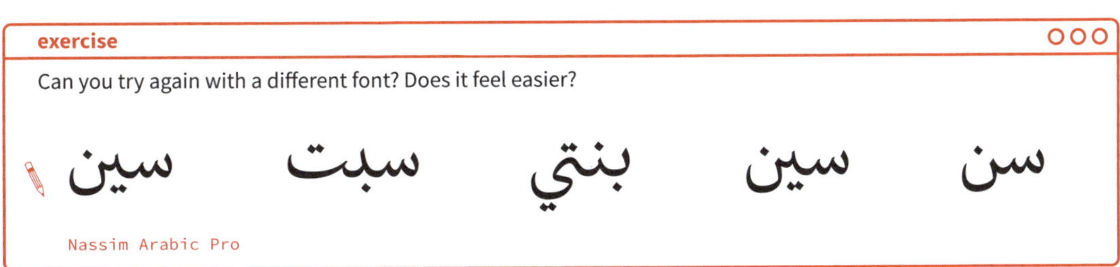

exercise ○○○

Can you try again with a different font? Does it feel easier?

سين بنتي سبت سين سن

Nassim Arabic Pro

Depending on the typeface, the shape of the teeth can be homogenous or greatly diversified in height and direction.

When Arabic letters have identical teeth, it is like Cyrillic handwriting and italic type with strokes slanting at the same angle. In some words, it can be hard to tell where a letter begins and ends.

HANDWRITING *пришил*

ITALIC *пришил*

Adobe Handwriting, Book Antiqua

Cordale Arbc, Tarif Arabic, Microsoft Sans Serif, Nassim Arabic Pro, Amiri

Arabic letter connections are more complicated than Cyrillic cursive linkage. It is mandatory, for example, to write la (l and a) as a ligature. The shape of this ligature can vary greatly across typefaces.

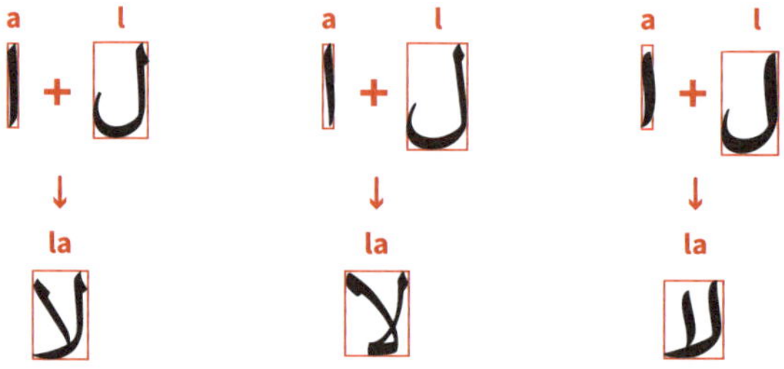

Adobe Arabic, Adobe Naskh, Layaan

Other two-letter combinations in Arabic may or may not be ligatures in a given font family.

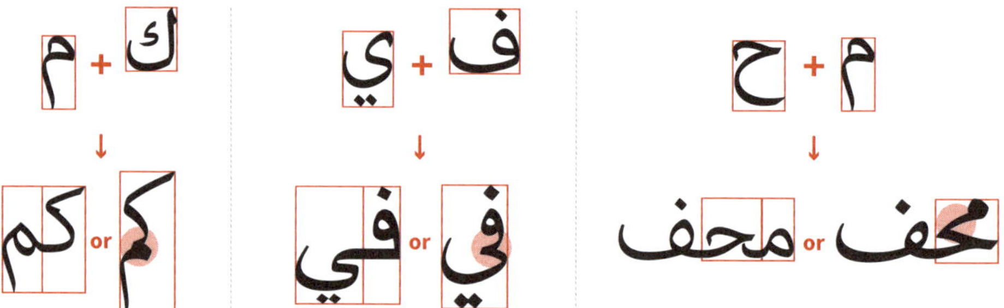

Adobe Arabic, Adobe Naskh, Arial

1. Onur F. Yazıcıgil, *Pergamon: A Greek Script Typeface Design* (YEM Yayınları, 2023), 27.

In the ligatures on the previous page, Arabic letters are stacked vertically. This typesetting is foreign to modern Latin script readers. Nevertheless, in Pergamon (modern-day Turkey) 2,200 years ago, Greek stone carvers employed stacking to be able to fit all necessary letters in a line on a monument.[1] Below is not a replica of a Greek inscription, but an example that demonstrates letter positioning.

MONUMENT

Like the Pergamon stone inscription, the number and the shapes of the ligatures affect the length of a sentence in Arabic.

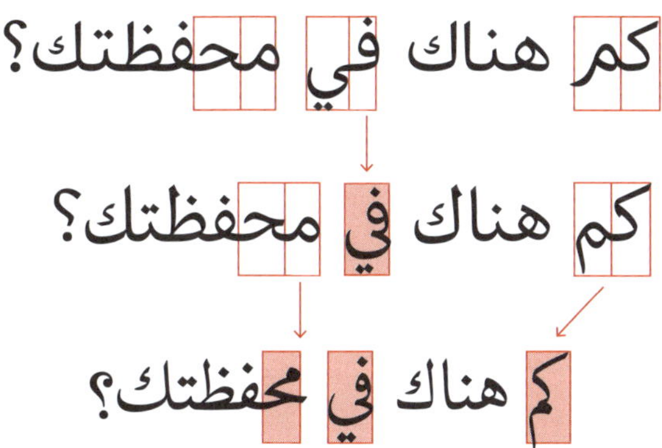

Athelas ARA var, Nassim Arabic Pro, Adobe Naskh

2. Titus Nemeth, ed., *Arabic Typography: History and Practice* (Niggli, 2023), 322.

An Arabic **b** at the beginning of a word can take at least seven forms depending on the letters that follow it.[2]

Adobe Naskh

An **m** in the middle or at the end of a word can also vary according to the letters that connect to it.

Adobe Naskh

CONJUNCTS

Devanagari consonantal conjuncts resemble ligatures: vowels are combined with consonants at different sides. In the illustration below, the short **i** is added to the left of the consonant, the long **ii** to the right, **e** on the top, and **u** at the bottom. All these combinations are designed as new glyphs.

Noto Serif Devanagari

Like Devanagari, vowels in Thai may connect to consonants in different directions. When the same vowel joins different consonants, it moves positions horizontally depending on the consonant's ascender.

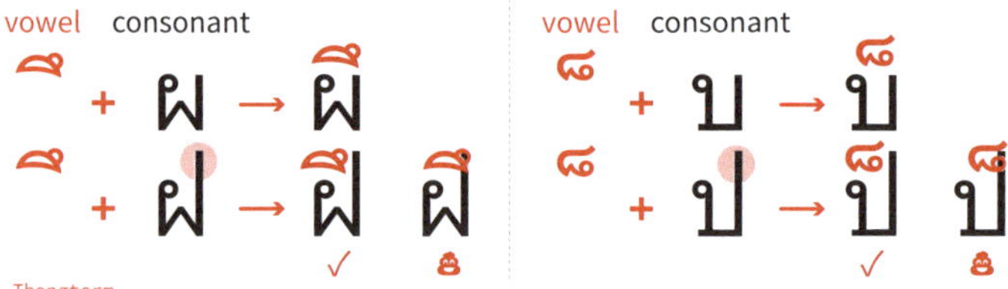

Thongterm

Without a vowel or tone mark, a tall Thai letter moves closer to the preceding letter.

Fahkwang

In Burmese, when **ha** is combined with **wa**, the little **h** is rotated ninety degrees and connected to the **wa**. Some typefaces stylistically rotate it forty-five degrees, as shown in the second example below.

A Burmese letter's shape may also change according to the letter that follows it. Below is an example of how two consonants change their bottom designs as new letters are attached to them.

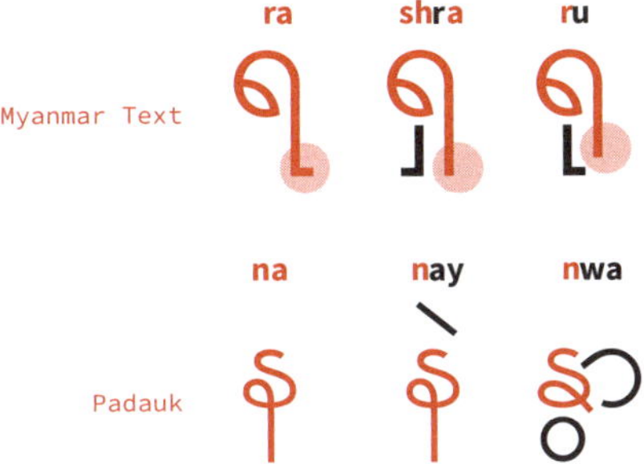

There are two medial diacritics with the **ya** sound. One looks like a saxophone; the other, like a tuba that wraps around the consonant. Both change lengths depending on which letter they are combined with.

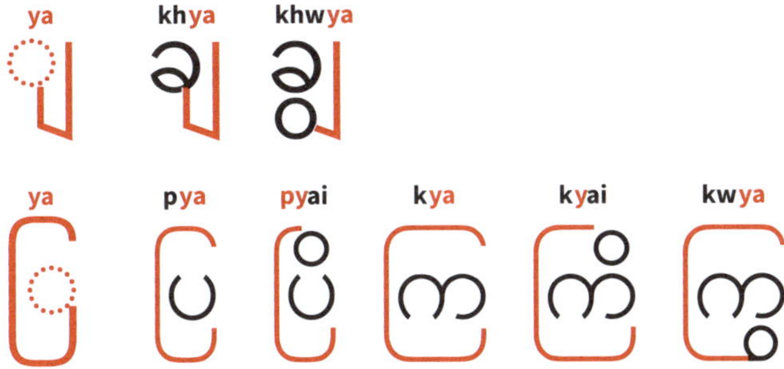

Burmese vowels can also take up more space horizontally and vertically; they can also change their form when combined with different letters. During type design, this requires a new glyph to be designed.

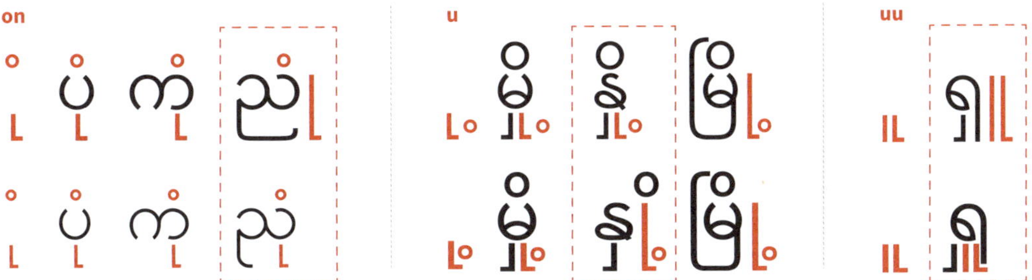

* The boxed ones have different positions for the vowels in different fonts.

Myanmar Text, Padauk, Noto Sans Myanmar

The small circle below consonants in Burmese can change its horizontal position according to the consonant and vowel it is combined with.

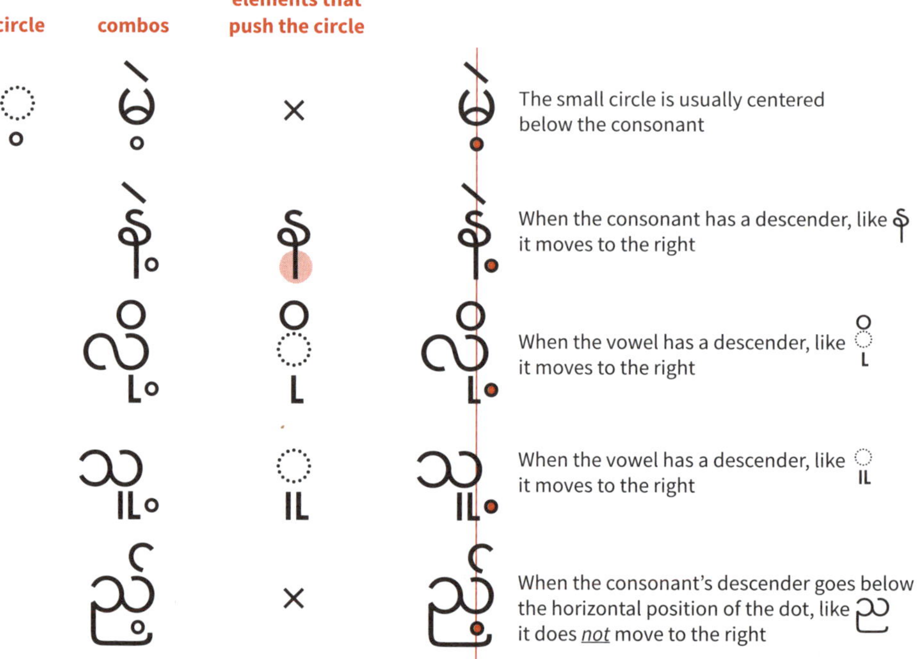

circle   **combos**   **elements that push the circle**

The small circle is usually centered below the consonant

When the consonant has a descender, like it moves to the right

When the vowel has a descender, like it moves to the right

When the vowel has a descender, like it moves to the right

When the consonant's descender goes below the horizontal position of the dot, like it does *not* move to the right

Myanmar Text

Like the tiny circle in Burmese, Thai tone marks are placed above vowels and consonants. Its position may also change depending on the height and width of the next letter. When the tone mark meets a letter that extends to the left, it may move horizontally; this varies from font to font. Below is an example of how a tone mark moves to the left to avoid clashing into a tall vowel.

Thongterm   Leelawadee

This is akin to the kerning pair **To** in Latin. To avoid a big gap, the **o** usually slides closer to the **T**. When there are diacritic marks above the **o**, the diacritic mark can clash with the **T**. Hence, the wider space between **T** and **ö**.

CLOSE / CLOSER

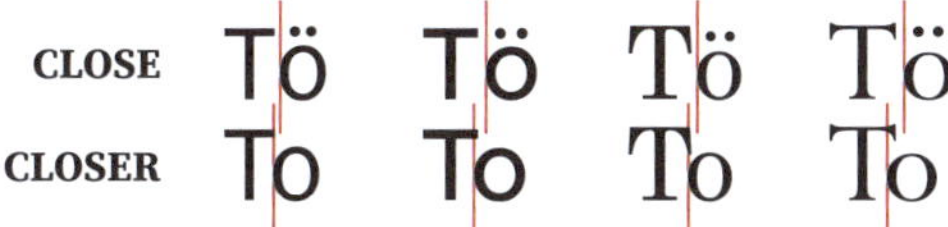

Franklin Gothic Book, Proxima Nova, Century, Perpetua

In Thai, vertical spacing also matters. In addition to appropriate horizontal spacing, there should be ample vertical space between the tone mark, vowel, and consonant.

GOOD SPACING

tone / vowel / consonant

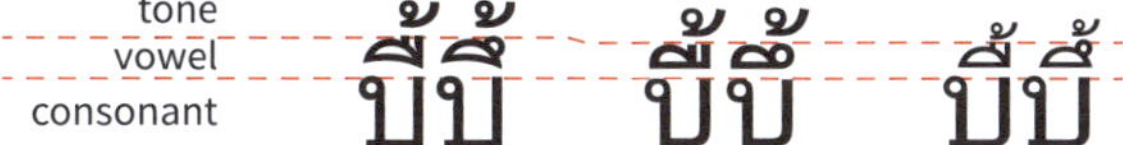

Thongterm, Noto Looped Thai, Microsoft Sans Serif

When there is not enough space (or no space at all), the vertical clashing of tone marks and vowels can cause confusion.

NO SPACING (EXAGGERATED)

tone / vowel

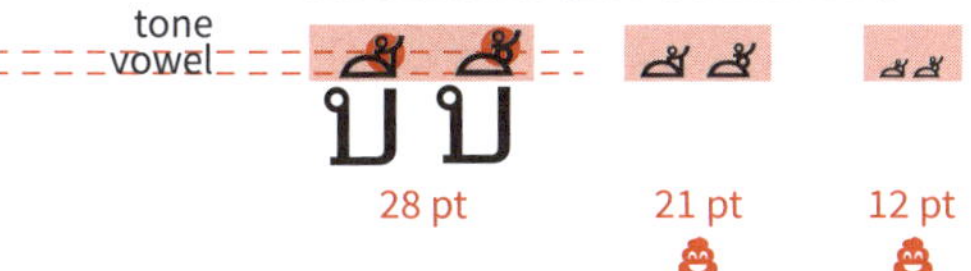

28 pt   21 pt   12 pt

In Latin, diacritical marks are rarely misplaced.

💩 **Kalsarıkännıt**
√ **Kalsarikännit**

💩 **Le perè aime les foretŝ interéssants**
√ **Le père aime les forêts intéressants**

Source Sans Variable

In Southeast Asian languages, however, it is common to see misplaced diacritics by nonnative designers. In Thai, vowels and tone marks can often be misaligned.

💩 ฉันไม่รู้สึกดี

√ ฉันไม่รู้สึกดี

Noto Looped Thai

In Khmer, vowels can be misplaced (as in 1 below), and the sub-consonant may be a plus sign and their consonant form (2).

Leelawadee UI

In Devanagari, conjuncts can be separated as their original consonants with a long dot (1); vowels can be misplaced like in Thai (2); and nasal sound dots can be crushed (3).

Nirmala UI

A well-developed program allows "Middle Eastern and South Asian Composers" to display the text in the correct ligature. However, users must select this option manually because South Asian languages are not displayed correctly by default.

The plus sign in Khmer and the dot in Devanagari were used to present half consonants. In metal type, this allows conjuncts to be set linearly, printing speed to be faster, and costs to be reduced. In the digital age, this should be avoided.

LINEARIZATION

CONJUNCT

Leelawadee UI, Nirmala UI

In Devanagari and Khmer, linearization was a temporary solution in the era of moveable type. When the temporary compromised solution was execcuted in printing, people wrote the correct conjuncts by hand without linearization. In the 1970s, the Malayalam script in India was simplified and linearized to sustain ongoing demands for printing. Unlike Devanagari and Khmer, this script reform changed people's writing habits. The following chapter will address more of this history.

08 ALTERNATE GLYPHS AND STRETCHING

Some scripts treat their letters as a stretchy pie dough, others, as crispy, baked crust. Stretching in Latin is rare because Latin letters do not connect like those in Arabic or Traditional Mongolian; they also do not stack inside square boxes like those of Korean Hangeul or Chinese.

Stretching is just one method of generating alternate glyphs, some scripts can also change the angles and lengths of specific strokes. In most languages, including English, alternates are rare; however, they do exist as sets of scripts in languages like Japanese and Georgian. This chapter redefines what is considered "acceptable" in modern-day typography and what should be addressed when transcending Western and non-Western divides in graphic design.

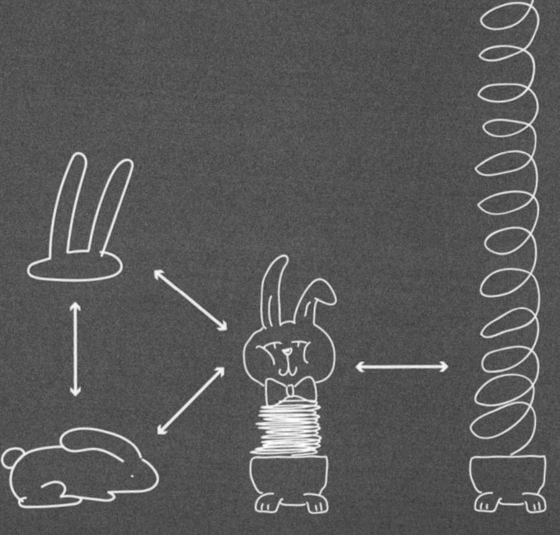

ALTERNATES

1. Erik Spiekermann, *Stop Stealing Sheep & Find Out How Type Works* (The Other Collection, 2022), 117.

Latin and Greek typefaces sometimes provide an alternative look for letters to diversify the aesthetics.[1]

Adobe Garamond   Source Sans

Q Q   α α   β B   φ φ   θ ϑ

Some Armenian typefaces also offer alternates.

Arek Armenian   զ զ   լ Լ   ղ ղ   վ վ

In Georgian, some alternates look less similar, especially the letter **j**.

ts'   **t'**   **j**

OmnesGeorgian   წ წ   თ თ   ჯ ჯ

Cyrillic is used in many languages including Russian, Ukrainian, Bulgarian, and Serbian. Most of the letters are identical across these languages, although some do have variations. The Bulgarian alphabet, for example, uses shapes more like handwriting than in Ukrainian and Russian.

UKRAINIAN/ RUSSIAN   Д   Л   В   Г   Д   И   Т   Ж

BULGARIAN   Д   Л   В   Г   Д   И   Т   Ж

Novel Sans Cy

2. David Březina, "Elements of Multi-Script Typography: Codes, Keys, and Word Shapes," *Design Regression*, March 21, 2022, https://designregression.com/essay/elements-of-multi-script-typography-chapter-2.

An extended Cyrillic typeface should include all these alternates as well as the letters that only exist in Serbian, just like a Latin typeface that includes diacritics, so it can be used for multiple languages that employ Latin script. It is up to the designer to decide which glyphs show up by default, but if the typeface is primarily used in Ukraine, the first row above should be the default.[2]

SERBIAN   Љ љ   Њ њ   Ћ ћ   Ђ ђ   Џ џ

Novel Sans Cy

DIFFERENT LETTERS

Some Georgian letters look very similar to one another.

Noto Serif Georgian, Loos Compressed

Some Armenian letters, like Gerogian, share close similarities. These groups of look-alike letters in Armenian and Georgian should not be confused with the alternates.

Arek Armenian

While Georgian and Armenian only have a few groups of letters like those shown above, Burmese is full of similar letters.

Padauk

Many consonants differ only slightly in the counters' closures and openings.

Padauk

In Devanagari, a few letters differ only by the closures of their counters (the space that is entirely or partially closed by forms inside a letter): full closures produce one letter, while partial closures generate another.

ध घ   भ म   थ श

Aktiv Grotesk Ex

REGIONAL VARIATION

Punjabi (also Panjabi) is spoken in the Punjab regions of Pakistan and India; two distinct scripts are used in each country. In Pakistan, Shahmukhi (developed from the Perso-Arabic alphabet) is used, while in India, the preferred script is Gurmukhi.

Shahmukhi

PAKISTANI

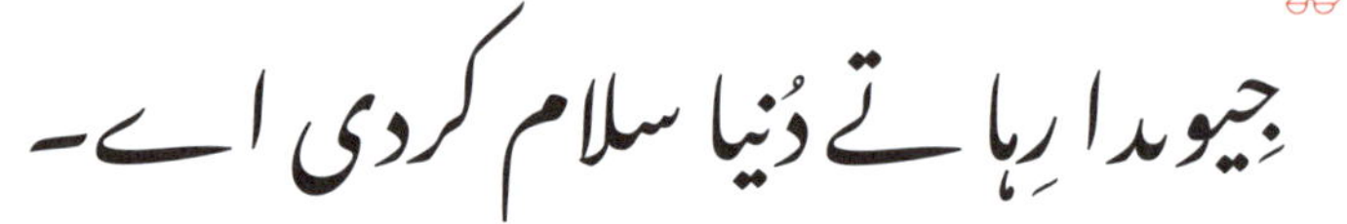

Gurmukhi

INDIAN

ਜਿਉਂਦਾ ਰਿਹਾ ਤੇ ਦੁਨੀਆ ਸਲਾਮ ਕਰਦੀ ਹੈ।

Noto Nastaliq Urdu, Nirmala UI

Mongolian is spoken both in Inner Mongolia (in China) and in Mongolia. In Mongolia, Mongolian is usually horizontally written in Cyrillic, but in China the traditional, vertical Mongolian script is exclusively used.

Mongolian

MONGOLIA

Би чамд хайртай.

Traditional Mongolian

INNER MONGOLIA

Droid Serif, Noto Sans Mongolian

In different parts of Asia, Chinese characters are standardized differently, but people can still easily read other regions' characters.

HONG KONG · SOUTH KOREA · TAIWAN · JAPAN · MAINLAND CHINA

Adobe Song Std L, Adobe Ming Std L, Source Han Serif K, Source Han Serif, Source Han Serif TC

You can think of this like the word **photograph** still being recognized if typed as **photo** being or **foto**. Take Simplified Chinese characters and Japanese kanji, for example. The same character can have one stroke more or less than its counterpart in another country, but the contour and identifiable particles remain the same and therefore recognizable to readers of both languages. In the image below, the characters in the first group have one more stroke in Japanese than in Chinese; in the second group, Chinese has the additional stroke.

JAPANESE KANJI · SIMPLIFIED CHINESE

Source Han Serif, NSimSun

In the examples below, the group on the left has one stroke that extends further in Chinese than in Japanese; in the group of characters on the right, Japanese has the extended strokes.

JAPANESE KANJI · SIMPLIFIED CHINESE

Source Han Serif, NSimSun

The first character shown below has a tiny square in the right corner of the frame in the Japanese. In the Chinese version, the square is attached to the left side. The second character has a longer top bar in Japanese; in Chinese, the bottom bar is longer.

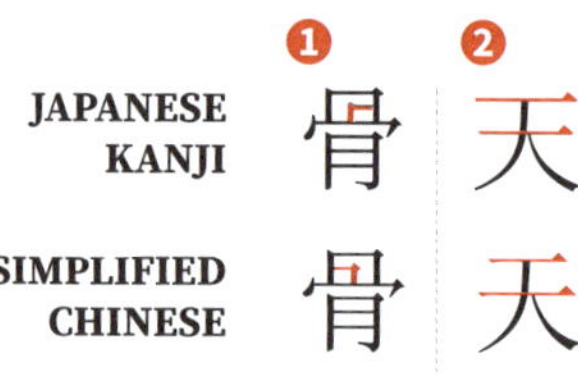

JAPANESE KANJI

SIMPLIFIED CHINESE

Source Han Serif, NSimSun

It usually takes ten years for a Chinese person to become literate—a bad time investment, especially compared to Spanish, for instance, with just twenty-seven letters that can be learned within a day. By the 1920s, 90 percent of the population in China was illiterate, and this posed the greatest threat in combating colonization.[3] In 1922, Qian Xuantong—a Chinese linguist, writer, professor of literature at National Peking University—proclaimed that the vast number of strokes in Chinese characters was a waste of citizens' brain power; he proposed that reducing the number of strokes would achieve greater information efficiency.[4]

3. Ulug Kuzuoglu, *Codes of Modernity: Chinese Scripts in the Global Information Age* (Columbia University Press, 2024), 89.

4. Kuzuoglu, *Codes of Modernity*, 118.

Initially, reformers called for **suzi** (Simplified Chinese characters then in circulation by common people), which was already widespread in novels, plays, letters, medical prescriptions, dictionaries, and account books.[5] Over the past two millennia, people had deliberately omitted and combined strokes to speed up writing in nonstandardized fashions that provided immense data for research toward script reform. All styles of Chinese calligraphy also offered formulas for this simplification project, which continued after the establishment of the People's Republic of China in 1949. In contrast to alphabetization, character simplification "domesticated global forces and changed from within."[6]

5. Kuzuoglu, *Codes of Modernity*, 119.

6. Kuzuoglu, *Codes of Modernity*, 151.

TRADITIONAL

SIMPLIFIED

Source Han Sans CN

In the traditional character for **bug**, three identical particles for **bug** were combined. In the simplified character, only one "bug" is left. In the character for **love**, the particle (a building block of a character) for **heart** was simplified to a dash and added to the bottom of the particle meaning **friend**.

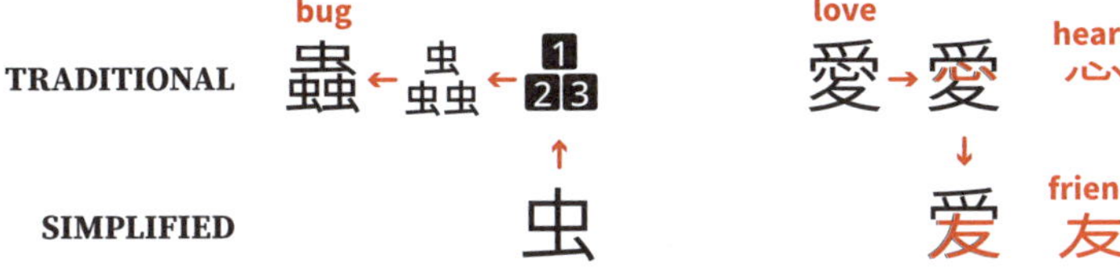

People in Taiwan continue to use Traditional Chinese characters today, but Singapore and Malaysia have adopted Simplified Chinese characters from mainland China. Aside from geopolitical tensions that influence which set of characters is used, there are benefits to both Traditional and Simplified Chinese. Simplified Chinese makes it easier to write fast, but to those accustomed to Traditional Chinese, some characters may appear off-balance.

SIMPLIFIED 

In the 1970s, the government in mainland China initiated another round of simplification. This second project resulted in too many groups of similar characters. Unlike the first round, which was based on existing written habits—suzi—this attempt did not connect with natural tendencies to reduce strokes. Consequently, instead of memorizing the new simplification methodology, people began inventing their own simplified versions. By the time teachers started teaching this new simplification, illiteracy had reduced significantly. Therefore, it was not as successful or necessary as the first round and was abandoned in the 1980s.

Pictographic Chinese characters enabled learners to connect intuitive drawing to systematic writing. However, the number of commonly-used characters was massive—it took half an hour to send a telegram in Morse code in Chinese, as opposed to two minutes in English, leaving China significantly behind in sharing information during the First Sino-Japanese war in 1894.[7]

7. Jing Tsu, *Kingdom of Characters: The Language Revolution that Made China Modern* (Riverhead books, 2023), 173.

Before Latin-based Pinyin, Arabic letters and diacritic marks were used to transcribe Mandarin sounds, known as **Xiao'erjin**, which has been dated as early as 1313.[8] It did not gain popularity and thus left little evidence for modern researchers to investigate.

8. Kuzuoglu, *Codes of Modernity*, 171.

Since the early twentieth century, scholars have been proposing that characters be abandoned completely. Some even supported using Esperanto—the most successful artificial international language—over of Chinese to overcome mass illiteracy.[9] In 1958, Zhou Youguang—a Chinese economist, linguist, and sinologist—led the invention of Pinyin, a system that used the Latin alphabet to Romanize the sound of Chinese character.[10]

9. Kuzuoglu, *Codes of Modernity*, 69.

10. Kuzuoglu, *Codes of Modernity*, 227.

Pinyin was disseminated as a replacement for Chinese characters and the new—and only writing system—in China. But in 1986, the State Council declared that it would not replace Chinese characters, thereby ending the century-long endeavor to Latinize Chinese.[11] Today, first graders in mainland China study Pinyin before moving on to Chinese characters. Pinyin is also a popular typing method on digital devices. Below is an example sentence written in both Pinyin and Chinese characters.

11. Kuzuoglu, *Codes of Modernity*, 23.

PINYIN   **Lái shēng zuò yī zhī tè lì dú xíng de zhū**

CHARACTERS   # 来生做一只特立独行的猪

Source Han Sans CN

Defeating all political and technological barriers, Chinese characters are still in use to this day. The computerized laser photocomposition system, invented by Wang Xuan in the 1980s, eventually closed the gap between digitized Latin and Chinese. The convoluted revision of Chinese scripts in the twentieth century, however, is a symbol of resilience and perseverance.

The standardization of strokes is only relevant to Chinese speakers, but the experiment of simplification can occur in any language. This history is an example of recognizing when to push boundaries and when to hold back.

HISTORICAL VARIATION

12. Robert Bringhusrt, "Voices, Languages and Scripts," in *Language Culture Type: International Type Design in the Age of Unicode*, ed. John Berry (AtypI Graphics, 2002), 8.

The script chosen for a language can be political. Turkish was written in Arabic script from the 1100s to 1928, when the Turkish government ordered Latin script to be used.[12] Since 1929, Turkish has been written in Latin.

900–1928   لِسانِ عُثمانی

↓

1929–CURRENT   Türkçe

Source Han Serif SC, Change

13. Sébastien Morlighem, "Modern Handwriting: Introduction Series 4 Cyrillic and Greek Handwriting," *Typoteque*, November 7, 2023, https://www.typotheque.com/articles/modern-handwriting-a-historical-survey-5.

14. Kuzuoglu, *Codes of Modernity*, 187.

In 1922, the Soviet Union attempted to replace Cyrillic and Arabic with Latin, believing that Latin had helped in the global spread of socialism. This change was, contrary to the Latinization in Turkish, not a long-lasting change.[13] In 1938, unable to meet the demand for Latin teachers, new typewriters, and linotype machines, Stalin ordered the Re-Cyrillization of all national scripts, abruptly terminating the Latinization process.[14]

1917–1922   УДАЛЬЦОВА улица

1922–1938   UDAL'TSOVA street

1938–CURRENT   УДАЛЬЦОВА улица

Droid Serif

In the early twentieth century, Vietnam, then under French colonization, switched its script from **Chữ Nôm** (Chinese characters) to Latin. In modern Vietnam, Chữ Nôm occasionally appears on signages, but Vietnamese people do not actively study it. Like the script change in Turkish, it created a dramatic typographic shift in their culture.

斷　腸　新　聲　傳　翹

↓　↓　↓　↓　↓　↓

Đoạn　Trường　Tân　Thanh　Truyện　Kiều

Source Han Serif SC, Change

15. Karthik Malli, "Malayalam Writing Script, History, Evolution and Changes in Traditional and Simplified Orthography," *Typoteque*, June 25, 2023, https://www.typotheque.com/research/malayalam-scripting-tradition-and-modernity.

The script choice for a language can also be technical. Malayalam, spoken in the Indian state of Kerala, has more than a thousand individual characters. In 1971, its script was reformed to create a Simplified Malayalam for printing, while the Traditional Malayalam was maintained for handwriting but people started to write in the Simplified script out of convenience.[15]

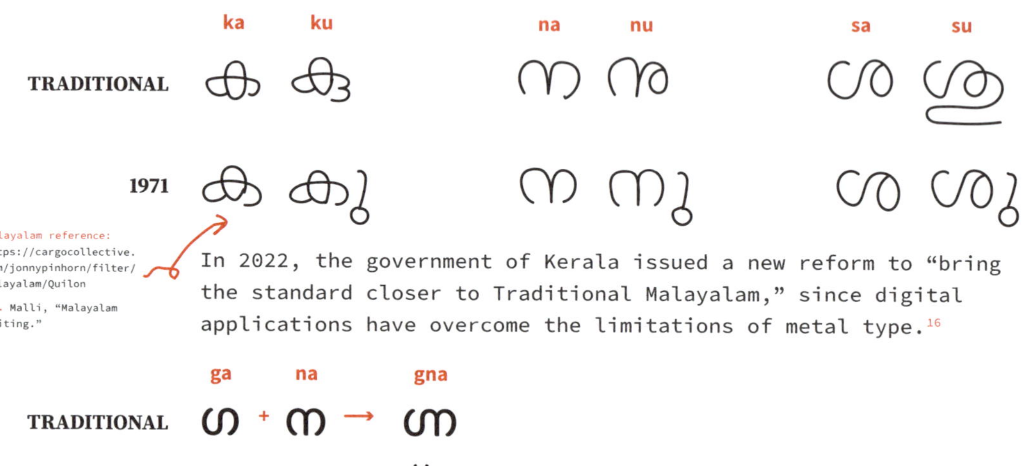

Malayalam reference: https://cargocollective.com/jonnypinhorn/filter/malayalam/Quilon

16. Malli, "Malayalam Writing."

In 2022, the government of Kerala issued a new reform to "bring the standard closer to Traditional Malayalam," since digital applications have overcome the limitations of metal type.[16]

Baloo Chettan 2

In other languages, the usage of a script evolved more naturally. Letters changed slowly over time. In Korean Hangeul, a dot used to be a letter, but is no longer used. This old shape is occasionally used in modern logo design. The triangle letter has also been replaced in standardized writing but can be found in display types.

The triangle letter has also been replaced in standardized writing but can be found in display type. It is a Middle Korean letter, not used in modern Korean, which produces a sound similar to "z."

Middle Korean reference: https://en.namu.wiki/w/%E3%85%BF

Source Han Sans KR

Middle Korean reference: https://en.namu.wiki/w/%E3%85%BF

These old letters can be found in modern display types and logo designs.

Source Han Sans KR

The triangle shapes can also be found in display types that highlight the geometric nature of Hangeul.

ㅅ ㅈ
오징어 게임은 전 세계적으로 큰 인기를 끌며 한국 드라마의 위상을 높였습니다.

▲ ㅈ
오징어 게임은 전 세계적으로 큰 인기를 끌며 한국 드라마의 위상을 높였습니다.

210 OmniGothic, 1HOONEorinigyosilOTF Regular

In Japanese language, kanji appeared before hiragana and katakana. In the Heian period (beginning in the 700s), only high-class women were taught to read and write hiragana; ordinary people could not read or write. For this reason, hiragana is also called **onade** (women's writing). Now, everyone can learn how to write in any script, so there is no longer gender and class distinctions among the three Japanese systems. Many words can be written in kanji, hiragana, or katakana.

	bear	**lie**	**vain**	**apple**	**sloth**
KANJI	熊	嘘	駄目	林檎	怠け者
HIRAGANA	くま	うそ	だめ	りんご	なまけもの
KATAKANA	クマ	ウソ	ダメ	リンゴ	ナマケモノ

Heisei Maru Gothic Std

Visually—and in terms of typographic choice—kanji seems complicated; hiragana, round and fluid; and katakana, which consists of more straight lines, more minimal. Linguistically, these three scripts also render a different atmosphere. Hiragana, used as grammatical particles, has a certain Japanese spirit; katakana, which is used for foreign words and onomatopoeia, feels more "Western;" and Kanji, the Chinese characters, has a sense of sophistication.

When typing, the input method editor will show all these options. Below are all the options to type the word **bear** in Japanese: 1) in hiragana, 2) in katakana, and 3) in kanji.

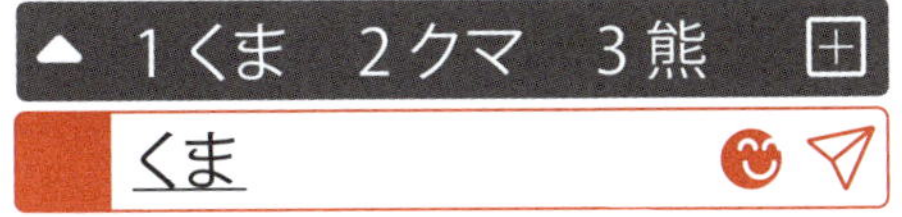

Kozuka Gothic Pr6N R

Beyond typography experimentation, switching from kana to kanji can be an educational choice. Contemporary first graders' books are typically printed in kana with a few basic kanji characters. As students progress through the school system, they are taught more and more kanji characters in their textbooks. Below is the same sentence in kana only and then in kana and kanji. Each has a different typography color (i.e., the density of a block of text).

1ST GRADE カーソンはさくひんにかいようどうぶつがくしゃならではのちしきをもりこみ、ストーリーにしんじつみをあえたのです。

6TH GRADE カーソンは作品に海洋動物学者ならではの知識を盛り込み、ストーリーに真実味を与えたのです。

BIZ UDPMincho

17. Peter Bilak, Sopio Kincurašvili, and Nino Kakiašvili, *New Georgian Type* (Typotheque, 2023), 8.

18. Christopher Calderhead and Holly Cohen, *The World Encyclopedia of Calligraphy. The Ultimate Compendium on the Art of Fine Writing: History, Craft, Technique* (Sterling, 2018), 264.

There are also three scripts in Georgian. Asomtavruli—or Mrgvlovani (rounded)—dates to the fifth century. Nuskhuri dates to the ninth century, but most inscriptions were still written in Asomtavruli until the 18th century.[17] Mkhedruli first appeared in the tenth century and had thirty-eight letters; the modern Mkhedruli alphabet only has thirty-three letters. Most Georgian typefaces focus on the Mkhedruli letters. A few typefaces include the letters of all three scripts. Asomtavruli, the earliest style, can still be found today in titles.[18] The adoption of one has not led to the death of others.

Asomtavruli

Nuskhuri

Mkhedruli

400 AD   900 AD   1800 AD

Sylfaen

The examples above shows that the adoption of one script does not always lead to the demise of another. In the example of Japanese and Georgian, the development of scripts accumulates and contributes to the typography diversity in the language.

STRETCHING

In a Latin-based type class, professors may denounce "stretching," because stretching letterforms disproportionally can create disturbing results. If done with care, however, stretching looks exciting.

Eurostile

Stretching can also be used effectively in other scripts. In Hebrew, for example, the bars in some letters can be stretched without misshaping the letter's anatomy.[19] This practice is common in religious texts for both decoration and justifying purposes.

19. Calderhead and Cohen, *World Encyclopedia of Calligraphy*, 91.

Narkissim

Below is an example of this kind of stretching in Hebrew words.

Narkissim

In Arabic, more common than in Hebrew, a typeface often has an elongated version of a letter as an alternate character.

Adobe Naskh

In Traditional Mongolian, the vertical length of a letter is also stretchy. The calligraphy typeface is notably characterized by its longer stroke at the end of a word. In some Mongolian textbooks for nonnative learners, authors include the two styles of typefaces side by side so readers can learn both.

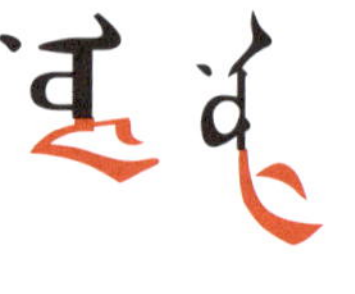

Mongolian White, Mongolian Writing

Stretched strokes are not only beautiful; they can also be useful in adjusting the length of a line of text. In English, the length of a line of text is adjusted by changing the number of letters in a line and the space between letters. In Arabic, line length can be changed by stretching letters or stretching the connections between two letters.

Nassim Arabic Pro, Bahnschrift

In Traditional Mongolian, the connection between letters can be stretched vertically, just like Arabic's horizontal stretching.

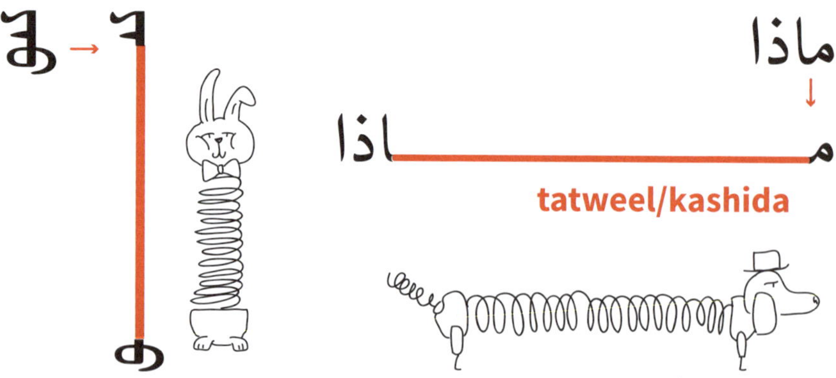

Mongolian White, Adobe Naskh

20. "29LT Okaso," *29LT*, accessed December 20, 2024, https://www.29lt.com/product/29lt-okaso.

As of 2024, some biscriptual typefaces tend to have the non-Latin characters matching the characteristics of their Latin counterparts. With more discussion and education on non-Latin scripts, a shift away from this Latin-centric approach is happening, as demonstrated in the typefaces designed by 29Letters Type Foundry S.L., a Madrid-based type company dedicated to creating multiscript typefaces. Their 29LT Okaso exemplifies this defiance by guiding the Latin letterforms according to standard Arabic ones. Notably, it includes stretched Latin letters that pair especially well with Arabic text.[20]

The stretching in CJK (Chinese, Japanese, and Korean) applies to the components inside the character's box. In Korean Hangeul, a letter's height and width vary according to the other letters that accompany it. Each letter shows its elasticity within the square composition.

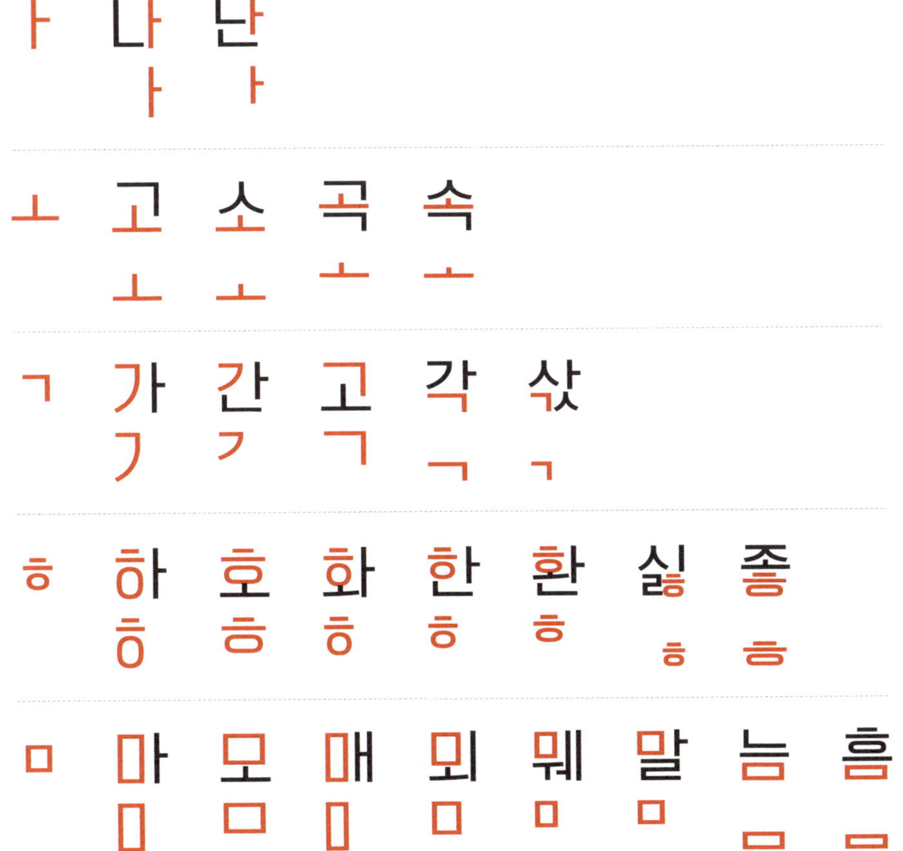

210 OmniGothic

The particles in Chinese share a similar elasticity.

干 平 刊 罕
干 干 干

女 好 委 嫩 赢
女 女 女 女

弓 弔 引 弛 弩 弱 彀
弓 弓 弓 弓 弓 弓

田 由 甲 思 画 甸 畔 畅 疆 叠
田 田 田 田 田 田 申

力 加 动 边 勇 努 另 穷 历 办
力 力 力 力 力 力 力 力 力

厶 私 么 篡 凶 内 窗 至 垒 強 圖
厶 厶 厶 厶 厶 厶 厶 厶 厶

口 和 哈 吴 另 史 嘉 哲 喜 周 同 嗣
口 口 口 口 口 口 口 口 口 口

Source Han Sans CN

In Japanese books, difficult kanjis are accompanied by their pronunciation in hiragana on a smaller scale. It looks best when the pronunciation text is short. When the pronunciation is long, the smaller hiraganas might be stretched to fit the kanji. A disproportionally stretched 6-pt font is more legible than an unstretched 4-pt font. Therefore, in this context, stretching is a reasonable solution for extremely small type.

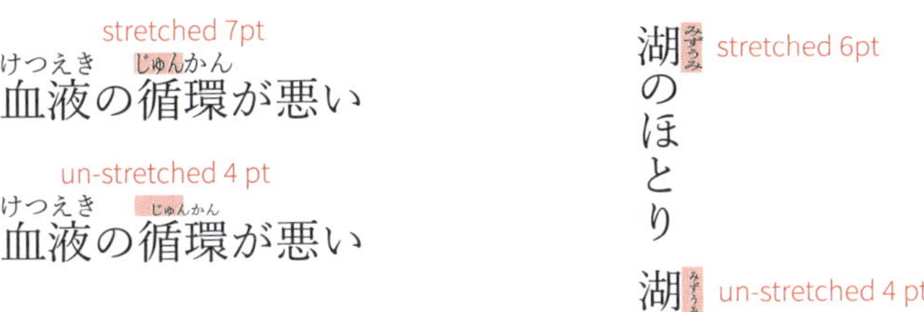

To offer a more elegant solution, some books increase the character space between the kanji to create a wider space for the pronunciation text.

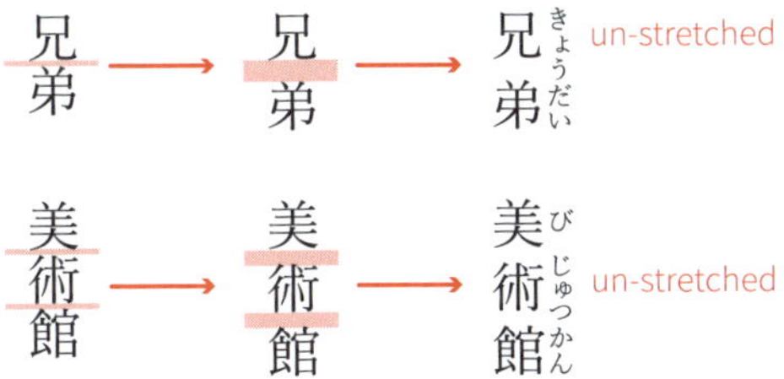

Another solution is to utilize the space next to the characters.

Other books use a narrower font for longer pronunciation texts.

All the strategies above avoid undesired stretching of Japanese kana used for indicating the pronunciation of kanji.

血液の循環が悪いのため、ライト兄弟と芥川賞作家は市原湖畔美術館へ行った

Yu Mincho

STRETCHING 2.0

So far, the stretches discussed in this chapter have all gone in the same reading direction as the script. Display type, however, can also be stretched perpendicularly to the reading direction.

Arabic can stretch downward as well as upward.

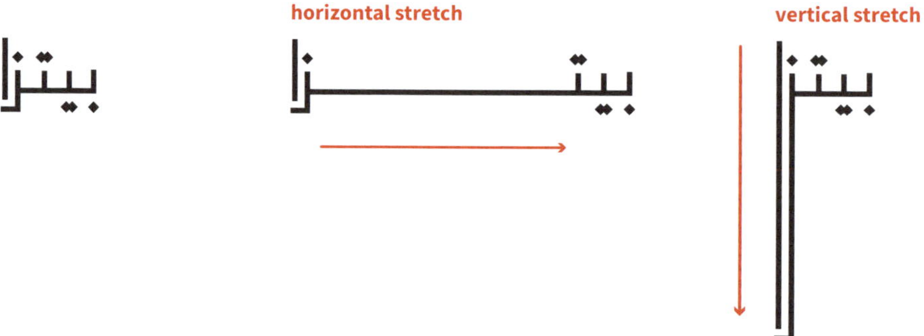

Chinese characters share this multi-directional stretchability, and stretching can be paired with duplications of the character particles to achieve the desired effect.

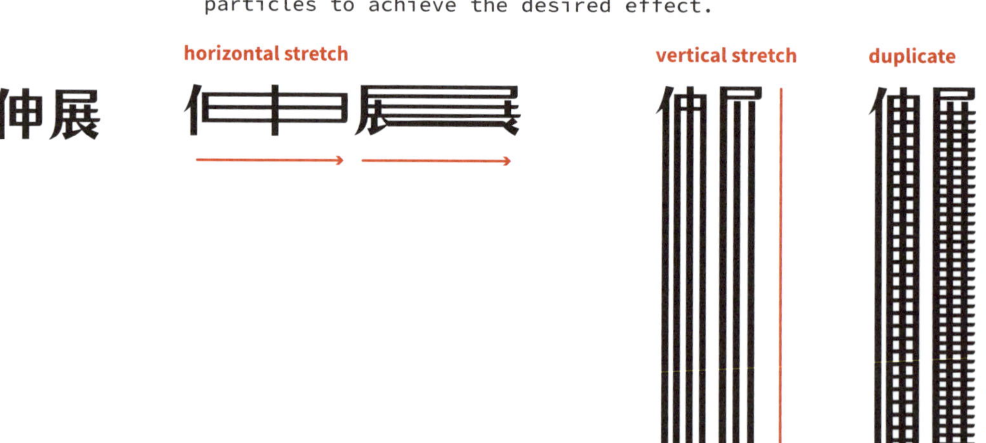

Hellofont ID MeiLingTi

09

SERIF

Typefaces are classified into "sans-serif" and "serif" because serifs are one of the most identifiable features of Latin typography. Dividing typefaces into serif and sans-serif beyond Latin scripts, however, is not optimal for understanding the features that differentiate non-Latin typefaces. In letters with unique terminals, serifs become secondary to the type's personality. This chapter explains different type categorization methods and uncovers distinctive details of non-Latin scripts.

Serifs, loops, headlines, and other embellishments at the terminals of a letter are like a character's headwear. Some wear baseball caps, with protrusions on only one side; some wear wide-brimmed sun hats, with the serifs being the most attention-grabbing elements; some wear hoodies, with the serifs being more subtle and coherent with the rest of the letterforms; some leave their heads uncovered.

PRINTED, NOT WRITTEN

Latin and Greek serifs date to the age of the Roman monument, when the text was only carved in capital letters without word spacing. While broad calligraphic brushes render serifs on one side, the other side of serifs does not appear in handwriting, only in moveable types.

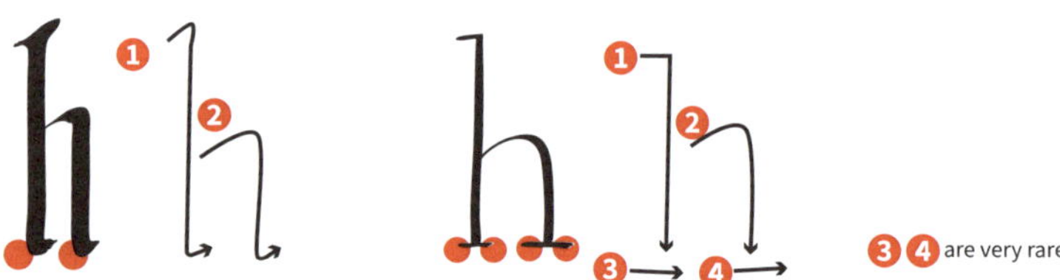

As the moveable types have progressed from old-style to transitional to modern, serifs have become thinner and thinner. The development of technologies that have enabled us to print delicate typographic elements helped realize this progression.

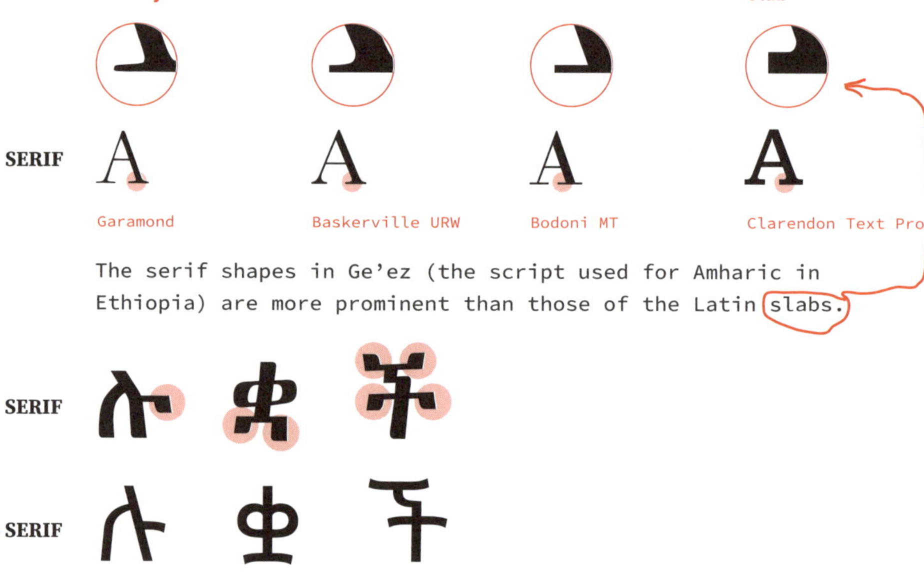

The serif shapes in Ge'ez (the script used for Amharic in Ethiopia) are more prominent than those of the Latin slabs.

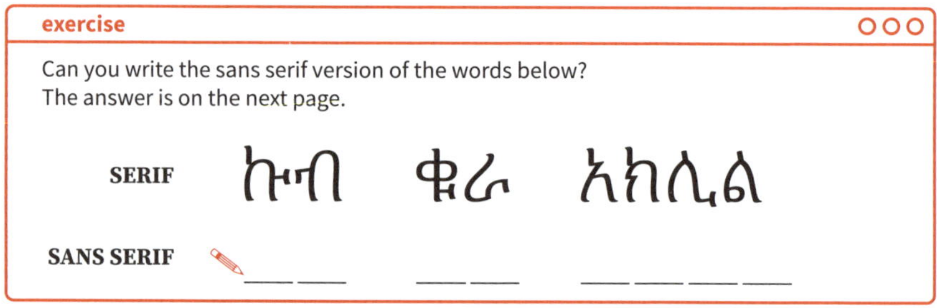

The serifs on the Ge'ez script are sometimes even larger than the shorter strokes in the sans-serif fonts. A nonnative Ahmaric learner who has only read Amharic in serifs might not have guessed all the sans-serif versions of the Ge'ez letters.

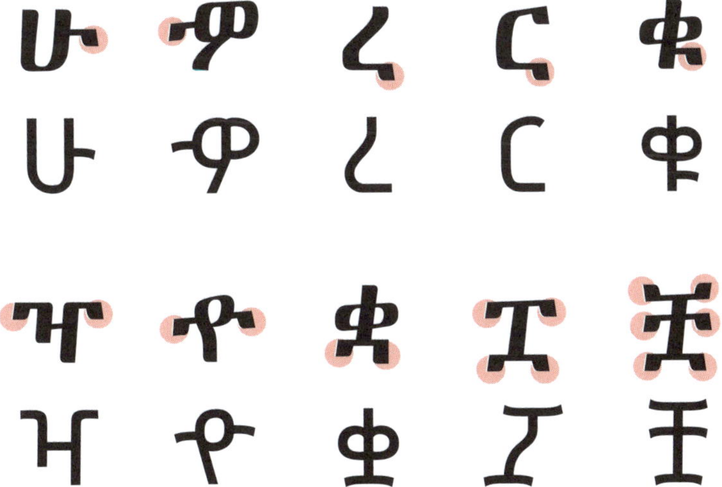

Tayitu, Shiromeda

The direction and shape of Ge'ez serifs are extremely diverse, contributing to the aesthetic features of different typefaces.

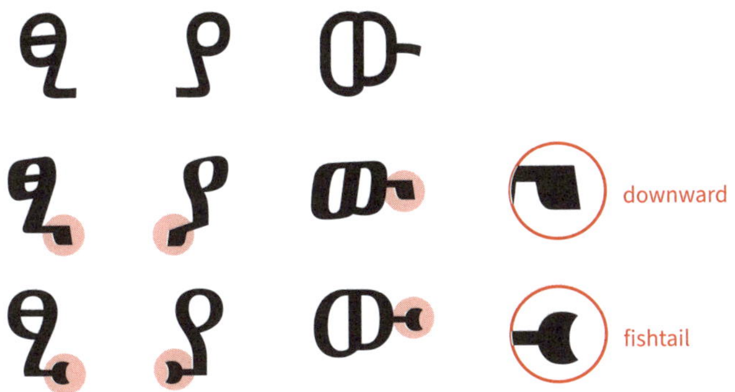

Shiromeda, Tayitu, Noto Serif Ethiopic

TERMINAL DESIGN

Some Armenian serif typefaces not only add serifs, but other flourishes.

SANS SERIF
SERIF

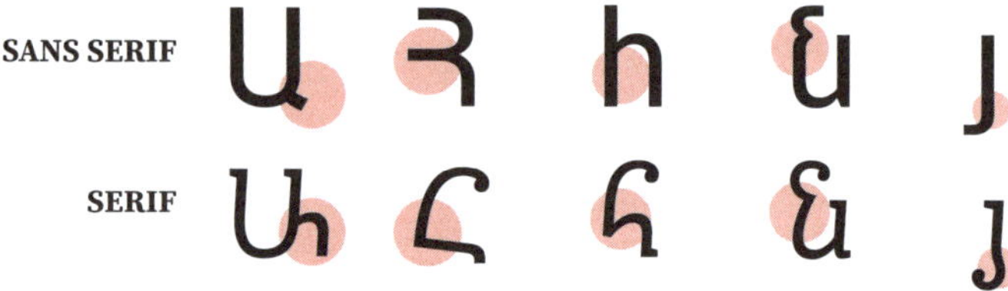

Trebuchet MS, Ernestine Pro

The terminals, for instance, can be more ball- than stick-shaped, and Armenian letters have more curvy strokes compared to Latin. Therefore, the typical Latin short-line serif does not work well with the terminals of many Armenian strokes.

SANS SERIF
SERIF

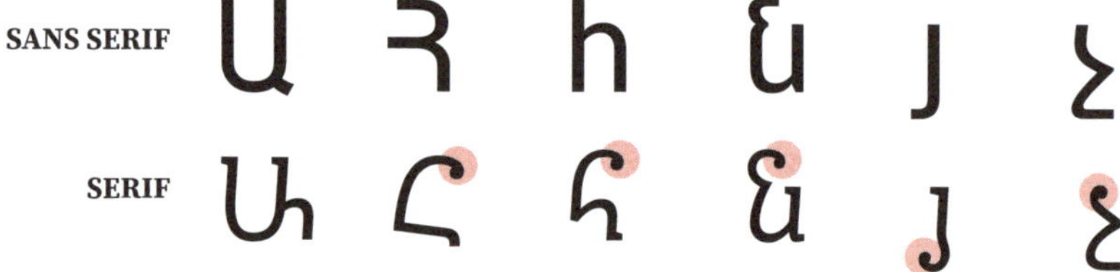

Trebuchet MS, Ernestine Pro

Such ball-shaped serifs are also used in Latin and Cyrillic type designs, on non-vertical strokes.

Bodoni MT, Baskerville Display PT, Yeseva One, Baskerville Display PT

1. Vladimir Yefimov, "Civil Type," in *Language Culture Type: International Type Design in the Age Of Unicode*, ed. John Berry (AtypI Graphics, 2002), 135.

2. Yefimov, "Civil Type," 134.

Scholars believe that when Peter I of Russia reformed Cyrillic in 1708, he sketched the letterforms himself without having any professional knowledge of a punchcutter's, and that he had the punches manufactured in Amsterdam.[1] Consequently, the serifs (usually unbracketed) entered the design of Cyrillic letterforms, albeit varying slightly from their Latin counterparts. Some serifs were criticized by contemporary designers and are therefore not found in modern Cyrillic typefaces, including the one-sided serifs for **A** and **X** as well as the curved serifs on the top left of **n** and **p**.[2]

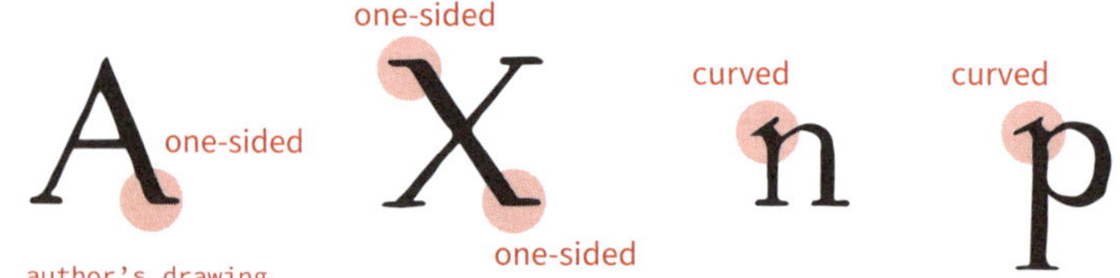

WRITTEN IN CALLIGRAPHY

Regular Script—known as **kaiti** in Chinese and **kaisho** in Japanese—was based on brush calligraphy. Its terminals, consequently, match the flow of brush strokes. The thick and thin line variations are the result of pressing down the brush with different pressures. The eight main strokes in calligraphy are illustrated in the **yong** character below.

Hellofont ID QingHuaKai

The "serifs" here follow the structure of calligraphic strokes.

KAITI 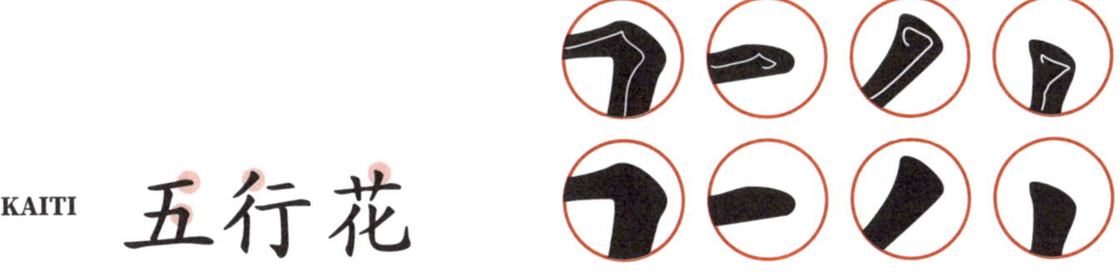

Hellofont ID QingHuaKai

As the demand for printed works grew, it was no longer efficient to produce books in this Regular Script—kaiti—so the angled strokes were flattened.

KAITI

"SERIF" 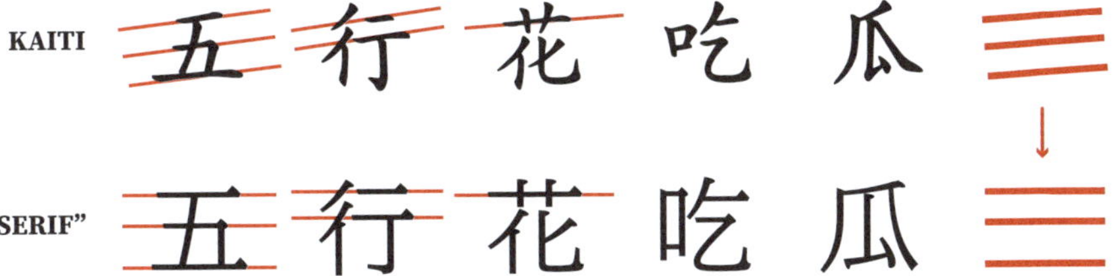

Hellofont ID QingHuaKai, BIZ UDPMincho

Along with the flattened strokes, the corners and terminals were simplified into triangles to honor the calligraphic strokes that inspired them.

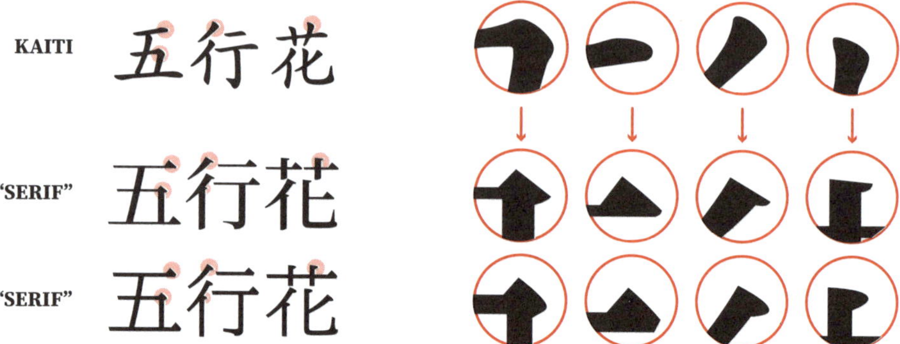

Hellofont ID QingHuaKai, Source Han Serif TC, BIZ UDPMincho

Arabic types also draw inspiration from their calligraphic origins. Unlike the Chinese calligraphy brush, which is made of animal hair, the Arabic calligraphy pen is made from reeds, a much more rigid material.

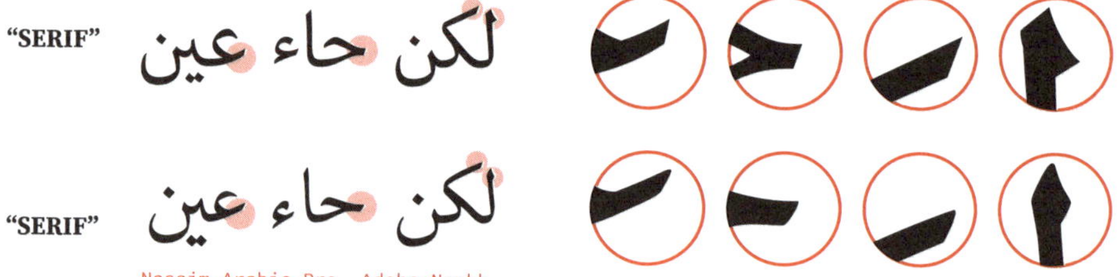

Nassim Arabic Pro, Adobe Naskh

3. Meir Sadan, "What Is a 'Serif' in Hebrew?" *Medium*, October 25, 2017, https://medium.com/@meirsadan/what-is-a-serif-in-hebrew-8014f1f63f63.

In Hebrew, **tags** are the decorative elements at the start of a letter, and the elaborate versions on the letters of Ashkenazi Torahs look like crowns. To directly translate **tag** to **serif**, however, is inaccurate.[3] In Hebrew typefaces that resemble sans-serif styles, serif-like head strokes are still present.

Times New Roman, Narkissim, Aktiv Grotesk Ex, Rubik

Like Hebrew's tag, **instroke** is a better way to introduce stroke transition and variation in Greek, than Latin's serif, because Greek letters are curvy and few letters have vertical strokes.

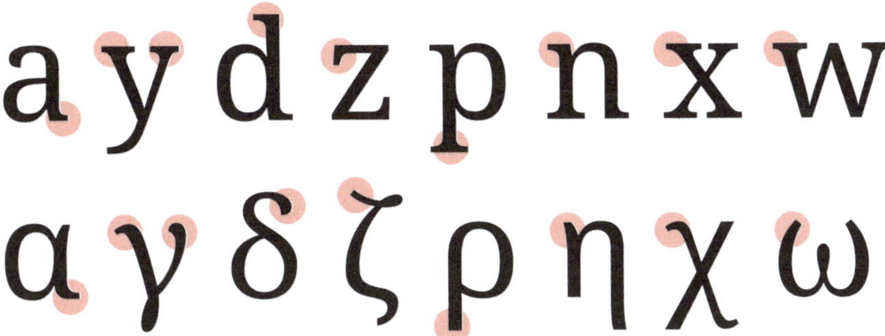

Droid Serif

In Hebrew, horizontal strokes are heavier than vertical strokes, which is the opposite of Latin.

HORIZONTAL EMPHASIS

VERTICAL EMPHASIS

Frank Ruhl Libre, Bodoni MT

4. Turkenich, Liron Lav, and Adi Stern, "Hebrew," in *Bi-scriptual Typography and Graphic Design with Multiple Script Systems: Arabic, Cyrillic, Greek, Hangeul, Hanzi, Hebrew, Devanagari, Kanji/Hiragana/Katakana*, ed. Ben Wittner, Sascha Thoma, Timm Hartmann (Niggli, 2019), 245.

5. Misah Beletsky, "Zvi Narkiss and Hebrew Type Design," in *Language Culture Type: International Type Design in the Age Of Unicode*, ed. John Berry (AtypI Graphics, 2002), 95.

In the nineteenth century, Hebrew printed letters evolved with the popularity of Didone (a modern typeface style famous for its high contrast between thick and thin strokes and hairline serifs), and this Latin style made vertical strokes too thin to support the heavy horizontal strokes on the top; legibility, in turn, also suffered.[4] In this style, vertical strokes were made inferior to the horizontal ones.[5] This example demonstrates how not all Latin aesthetics are appropriate for other scripts.

SOLID UNIVERSITY

Bodoni MT

FRAGILE

WRITTEN, BUT OMITTED IN FAST WRITING

Serifs do not exist in common Thai fonts. A better method of classifying Thai typefaces is according to the presence or absence of loops.

Noto Looped Thai    

Noto Sans Thai   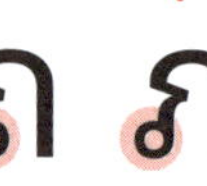

Making a loopless version of a looped letter usually follows a predictable pattern. However, due to the large number of consonants in the Thai alphabet, changing the position of the loop itself can transform one consonant into another.

g	t	p	p (high)	p (low)	k	d

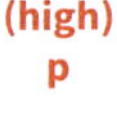   

Noto Looped Thai

---

exercise ○ ○ ○

With the looped letters, can you guess their loopless forms?

LOOPED      

LOOPLESS  — — —   — —   — —

The first group above is the easiest to guess the loopless forms for, as each loop can be simplified into to a short stroke. The second set can be challenging because the second letter looks like the English **w**. The third set is likely the most challenging among the three, since the last letter barely hints at the position of the loop.

Noto Looped Thai    

Noto Sans Thai   

The Thai simplification process makes some loopless Thai letters resemble the letters in the Latin alphabet. The loopless Thai letters below do not read phonetically as **sankuu**.

LOOPLESS ร ล ก ห บ น

LOOPED ร ล ท ห บ น

Noto Sans Thai, Noto Looped Thai

Below is the same Thai sentence presented in a looped and loopless typeface.

LOOPED สาวโสดแสนสวยใส่เสื้อสีแสดสวมส้นสูงสีส้ม

LOOPLESS สาวโสดแสนสวยใส่เสื้อสีแสดสวมส้นสูงสีส้ม

Noto Looped Thai, Noto Sans Thai

"Looped" cannot be defined as the equivalent of a serif; neither can "loopless" cannot be defined as the equivalent of a sans-serif. A loopless typeface can still have serif-like elements. The loop is another example of the unique typographic elements in non-Latin scripts that get neglected when most of the world adopts Latin type terminologies.

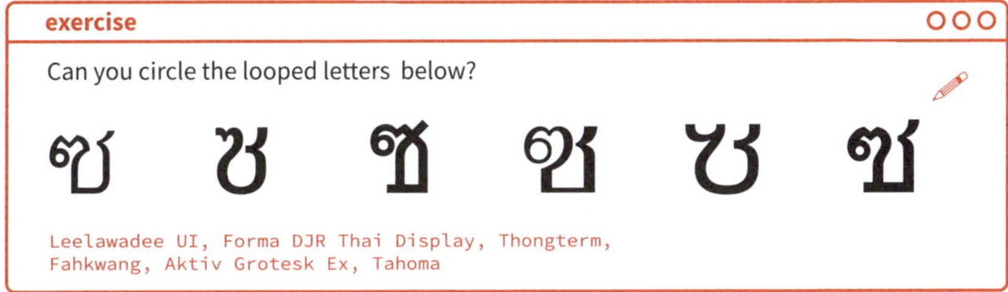

LOOPLESS

Zahrah Thai   Chonburi

exercise ○○○

Can you circle the looped letters below?

ซ ช ซ ช ช ซ

Leelawadee UI, Forma DJR Thai Display, Thongterm, Fahkwang, Aktiv Grotesk Ex, Tahoma

Google's Noto Lao typefaces show the irrelevance of loops and serifs in Lao and Thai typefaces.

		LOOP	SERIF
noto sans	ຜ ຟ		
noto sans looped	ຜ ຟ	√	
noto serif	ຜ ຟ	√	√

In Lao, unlike in Thai, few letters will come to resemble another letter because of the loop's position. Those that do are highlighted below.

Leelawadee UI

Therefore, the Latinization of loopless forms is less necessary in Lao type design.

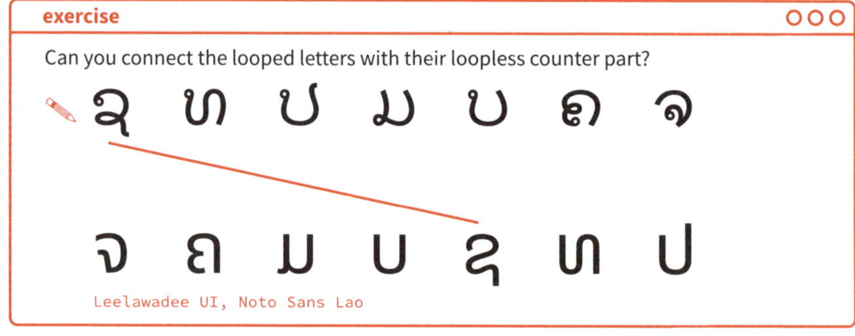

Lao

Thai

LOOPED

LOOPLESS

Leelawadee UI,
Noto Sans Lao

Noto Looped Thai,
Noto Sans Thai

exercise   ○○○

Can you connect the looped letters with their loopless counter part?

Leelawadee UI, Noto Sans Lao

In many Khmer typefaces, the loops resemble an oval more than a circle, and some loops are filled rather than hollow.

LOOPLESS

LOOPED

LOOPED

Dangrek Regular, Noto Serif Khmer, Siemreap

In Khmer, like in Thai, a few pairs of consonants also differ only in the existence or direction of loops.

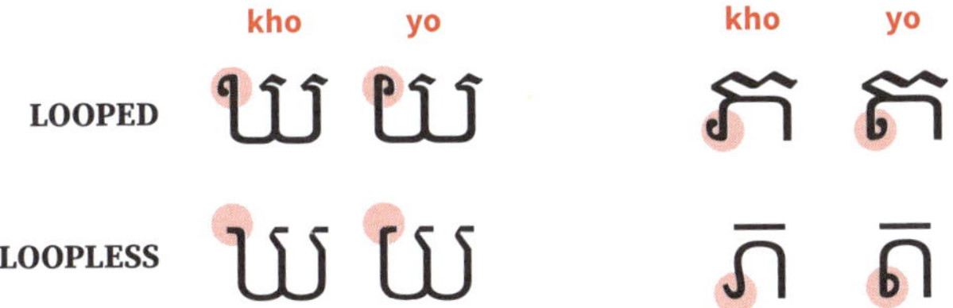

Leelawadee UI, Noto Sans Khmer

Beyond the loop, the "wavy hair" on some consonants can be simplified into a straight line. When line simplification occurs, the type may still retain the loops on most consonants.

LOOPED

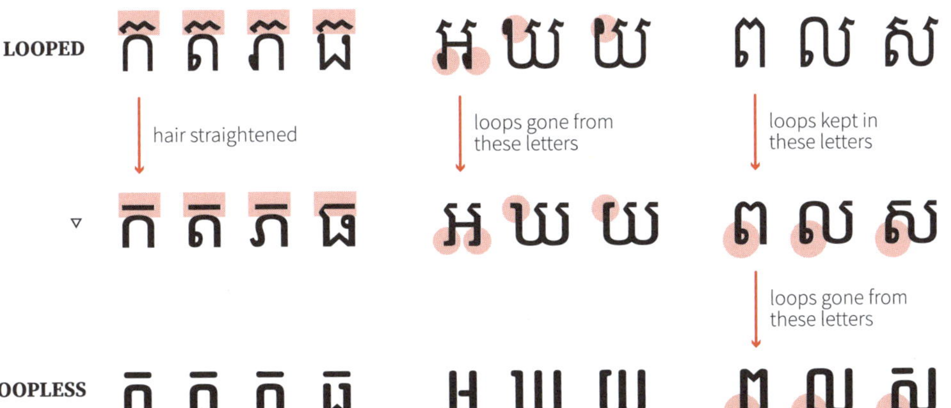

LOOPLESS

Siemreap, Nokora, Dangrek

HEAD, ANOTHER CLASSIFICATION ELEMENT

There are many different writing styles in Tibetan. The two most common are **uchen** (with a head) and **ume** (without a head). Uchen is used in more formal situations and is treated as the equivalent of a serif. Ume is closer to handwriting and is treated like a sans-serif typeface, although it bears a distinctive style from Latin sans-serif styles.

WITH A HEAD   བཀྲ་ཤིས་བདེ་ལེགས

HEADLESS   བཀྲ་ཤིས་བདེ་ལེགས

Microsoft Himalaya,
author's handwriting (not very good, sorry...)

Among scripts in India, nonetheless, the existence of the head or headline distinguishes different writing systems throughout the country. Hindi (written in Devanagari script) uses a headline, and Gujarati does not. Below are words that share similar pronunciations and spellings in both scripts.

	forest	love	bus	route	doctor
HINDI	वन	प्रेम	बस	मार्ग	डॉक्टर
GUJARATI	વન	પ્રેમ	બસ	માર્ગ	ડોક્ટર

Nirmala UI

exercise

Can you circle the words in Gujarati?

ભાષા   भोजन   दुकान   मित्रो

भाषा   ભોજન   ६કાન   मित्र

CONTRASTY VS. MONOLINEAR

From the 2000s to early 2010s, some designers believed that sans-serif fonts were better than serif fonts on screens. Screen quality was low then, but with the upgraded technology that displays serifs sharply on digital devices today, serifs no longer affect a font's legibility compared to other micro-typographic factors.[6]

Serifs are not omnipresent in all scripts globally. In the case of Thai, loops are more necessary than serifs. But, as English is still the dominant international language, designers take shortcuts and combine some features to assign different non-Latin typefaces to the categories of "serif" and "sans-serif."

The most common feature for categorizing some scripts, however, is the contrast between thick and thin strokes.[7] When this contrast is low or nonexistent, the typeface is classified as "sans-serif"; when the contrast is high, "serif." Another term to describe a typeface with little or no contrast in strokes is "monolinear," which is much more precise than "sans-serif."

6. Linda Kudrnovská, *Building Ligatures: The Power of Type* (TypeTogether, 2022), 215-16.

7. Vaibhav Singh, "Devanagari," in *Bi-scriptual Typography and Graphic Design with Multiple Script Systems: Arabic, Cyrillic, Greek, Hangeul, Hanzi, Hebrew, Devanagari, Kanji/Hiragana/Katakana*, ed. Ben Wittner, Sascha Thoma, Timm Hartmann (Niggli, 2019), 107.

Noto sans serif	ლამაზი	ဗောဆလုံး	भारतीय
Noto serif	ლამაზი	ဗောဆလုံး	भारतीय

The first sans-serif font was designed much later than serif fonts in Latin typesetting history. Latin sans-serif typefaces are typically more minimal, while serif typefaces have more delicate elements, including serifs. However, it is unfair to call the sans-serif style a product of "modernity" or "minimalism." In Georgian, a few delicate elements are present regardless of whether there are serifs at the terminal of the strokes. The example below demonstrate how "sans-serif" does not inherently imply a more minimalistic design than "serif."

SANS SERIF	უ	ზ	ხ	კაპუჩინო
SANS SERIF	უ	ზ	ხ	კაპუჩინო
SERIF	უ	ზ	ხ	კაპუჩინო
SERIF	უ	ზ	ხ	კაპუჩინო

OmnesGeorgian, Microsoft Sans Serif,
Noto Serif Georgian, Sylfaen

Opposite to Peter's Cyrillic reform that included serifs, the Korean Hangeul began without "serifs" in the 1440s, when King Sejong designed the letters. Over the years, it has developed various styles, some of which can be considered the stylistic equivalent of serifs.

The "serif" style in mainland China is known as "Song," because it started during the Song Dynasty. In Japan, it is known as "Mincho," in Korea as "Myungjo," and as "Ming" in Taiwan, because the style flourished during the Ming Dynasty. Song/Ming is the most common style of Chinese characters' typefaces for printed materials.

Song ti / **Mincho** / **Ming ti**

宋体 / 明朝 / 明體

Myungjo

명조체/明朝體

Adobe Song Std L, Adobe Ming Std L, Adobe Myungjo Std M

Unlike Korean Hangeul, the sans-serif style for Japanese and Chinese is a relatively modern phenomenon among the styles developed after the invention of movable types. (When Chinese characters were engraved on animal shells, they did not have serifs, unlike Latin letters carved on the Roman stone.) Inspired by Latin sans-serif typefaces, East Asian sans-serif typefaces (outside Korea) first appeared in Japan, where in typography they are named "Gothic."

MINCHO/ "SERIF" 五つの花

GOTHIC/ "SANS SERIF" 五つの花

BIZ UDMincho Medium, BIZ UDGothic

In the early and mid-twentieth century, printing presses in Shanghai developed a low-contrast style for Chinese characters, known as "Heiti/Hei style."

HEI STYLE/ "SANS SERIF" 五行花

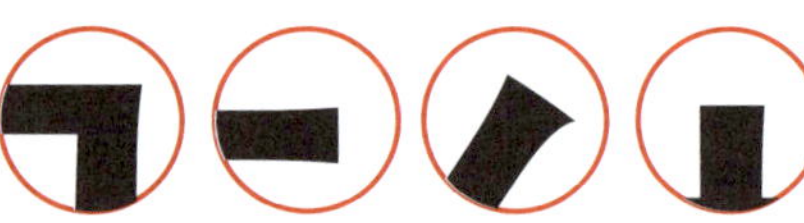

SimHei

In Heiti/Hei style, the contrast is low but nonetheless present; terminals are slightly wider, like the bell of a trumpet. Therefore, there is a difference between the Japanese Gothic style and the Chinese Hei style.

Japanese: little contrast

GOTHIC/ "SANS SERIF"

Chinese: more contrast

HEI STYLE/ "SANS SERIF"

BIZ UDGothic, SimHei

The sophistication of Chinese characters enables the freedom to exaggerate the contrast between horizontal and vertical strokes, especially in the so-called serif typefaces: a "serif" type family can change only the weight of its vertical strokes; horizontal strokes remain the same thickness, regardless of the font weight, be it thin or bold.[8]

8. But Ko and Winston Su, *A Chinese Font Walk Next* (Faces Publications, 2019), 62.

thin ⟵⟶ heavy   heavy

Source Han Sans CN

"SANS SERIF"
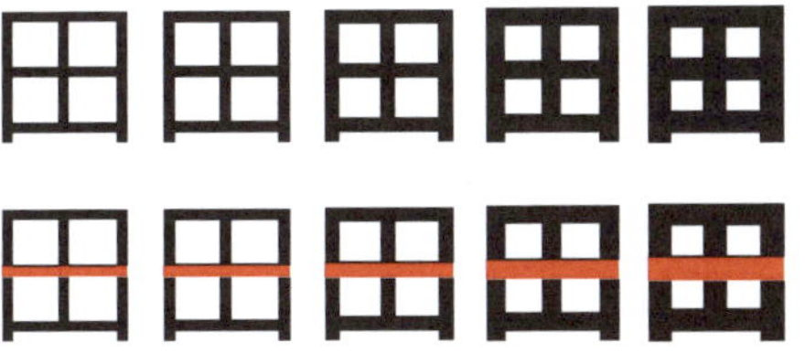

Source Han Serif TC

"SERIF"
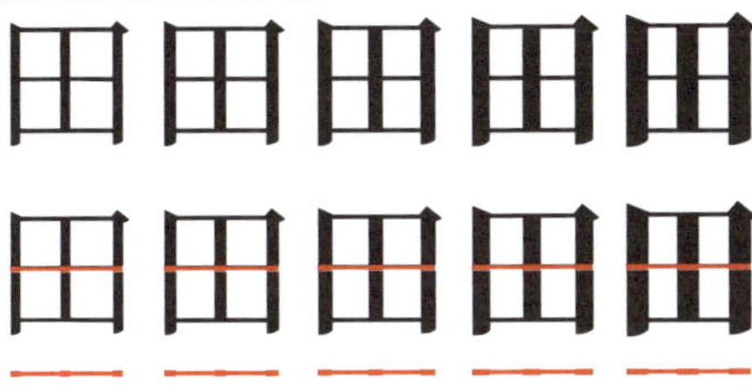

Most bold, high-contrast Chinese characters remain recognizable without the horizontal strokes.

水光潋滟晴方好
山色空濛雨亦奇
欲把西湖比西子
淡妆浓抹总相宜

Source Han Serif TC

10 | ITALIC AND HANDWRITING

In modern typefaces, upright letters come, by default, with italic counterparts that can be used to add emphasis. Italics have existed for centuries, but its usage in the sixteenth century differed from contemporary usage. Most non-Latin languages do not use italics as a secondary style. Instead, lines, shapes, colors, and other typefaces serve the same purpose. It is especially rare to see italics in Chinese, Japanese, and Korean, both because of the large number of characters and the complicated distortion required. This chapter covers the design, usage, and application of secondary styles known as "italic" in Latin typography.

This chapter also inspects a calligrapher's interpretation of written letters' structures, which fuse and sever forms creatively. Especially in countries where italic forms lack the context of local readership, calligraphy plays a vital role in diversifying style. Even though many people prefer the efficiency and clarity of typing over writing by hand, handwriting also deserves attention in type design discussions as it pushes the boundaries between readability and unreadability and unlocks the potential for diverse creative expression for mechanical and digital type design.

DEVELOPMENT, USAGE, AND ALTERNATIVES

In the early sixteenth century, the italic form was regarded as an independent book type not to be mixed with upright forms of text.[1] Between 1501 and 1515, Italian printer Aldus Manutius printed entire books in only italics to save space and reduce the cost.[2] Before the late Renaissance, roman type was used for main texts and italics for prefaces and notes; no paragraphs contained both forms.[3] Today, it takes us longer to read a Latin paragraph set entirely in italics because we are not used to it as a standard form.

In **The Elements of Typographic Style**, Robert Bringhurst describes the asynchronous development of italic lowercase and italic uppercase in Latin, and emphasizes how roman and italic types represent different genes.[4]

When the early analog typewriters were invented, Latin text could be marked with spacing, underlining, or uppercase.[5] Until around 1910, when inclined typefaces became considered secondary to upright text, interletter spacing was also used by Greek typesetters for emphasis.[6] Outside the development of typewriters, the Greek type has adopted both upright and cursive forms since 1475, but each form was used separately until the late twentieth century.[7]

Coronette, Cascadia Code

In Germany, it was common until the 1980s to accentuate words by widening the letter spacing, due to the convention of using Blackletter typefaces.[8]

Amador

It is easier to find italics in loopless Thai typefaces thanks to their Latinized forms; however, it is also common to see an entire paragraph in Thai set in italics, rather than just a word or two.[9]

---

1. Jost Hochuli, *Detail in Typography Letters, Letterspacing, Words, Wordspacing, Lines, Linespacing, Columns* (Éditions B42, 2015), 20.

2. Hendrik Weber, *Italic: What Gives Typography its Emphasis* (Niggli, 2021), 30.

3. Robert Bringhurst, *The Elements of Typographic Style* (Hartley & Marks Publishers, 2019), 57.

4. Bringhurst, *Elements of Typographic Style*, 59.

5. Robert Steinmuller, *Mono is the New Black: Monospace Fontionary* (Niggli Verlag, 2024), 116.

6. Gerry Leonidas, "Greek Type Design," in *Language Culture Type: International Type Design in the Age Of Unicode*, ed. John Berry (AtypI Graphics, 2002), 83.

7. Robert Bringhurst, "Voices, Languages and Scripts," in Berry, *Language Culture Type*, 8.

8. Weber, *Italic*, 18.

9. Ben Mitchell, "Thai Italics 1," *The Fontpad*, accessed February 23, 2015, https://www.fontpad.co.uk/thai-italics-1/.

10. Karthik Malli, "Devanagari - The Makings of a National Character," *Typoteque*, March 21, 2022, https://www.typotheque.com/research/devanagari-the-makings-of-a-national-character.

In Devanagari, manuscript-style lettered words with disjointed headlines contrast words with jointed headlines and can mark emphasis.[10]

disjointed

मनोरंजनात्मक

Amita

jointed

मनोरंजनात्मक

Noto Serif Devanagari

11. Huda Smitshuijzen AbiFarès and Kameel Hawa, *Kameel Hawa: The Art of Shaping Arabic Letters* (Khatt Books, 2019), 155.

12. Khajag Apelian and Wael Morcos, "Arabic Typography," in *Thinking with Type: A Critical Guide for Designers, Writers, Editors, and Students*, ed. Ellen Lupton (Princeton Architectural Press, 2024), 174.

Tashkeel—an Arabic typeface developed by Lebanese designer Kameel Hawa for the fine arts magazine **Tashiliyun**—disjoints letters to suggest an Arabic "all-caps" style for the magazine's mastheads and large headlines.[11] There is no true italic in traditional Arabic writing. Modern bilingual Arabic typefaces include italic styles to match Latin scripts, but Arabic designers generally use another font style in place of italics.[12] For example, **Naskh** style and **Kufi** style can be used to add emphasis to Arabic text. Other practical methods include changing font color, weight, or size, which are also common in CJK.

In recent years, one can find books translated into Korean that use oblique Hangeul type to imitate Latin italics from the original language. Traditionally—due to the large quantity of characters in CJK—most typefaces do not come with italics. Culturally, people are more familiar with other visual elements that create emphasis.

we do it like this, or this, or this, or this, or this, or this

Bahnschrift

Therefore, in bilingual publications, one language might use italics while CJK-language texts use other methods. Below is an example from a bilingual document. The word that is italicized in Thai is underlined in color in Japanese.

ส่งผลให้คีคนที่อพยพไป ญี่ปุ่น[โตะไรจิน]มากขึ้น

その結果、日本に移住する人 [渡来人]が増えた。

Aktiv Grotesk Ex, Meiryo

Another bilingual example with English and Chinese, uses italics in the English and bolded text in the Chinese:

The people who interviewed us were *remarkable*. First she told the audience that we had never met. Then she turned to us and asked what we thought of each other.

採訪我們的人真是**卓越**。首先她告訴觀眾們, 我們從來沒有見過面。接著她轉向我們, 問我們對對方有什麼看法。

Adobe Garamond Pro, Source Han Serif SC

13. But Ko and Winston Su, A Chinese Font Walk Next (Faces Publications, 2019), 67.

In some Chinese books, the main body text is set in Song while citations and notes are set in **Fangsong** (Imitation Song).[13] Both are considered the equivalent of serif typefaces in Latin, but Fangsong has a different texture than Song.

COMPARISON

SONG

宋体的设计源自宋朝的雕版印刷术,字体结构方正。宋体的特点是横细竖粗,笔画有明显的起笔和收笔。仿宋体的设计模仿了宋朝的手写体。仿宋的特点是笔画较为流畅,带有手写的风格

FANGSONG / IMITATION SONG

宋体的设计源自宋朝的雕版印刷术，字体结构方正。宋体的特点是横细竖粗，笔画有明显的起笔和收笔。仿宋体的设计模仿了宋朝的手写体。仿宋的特点是笔画较为流畅，带有手写的风格。

SAMPLE PARAGRAPH

《世梨说新语》是一本非传统意义上的字体书。除了对不同语言的文字形态和视觉传达的探索和剖析,作者尝试在人类文明历史上不同的时间点找出世界各种文化碰撞的瞬间。书中关于衬线的章节阐述到:

> 虽然主流设计软件将字体分成有衬线字体和无衬线字体两大类，衬线作为装饰字型的工具之一并不能广泛应用于非西方文字。书法历史丰富的阿拉伯文和汉字运用的是旋转或者按压书法工具，从而制造粗细变化和笔画韵律。

Source Han Serif SC, FangSong

Modern Chinese books sometimes use Regular Script/Kaiti instead of Fangsong/Imitation Song for block quotes. More of the history and stylistic development of Regular Script/Kaiti will be covered later in the chapter.

SAMPLE PARAGRAPH

《世梨说新语》是一本非传统意义上的字体书。除了对不同语言的文字形态和视觉传达的探索和剖析,作者尝试在人类文明历史上不同的时间点找出世界各种文化碰撞的瞬间。书中关于衬线的章节阐述到:

> 虽然主流设计软件将字体分成有衬线字体和无衬线字体两大类，衬线作为装饰字型的工具之一并不能广泛应用于非西方文字。书法历史丰富的阿拉伯文和汉字运用的是旋转或者按压书法工具，从而制造粗细变化和笔画韵律。

Source Han Serif SC, KaiTi

DESIGNING ITALICS

In many languages, it is rare to find italics, but that does not mean italic fonts do not exist in corresponding scripts. The key to italics is slanting a letter without losing its balance. The Devanagari word **hun** is typed below. **H** is vertically positioned in the center (1), **u** on the bottom (2), and the nasal sound on the top (3).

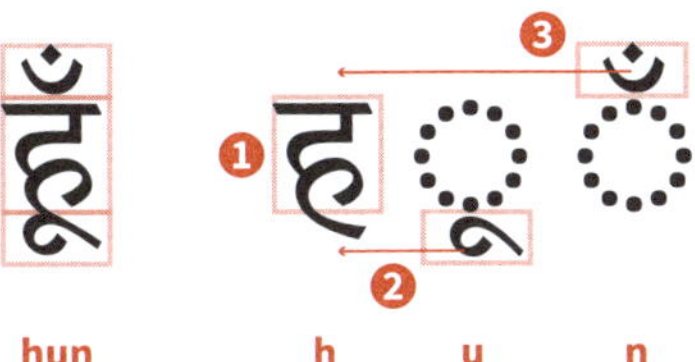

If we push each sound block to the right with the same strength, eventually the letters will tip over.

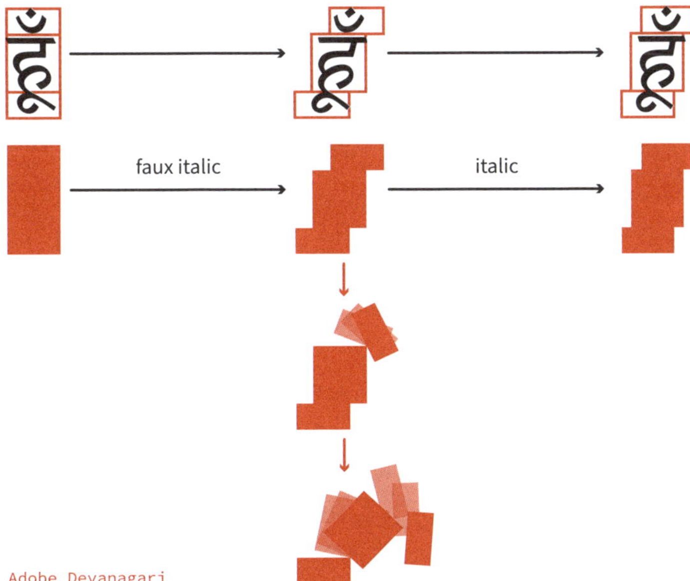

Adobe Devanagari

To achieve a stable stance, the building blocks of each word cannot lean too far forward.

Adobe Devanagari

14. Vladimir Yefimov, "Civil Type," in Berry, *Language Culture Type*, 143.

Cyrillic italics developed later than upright forms, appearing first in 1730, twenty years after the Petrine reform; it was based on engraved inscriptions.[14] The most striking example of the structural difference between the upright and italic is the lowercase **т**.

| REGULAR | б | Д | Т | М | Ж |

| ITALIC | б | д | т | м | ж |

| HANDWRITING | б | д | т | м | ж |

Droid Serif, Adobe Handwriting

As shown below, the italic form is not completely derived from the upright. The angles contribute to different aesthetics, but that is only part of its genes; there are also more curves.

| CURSIVE | л и ш | лишился |

| ITALIC | л и ш | лишился |

| REGULAR | Л И Ш | ЛИШИЛСЯ |

Adobe Handwriting, Droid Serif

As in Cyrillic, Greek italic letters follow the motion of handwriting, making it easier to connect the strokes between letters.

| REGULAR | θ β k κ φ | θαλάσκαφος |

| ITALIC | ϑ β k κ φ | θαλάσκαφος |

Change

Armenian offers another example of italic letters that resemble handwriting more than the upright letters.

| REGULAR | Ս զ ձ ճ Ց ք |

| ITALIC | Ս ղ ջ հ ՠ ք |

| HANDWRITING | Ս ղ ջ հ ՠ ք |

Arek Armenian, Poqrik dzeragir

In the 1950s, the Cathod Ray Tube (CRT) photo-typesetting technology enabled slanting upright roman letters mechanically to generate italics due to the lack of real italic fonts available for these machines.[15] By the time these machines improved, "faux italics" had become standard in newspapers.[16] Word processor programs allow the users to apply a faux italic that manually slants the upright version of the font. Most of these were not visually appealing.

15. Weber, *Italic*, 80.

16. Weber, *Italic*, 80.

true *faux*   true *faux*   true *faux*   true *faux*   true *faux*   true *faux*

a *a*   p *p*   f *f*   g *g*   y *y*   v *v*

Adobe Garamond Pro

The italics of Adobe Garamond were based on the creation of French punchcutter and master printer Robert Granjon.[17] The italic **a** becomes single-story form from a double-story, upright **a**; the italic **p's** stem shoots above the x-height line; the italic **f** extends an outstroke; the italic **g** has two skinnier circles; the italic **y** has a ball-shaped terminal on the bottom that is directed slightly upward; and the italic **v** has swashes instead of serifs.

17. Weber, *Italic*, 56.

a *a*   p *p*   f *f*   g *g*   y *y*   v *v*

Adobe Garamond Pro

A similar contrast between the upright and italic forms is found in other serif typefaces, such as Bodoni.

a *a*   p *p*   f *f*   g *g*   y *y*   v *v*

Bodoni MT

In the nineteenth century, sans-serif italics were only expressed through the slope because using traditional elements worked against the clean nature.[18] Today, traditional elements have often been reintroduced to sans-serif italics.

18. Weber, *Italic*, 104.

upright   italic   italic above slanted upright

handgloves *handgloves* *handgloves*

handgloves *handgloves* *handgloves*

Museo Sans, Adelle Sans

DESIGN CHALLENGES

19. Peter Bilak and Michal Sahar, *Designing Hebrew Type* (Typotheque, 2017), 5.

Hebrew is a relatively homogenously structured script.[19] Its legibility benefits from angling certain strokes in the upright fonts.

	yod	zayin	gimel	tsadi	tav	chet
OmnesHebrew						
Aktiv Grotesk Ex						
Adapter Hebrew Display						
Adobe Hebrew						
Henri						
Narkissim						

In Ge'ez (the script used for Amharic in Ethiopia), slanting certain strokes can change the vowel of the letter.

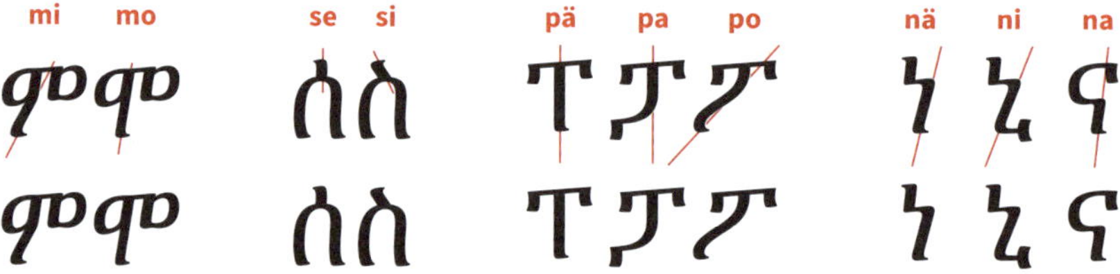

Kigelia Ethiopic

This makes Ge'ez a unique writing system, but the process of designing italic fonts for it much trickier. Like Ge'ez, Arabic letters have slanted components in the upright fonts.

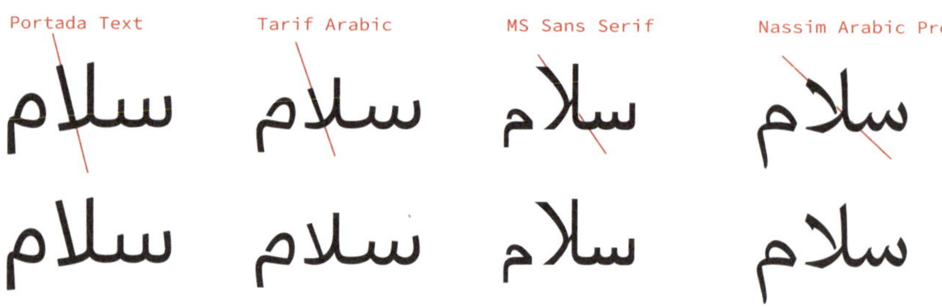

Many Arabic typefaces place the teeth at slightly different angles to increase a letter's legibility. The second typeface below uses more diverse angles so readers can distinguish the letters more quickly. These angles also make designing italic forms more challenging.

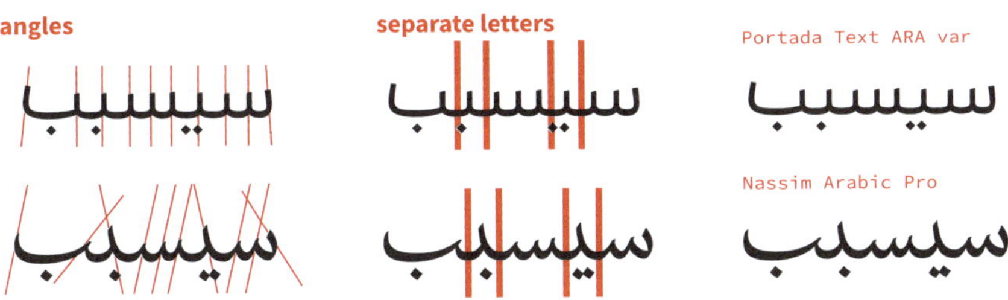

Mongolian calligraphic typefaces have downward-facing teeth, as if drawn by gravity. If a designer were to create an italic style for Mongolian, what do you think it would look like?

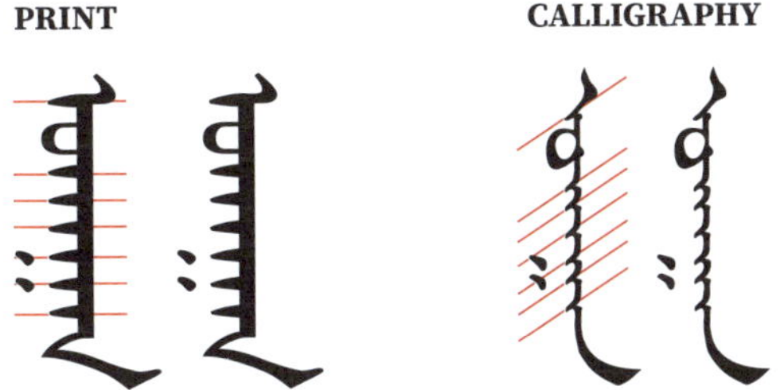

Mongolian White, Mongolian Writing

When CJK is typed vertically, slanting each character to the right horizontally interferes with the reading experience. To ease the flow, it is preferred to slant the characters vertically.

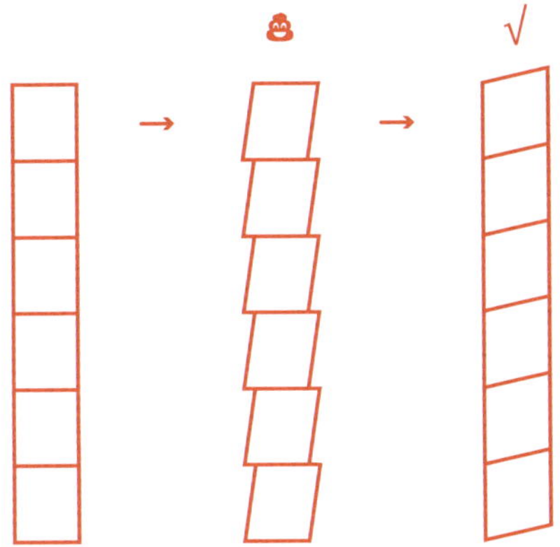

SLANTING DIRECTION

In Latin typography, left-leaning italics are labeled "backward slanting," but left is not backward for Arabic or Hebrew, which are read from right to left rather than left to right. Another factor is that although Hebrew reads from right to left, the writing of each stroke goes left to right.

In the 1950s, German-born Hebrew calligrapher Ismar David created David Cursive, the first attempt to design a secondary text style that leaned leftward to mirror the Latin italic.[20] Contemporary bilingual Hebrew typefaces tend to lean rightward to pair well with Latin script.

20. Bilak and Sahar, *Designing Hebrew Type*, 65.

RIGHT-LEANING

Adobe Hebrew

חָבְרוּתְיוּת

Aktiv Grotesk Ex

חָבְרוּתְיוּת

Kameel Hawa initiated the typeface Hakaya for Arabic, which has a handwritten quality. Letters lean gently to the left, following the direction of the pen.[21] Modern Arabic italic fonts slant in both directions, while retaining the diverse angles of Arabic strokes.

21. AbiFarès and Hawa, *Kameel Hawa*, 153.

RIGHT-LEANING

Aktiv Grotesk Arbc

صداقة الى الأبد

LEFT-LEANING

Amiri

صداقة الى الأبد

Adobe Arabic

صداقة الى الأبد

The bi-scriptual typeface 29LT Ada (Arabic and Latin) slants the baseline of Latin letters by five degrees leftward because its Arabic type design is based on the Ruqʿah Arabic calligraphic style, which leans slightly toward the writing direction.[22] This design choice proves the ingenuity of non-Latin-centric recipes for success.

22. "29LT Ada : A Ruqʿah Type System," *29LT BLOG*, accessed December 1, 2024, https://blog.29lt.com/2023/02/28/29lt-ada-ruqah-fonts.

SLANTED COMPOSITION AND STROKES

Like the Devanagari **hun** at the beginning of this chapter, words in any language can be beautifully slanted to the right or the left. In complicated languages like CJK, they are usually stylized typefaces rather than a style meant as a subordinate to an upright form. Below is a Chinese font that slants in accordance with the writing direction.

得意黑: 字身窄斜, 似美术字, 好用 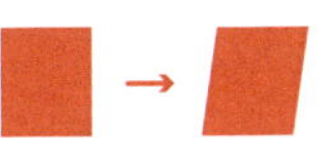

Smiley Sans Oblique

Below are some Japanese examples that slant in both directions.

Potta One Regular

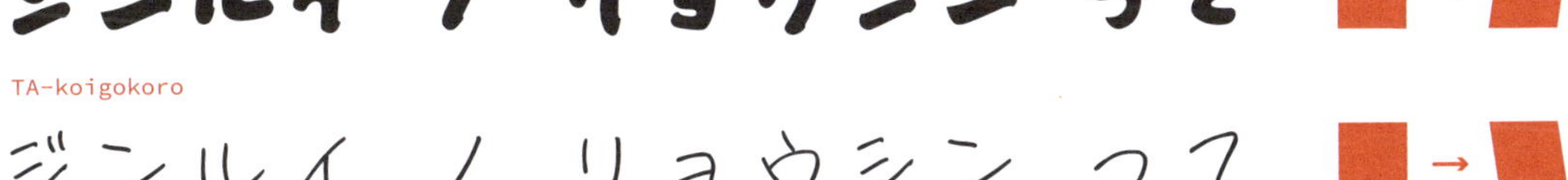

TA-koigokoro

ジンルイ ノ リョウシン って

Likewise, Korean typefaces can slant in either direction.

RixSuperRobot_Pro ObliqueShadow

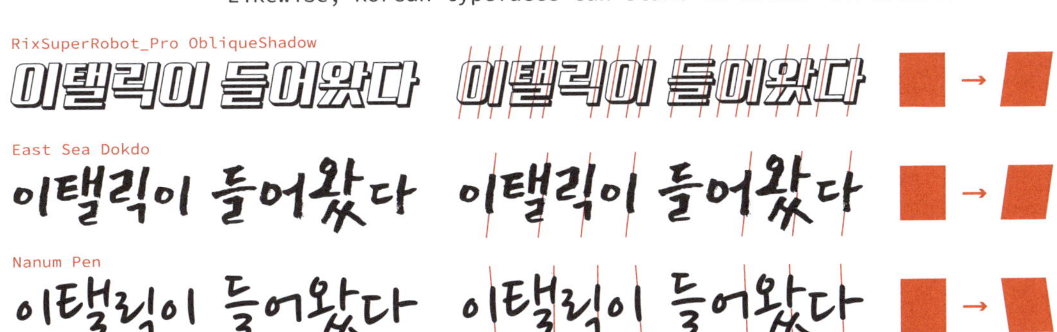

East Sea Dokdo

이탤릭이 들어왔다 이탤릭이 들어왔다

Nanum Pen

이탤릭이 들어왔다 이탤릭이 들어왔다

Another method is to selectively slant certain strokes rather than all of them. The second example below demonstrates how some strokes may not slant while other strokes do.

RixJongno_Pro

무슨 일이야  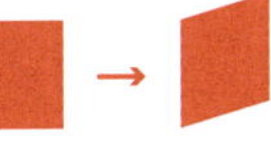

Sandoll BlueNight

무슨 일이야  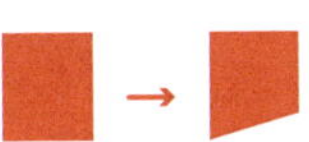

Some Khmer typefaces have subscripts upright, while others slant their subscripts without changing the angles of the consonants.

Kantumruy Pro

Noto Sans Khmer

Leelawadee UI

Hanuman

Noto Serif Khmer

Chenla

In Chinese, one common style—**kaiti** (Regular Script)—slants horizontal strokes by default; it was developed from handwritten styles. Unlike the much abhorred Comic Sans that mimics handwriting in English, kaiti is commonly used in children's books and in elementary school textbooks because it makes it easier for young learners to identify where a stroke begins and ends. Mahjong commonly uses kaiti for its tiles.

AR WeiBeiB5Std BD

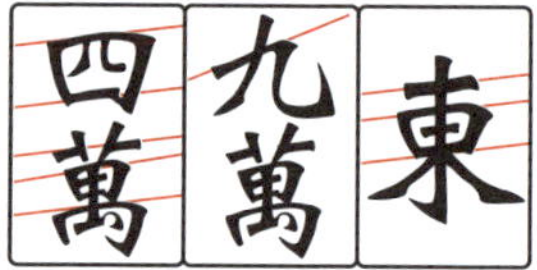

When people more commonly wrote with a brush and ink, they used these angles to bring a dynamic and energetic feel to calligraphy. That is why, even though kaiti is not an italicized form, each horizontal stroke is slanted upwards and to the right.

HelloFont ID JuanYong

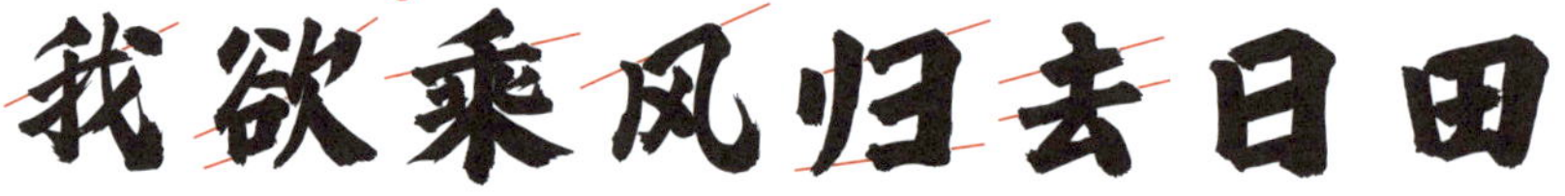

Hellofont ID DanMoXingKai

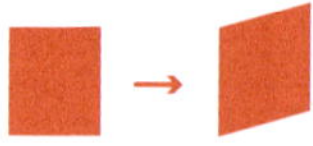

HelloFont ID QingHuaXingKai

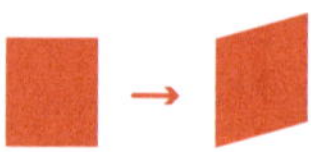

Hellofont ID QingHuaKai

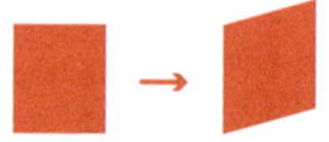

What separates the kaiti from Song/Ming and Hei/Gothic is not only the angled strokes, but the distribution of space among the particles in each glyph box. Kaiti uses more negative space in the composition, which leaves readers with more breathing room.

	composition	angle	negative space	composition	angle	negative space
KAITI	啼	啼		意	意	
SONG/MING	啼	啼		意	意	
HEI/GOTHIC	啼	啼		意	意	

KaiTi, Source Han Serif TC, Microsoft JhengHei

exercise

Can you circle the Regular Script/Kaiti in the following text?

Not in order:
Klee One, MS Gothic, Microsoft YaHei
Hellofont ID QingHuaKai, HelloFont ID JianSong,
Hellofont ID QingHuaKai

Some people criticize Song/Ming for having lost the energy of calligraphy. However, it is more legible than kaiti, especially when printing quality is compromised. As a result, it enjoys the same popularity as Times New Roman in Latin contexts.

	8 pt	**6 pt**	**6 pt 30% grey**
SONG/MING	朝辞白帝彩云间， 千里江陵一日还。 两岸猿声啼不住， 轻舟已过万重山。	朝辞白帝彩云间， 千里江陵一日还。 两岸猿声啼不住， 轻舟已过万重山。	朝辞白帝彩云间， 千里江陵一日还。 两岸猿声啼不住， 轻舟已过万重山。
KAITI	朝辞白帝彩云间， 千里江陵一日还。 两岸猿声啼不住， 轻舟已过万重山。	朝辞白帝彩云间， 千里江陵一日还。 两岸猿声啼不住， 轻舟已过万重山。	朝辞白帝彩云间， 千里江陵一日还。 两岸猿声啼不住， 轻舟已过万重山。

Source Han Serif TC, KaiTi

HANDWRITING AND CURSIVE

Fonts for Baybayin—the less frequently used script for Tagalog—are primarily based on handwriting. The "upright" style therefore retains a particular human touch in its design.

Noto Sans Tagalog

In Korean Hangeul, some people connect adjacent strokes into one to speed up the writing process.

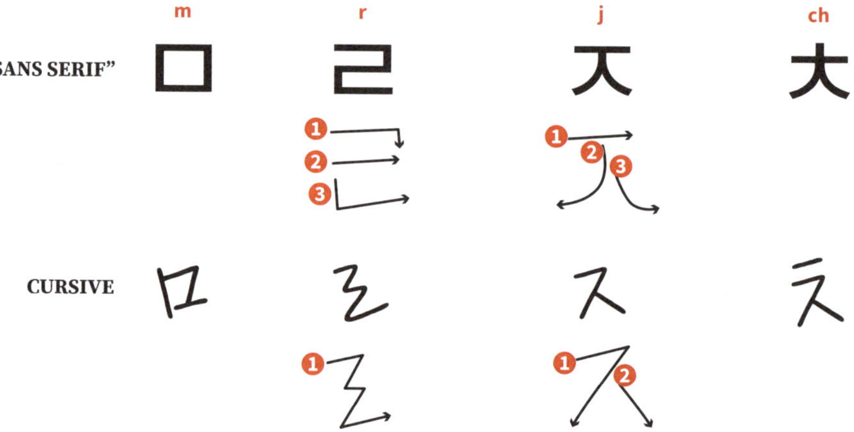

Source Han Sans CN, 210 Epilogue

In Thai, cursive forms simplify loops, as writing letters without them is much faster. However, the **k** (highlighted below) is simplified into a **v** shape in cursive. Spicy!

LOOPED ขอบคุณ ครับ ไก่เห็นตีนงู

LOOPLESS ขอบคุณ ครับ ไก่เห็นตีนงู

CURSIVE ขอบคุณ ครับ ไก่เห็นตีนงู

Thongterm, Forma DJR Thai Text, Sriracha

Exemplified by Korean and Thai typefaces, letters do not stay upright when written rapidly. Slanting occurs hand in hand with the simplification of letterforms, so one cannot conclude that slanting styles are colonial impositions. However, slanting is not used for the same purpose in scripts like Thai in as the italic is in Latin.

There are many ways to treat the loops in the Arabic letter **ha**.

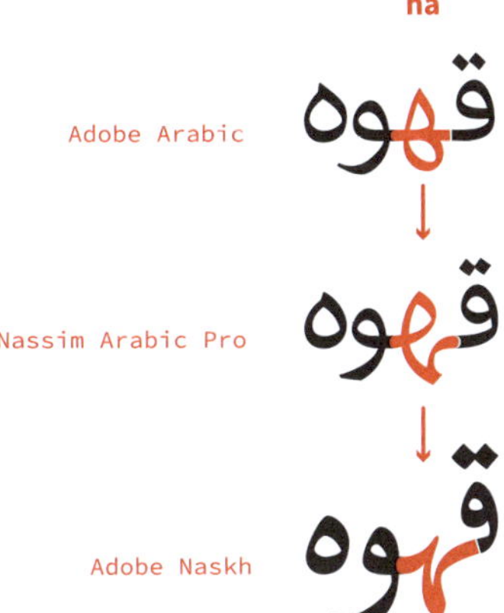

In Arabic, drawing out every tooth and dot of a letter takes a long time. Habitually, many people replace the two dots with a dash (-), three dots with a carat (^), and the three teeth with an elongated line (-).

Adobe Naskh, Layaan

This simplification, though, does not work in Hebrew as a dash and two dots represent two different vowel sounds.

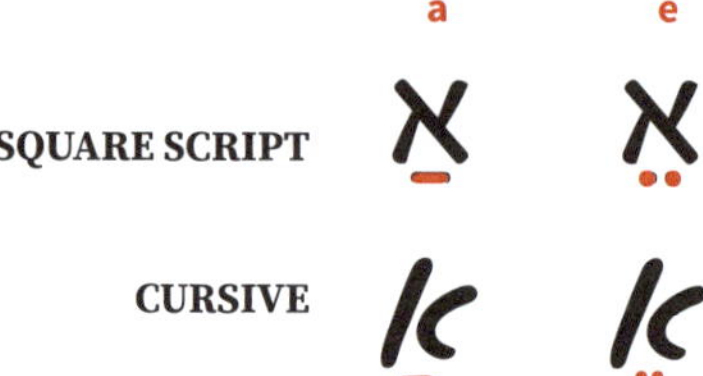

SQUARE SCRIPT

CURSIVE

OmnesHebrew, Gveret Levin AlefAlefAlef

In Hebrew, some cursive letters resemble their printed forms.

SQUARE SCRIPT

CURSIVE

OmnesHebrew, Gveret Levin AlefAlefAlef

But some look very different, and both forms are used commonly.

SQUARE SCRIPT

CURSIVE

OmnesHebrew, Gveret Levin AlefAlefAlef

The Canadian Syllabic script used for Indigenous Canadian languages like Algonquian and Inuit has not established a cursive form or calligraphic tradition, because these missionary scripts were initially intended for printing hymns and gospels rather than for indigenous content.[23] Before Indigenous peoples set a defined human touch to it, they engaged in type more frequently through keyboards and computers.[24] As a result, the syllabics have not yet standardized a form secondary to its upright version.[25]

Noto Sans Canadian Aboriginal

Communities adopting these syllabics have produced manuscripts for thousands of years, using styluses to incise non-phonetic pictographic marks into birchbark scrolls.[26] They did not use the syllabics, created in the 1840s, to form another writing culture.

23. Bringhurst, "Voices, Languages and Scripts," 11.

24. Bringhurst, "Voices, Languages and Scripts," 11.

25. Bringhurst, "Voices, Languages and Scripts," 11.

26. Kevin King and Peter Bilak, *Indigenous North American Type* (Typotheque, 2023), 38–39.

EPILOGUE

Reading is the process of converting letters into thoughts. Much research has been dedicated to achieving higher accessibility through forms within and between letters; however, there will never be a universal checklist or a one-size-fits-all analytical approach to script. The examples from non-Latin scripts discussed in this book demonstrate the importance of personalized and customized approaches geared toward serving a specific, target audience. Unified Arabic and Hangeul, for example, prove the importance of addressing accessibility by customizing type to the language, as both scripts' successes resulted from pointed modification and reform. Accessibility can be further enhanced through letterform distinction seen in fonts like Atkinson Hyperlegible and Japanese Universal Design. In addition to vision differences and neurodiversity, accessibility is highly subject to gender, ethnicity, nationality, politics, economy, and technology. It is crucial that designers identify the communities using a given script and establish conversations with native readers to achieve successful levels of accessibility beyond surface levels. With empathy, innovation, courage, and persistence we can cultivate more diversity in the world of digital literacy.

Complexity in design is comparable to spice levels in food. Building up tolerance opens up more opportunities for diverse experiences. With the current computational capacity to support glyphs as complicated as the Chinese character **biang** (noodle) addressed in chapter 2, there should be increased analysis of minimalism and complexity across cultural contexts. While we continue to digitize endangered scripts, we also need more research into non-Latin scripts that can be made widely available in English and other languages.

Although technology has improved immensely over the last decade, more must be done to ensure inclusion. Scripts that are currently not represented properly suffer from unintentional suppression. As of 2024, scripts like Mongolian remain compromised digitally. As in the examples of left-to-right printed Arabic discussed in chapter 3 and linearized Devanagari covered in chapter 7, even the most sophisticated design software requires extra, manual steps to display minority languages accurately. Technology is like an escalator that assists many people in moving up in one direction. For those whose destination is in another direction, moving against the escalator's set trajectory is a struggle. As analog writing is gradually replaced by digital typing, displaying each language correctly by default becomes increasingly critical.

When importing Western technology, contemporary non-Western cultures simulate Western aesthetics for communication and economy through numerals (chapter 6), serifs (chapter 9), and italics (chapter 10). To fulfill the global market demand in which English dominates the economy of knowledge, non-Latin scripts default to the standards of Latin, such as right-leaning italics for Arabic and Hebrew. For a more vibrant design community, we need less Western-centric policing on the development of non-Latin types. A "crime" in Latin can be a convention in other scripts, and that should be celebrated, not suppressed.

Biscriptual type design with Latin should give equal voice to Latin aesthetics and the non-Latin cultural perspectives. Instead of asking, "where is the x-height line in script A," try "how do we give script A an optically equal height?" The current typography community needs more bi-scriptual type collaborations among non-Latin scripts. For instance, Japanese kana and Filipino Baybayin, which have similar vowels; or Korean Hangeul and Berber Tifinagh, which both use circular, square, and triangular letters; or Armenian and loopless Thai, which both have curves in most letters.

Through more communication and exploration, a more inclusive and diverse typography culture will allow us to sustain long-term cultural preservation in the global community.

Now this book has come to an end. If you like it, please rate it five stars. You can fill it left to right, or right to left.

If by the time this book reaches you, digital applications have been compatible for vertical text, you can fill it downward.

typeface	designers	foundry
210 Epilogue		Design210
210 Mamablock		Design210
210 OmniGothic	Kwak Doo-Yul	Design210
AB-andante	Aki Toyoshima	FONT1000
Acumin	Robert Slimbach	Adobe Originals
Adapter Hebrew Display	Sláva Jevčinová	Rosetta Type Foundry
Adelle Sans	José Scaglione and Veronika Burian	TypeTogether
Adobe Arabic	Robert Slimbach and Tim Holloway	Adobe Originals
Adobe Caslon	Carol Twombly	Adobe Originals
Adobe Devanagari	Fiona Ross, Robert Slimbach, and Tim Holloway	Adobe Originals
Adobe Garamond	Robert Slimbach	Adobe Originals
Adobe Handwriting	Ernest March, Frank Grießhammer, and Tiffany Wardle de Sousa	Adobe Originals
Adobe Hebrew	John Hudson and Robert Slimbach	Adobe Originals
Adobe Ming		Adobe Originals
Adobe Myungjo		Adobe Originals
Adobe Naskh	Muhammad Zuhair Ruhani Bazi and Robert Slimbach	Adobe Originals
Adobe Song		Adobe Originals
Adobe Text Pro	Robert Slimbach	Adobe Originals
Adobe Thai	Fiona Ross, John Hudson,	Adobe Originals

	Robert Slimbach, and Tim Holloway	
Adriane Text	Marconi Lima	Typefolio
akabara-cinderella		Open Source
Akhand Devanagari	Sanchit Sawaria	Indian Type Foundry
Aktiv Grotesk		Dalton Maag
Amador	Jim Parkinson	Parkinson Type Design
Amiri	Khaled Hosny and Sebastian Kosch	
Amita	Eduardo Tunni	
	and Brian Bonislawsky	
Anaqa Variable	Kourosh Beigpour	Canada Type
AR WeiBeiB5Std BD	Arphic Font Design Team	Arphic Types
Arek Armenian	Khajag Apelian	Rosetta Type Foundry
Arial		Monotype
Athelas Arabic Variable	Sahar Afshar	TypeTogether
Atkinson Hyperlegible	Elliott Scott, Megan Eiswerth,	Applied Design Works
	Linus Boman, and Theodore Petrosky	
Bahnschrift	Aaron Bell	Microsoft
Baloo Chettan 2		Ek Type
Baskerville PT	Arina Alaferdova	Paratype
	and Dmitry Kirsanov	
Baskerville URW		URW Type Foundry
BIZ UDMincho		Morisawa Inc.
BIZ UDPGothic		Morisawa Inc.

BIZ UDPMincho		Morisawa Inc.
Bodoni MT		Monotype
Book Antiqua		Agfa Monotype
Brandon Grotesque	Hannes von Döhren	HVD Fonts
Cairo	Mohamed Gaber	Google
Calibri	Luc(as) de Groot (Standard Latin, Cyrillic, Greek, and Hebrew), Mamoun Sakkal (Arabic); Armenian and Georgian (Ruben Tarumian)	Microsoft
Cambria	Monotype Imaging and Tiro Typeworks	Microsoft
Cascadia Code		Microsoft
Catamaran	Pria Ravichandran	Open Source
Century	Morris Fuller Benton	Monotype
Change	Mateusz Machalski	MACHALSKI
Charmonman		Cadson Demak
Chenla	Danh Hong	
Chonburi		Cadson Dema
Clarendon Text	Patrick Griffin	Canada Type
Co Arabic		Dalton Maag
Comic Sans	Vincent Connare	Microsoft
Constantia	John Hudson	Microsoft

Cordale Arabic		Chank Co
Dangrek	Danh Hong	
DIN 2014	Vasily Biryukov	Paratype
DIN Condensed	Manvel Shmavonyan	Paratype
	and Tagir Safayev	
DINosaur	José M. Urós	Type-Ø-Tones
Dongle	Yanghee Ryu	
Droid Serif		Open Source
East Sea Dokdo	YoonDesign Inc	
EB Garamond	Georg Mayr-Duffner	Google
	and Octavio Pardo	
Ebrima		Microsoft
Eurostile		URW Type Foundry
Fahkwang		Cadson Demak
FangSong	Changzhou SinoType Technology Co	
FF Ernestine	Hrant Papazian and Nina Stössinger	FontFont
FF Karbid	Verena Gerlach	FontFont
Forma DJR Thai	David Jonathan Ross	DJR
	and Knaz Uiyamathiti	
Frank Ruhl Libre	Yanek Iontef	
Franklin Gothic	Victor Caruso	The International Typeface Corporation
Futura PT	Isabella Chaeva, Paul Renner,	Paratype
	Vladimir Andrich,	

	and Vladimir Yefimov	
Garamond	Claude Garamond	Monotype
Georgia	Matthew Carter	Monotype
Gill Sans MT	Eric Gill	Agfa Monotype
Greycliff CF	Connary Fagen	Connary Fagen
Gulzar	Borna Izadpanah, Fiona Ross,	
	Alice Savoie, Simon Cozens	
Gveret Levin AlefAlefAlef	Shavit Yaacov	
Hanuman	Danh Hong	
Heisei Maru Gothic Std		Adobe Originals
HelloFont FangHuaTi		HelloFont
Hellofont ID DanMoXingKai		HelloFont
HelloFont ID DaZiBao		HelloFont
HelloFont ID JiangHuTi		HelloFont
HelloFont ID JianSong		HelloFont
HelloFont ID JuanYong		HelloFont
Hellofont ID MeiLingTi		HelloFont
HelloFont ID MingKeBenWanSong		HelloFont
Hellofont ID QingHuaKai		HelloFont
HelloFont ID QingHuaXingKai		HelloFont
Hellofont ID XiaoLiShu		HelloFont
HelloFont ID YongShengCuSong		HelloFont
HelloFont ID YouQiTi		HelloFont

Henri	Henri Friedlaender and Yanek Iontef	Fontef
Hind Madurai		Indian Type Foundry
Hiragino Kaku Gothic ProN		SCREEN GA
HOONEorinigyosil		ziwoosoft
KaiTi		Beijing ZhongYi Electronics Co.
Kantumruy Pro	Tep Sovichet, Wei Huang	
Khmer	Danh Hong	
Kigelia Ethiopic	Mark Jamra and Neil Patel	JamraPatel
Kim jung chul Gothic	JUNGLIM Architecture	YoonDesign Inc
Kinkakuji	Mojiwaku Kenkyu	
Kohinoor Devanagari	Satya Rajpurohit	Indian Type Foundry
Kozuka Gothic	Masahiko Kozuka	Adobe Originals
Kurale	Eduardo Tunni	Google
Laila		Indian Type Foundry
Larabiefont	Ray Larabie	Typodermic
Lato	Adam Twardoch, Botio Nikoltchev, and Łukasz Dziedzic	Open Source
Layaan	Jawaher Alali	Universal Thirst
Leelawadee UI		Microsoft
Loos	Ilya Ruderman and Yury Ostromentsky	CSTM Fonts
Magpie	Vincent Connare	Dalton Maag

Malgun Gothic		Microsoft
Meiryo	C&G Inc.; Eiichi Kono;	Microsoft
	Matthew Carter	
Microsoft Himalaya	Founder	Microsoft
Microsoft JhengHei	Monotype	Microsoft
Microsoft Sans Serif		Microsoft
Microsoft YaHei	Founder	Microsoft
Mongolian Baiti		Almas
Mongolian White		Almas
Mongolian Writing		Almas
Montserrat	Julieta Ulanovsky, Sol Matas,	
	Juan Pablo del Peral,	
	Jacques Le Bailly	
MS UI Gothic		Microsoft
Mukta Malar		Ek Type
Museo Sans	Jos Buivenga	exljbris Font Foundry
Myanmar Text	John Hudson	Microsoft
Nanum Pen	Hyunghwan Choi, Kwak Doo-Yul,	NAVER
	and Nicholas Noh	
Narkissim	Daniel Grumer, Yanek Iontef,	Fontef
	and Zvi Narkiss	
Nassim Arabic Pro	Titus Nemeth	Rosetta Type Foundry
NextExit Variable		Fontef

Nirmala UI	Tiro Typeworks:	Microsoft
	David Brezina (Gujarati),	
	Valentin Brustaux (Telugu & Kannada),	
	Jo De Baerdemaeker (Bengali),	
	John Hudson (Devanagari),	
	Odia (Gurmukhi)	
Noam Text	Adi Stern	TypeTogether
Nokora	Danh Hong	
Noto Looped Thai		Google
Noto Nastaliq Urdu		XXXXXXXXXXXXX
Noto Sans Arabic		Google
Noto Sans Canadian Aboriginal		Google
Noto Sans Devanagari		Google
Noto Sans Ethiopic		Google
Noto Sans Georgian		Google
Noto Sans Javanese		Google
Noto Sans Khmer		Google
Noto Sans Lao		Google
Noto Sans Lao Looped		Google
Noto Sans Mongolian		Google
Noto Sans Myanmar		Google
Noto Sans Tagalog		Google
Noto Sans Thai		Google

Font	Designer	Foundry
Noto Serif Devanagari		Google
Noto Serif Ethiopic		Google
Noto Serif Georgian		Google
Noto Serif Khmer		Google
Noto Serif Lao		Google
Novel Sans Cy	Christoph Dunst	Atlas Fonts
NSimSun		Beijing ZhongYi Electronics Co
Nunito Sans	Vernon Adams, Jacques Le Bailly, Manvel Shmavonyan, Alexei Vanyashin	
OmnesGeorgian	Eben Sorkin, Joshua Darden, and Raymond Bobar	Darden Studio
OmnesHebrew	Daniel Grumer, Eben Sorkin, Joshua Darden, and Yanek Iontef	Darden Studio
Orbit	Sooun Cho, JAMO	
Padauk	SIL International	
Perpetua	Eric Gill	Agfa Monotype
Poppins	Jonny Pinhorn, Ninad Kale	Indian Type Foundry
Poqrik dzeragir	poqrik.am	
Portada Text ARA var	José Scaglione and Veronika Burian	TypeTogether
Potta One	Font Zone 108	
Proxima Nova	Mark Simonson	Mark Simonson Studio
Reem Kufi	Khaled Hosny, Santiago Orozco	

RixJangs_Pro	Sangmin Lee and Yong-rak Park	RixFont
RixJongno_Pro		RixFont
RixSuperRobot_Pro ObliqueShadow		RixFont
Rozha One		Indian Type Foundry
Rubik	Hubert and Fischer, Meir Sadan, Cyreal, Daniel Grumer, Omaima Dajani	
Sandoll BlueNight	Boomi Park and Jiin Park	
Segoe UI		Agfa Monotype
Shiromeda	Abraham Abebe	
Siemreap	Danh Hong	
SimHei		Beijing ZhongYi Electronics Co
Smiley Sans	atelierAnchor	
Source Code Pro	Paul D. Hunt	
Source Han Sans	Joo-Yeon Kang, Paul D. Hunt, Ryoko Nishizuka, Sandoll Communications, and Soo-Young Jang	Adobe Originals
Source Han Serif	Frank Grießhammer, Ryoko Nishizuka Soohyun Park, Wenlong Zhang, and Yejin We	Adobe Originals
Source Sans Pro	Paul D. Hunt	Adobe Originals
Source Serif 4 Variable	Frank Grießhammer	Adobe Originals

Sriracha		Cadson Demak
Stadio Now Variable	Cosimo Lorenzo Pancini	Zetafonts
Sunflower	JIKJISOFT	Microsoft
Sylfaen	John Hudson/Geraldine Wade	
TA_kasanemarugo		Gradeo Fonts
TA-koigokoro	Tegakiya Honpo	
Tahoma	Matthew Carter	Microsoft
Tarif Arabic	Andrea Tartarelli,	Zetafonts
	Cosimo Lorenzo Pancini,	
	and Francesco Canovaro	
Tayitu	Abraham Abebe	
Thonglor	Anuthin Wongsunkakon, Chorong Kim,	Cadson Demak
	and Ekaluck Peanpanawate	
Thongterm	Smich Smanloh, Stawix Ruecha,	Cadson Demak
	and Thongterm Smerasut	
Tiffin Devanagari	Salomi Desai	Universal Thirst
Times New Roman	Monotype	Agfa Monotype
Trebuchet MS	Vincent Connare	Microsoft
Uchen	Christopher J. Fynn	
UD Digi Kyokasho		Morisawa
Yeseva One	Jovanny Lemonad	
Yu Gothic UI		JIYUKOBO Ltd.
Yu Mincho		JIYUKOBO Ltd.

	Zahrah Thai	Michelle Parmar	Indian Type Foundry
	ZW MogujasusimgyeolOTF		ziwoosoft
	TOFU ON THE COVERS		
	Active	Adam Ladd	Adam Ladd
	Adelle	José Scaglione and Veronika Burian	TypeTogether
	Azo Sans	Rui Abreu	Rui Abreu
	Bahnschrift	Aaron Bell	Microsoft
	Brandon Grotesque	Hannes von Döhren	HVD Fonts
	Calluna Sans	Jos Buivenga	exljbris Font Foundry
	Cascadia Code		Microsoft
	Gemunu Libre		Mooniak
	Goodlife		HVD Fonts
	Ingeborg	Michael Hochleitner	Typejockeys
	Lust Sans	Neil Summerour	Positype
	Myriad	Carol Twombly and Robert Slimbach	Adobe Originals
	New Order	Miles Newlyn	Newlyn
	Oi	Kostas Bartsokas	
	Operetta	Jan Tonellato	Synthview
	Stadio Now Devanagari Variable	Aldo Novarese, Andrea Tartarelli,	Zetafonts
		Cosimo Lorenzo Pancini,	
		and Shrishti Vajpai	
	Trebuchet MS	Vincent Connare	Microsoft

BODY TEXT

Source Code	Paul D. Hunt and Teo Tuominen	Adobe Originals
Source Sans	Paul D. Hunt	Adobe Originals
Source Serif 4 Variable	Frank Grießhammer	Adobe Originals

BIBLIOGRAPHY

"29LT Ada : A Ruqʿah Type System," **29LT BLOG**, accessed December 1, 2024, https://blog.29lt.com/2023/02/28/29lt-ada-ruqah-fonts.

"29LT Okaso," 29LT, accessed December 20, 2024, https://www.29lt.com/product/29lt-okaso.

AbiFarès, Huda Smitshuijzen, and Kameel Hawa. **Kameel Hawa: The Art of Shaping Arabic Letters.** Amsterdam: Khatt Books, 2019.

Apelian, Khajag, and Wael Morcos. "Arabic Typography," in **Thinking with Type: A Critical Guide for Designers, Writers, Editors, and Students**, ed. Ellen Lupton. New York: Princeton Architectural Press, 2024.

Apelian, Khajag, and Wael Morcos. "Arabic Typography," in **Thinking with Type: A Critical Guide for Designers, Writers, Editors, and Students**, ed. Ellen Lupton. New York: Princeton Architectural Press, 2024.

Argur, Syhan. "The Gutenberg Bible," in **ABC of Typography**, ed. David Rault. Lonson: SelfMadeHero, 2019.

Beletsky, Misah. "Zvi Narkiss and Hebrew Type Design," in **Language Culture Type: International Type Design in the Age Of Unicode**, ed. John Berry. New York: AtypI Graphics, 2002.

Bilak, Peter, and Michal Sahar. **Designing Hebrew Type.** Den Haag: Typotheque, 2017.

Bilak, Peter, Sopio Kincurašvili, and Nino Kakiašvili. **New Georgian Type.** Den Hagg: Typotheque, 2023.

Březina, David. "Elements of Multi-Script Typography: Codes, Keys, and Word Shapes," **Design Regression**, March 21, 2022, https://designregression.com/essay/elements-of-multi-script-typography-chapter-2.

Bringhurst, Robert. **The Elements of Typographic Style.** Seattle, WA: Hartley & Marks Publishers, 2019.

Bringhusrt, Robert. "Voices, Languages and Scripts," in **Language Culture Type: International Type Design in the Age Of Unicode**, ed. John Berry. New York: AtypI Graphics, 2002.

But Ko and Winston Su. **A Chinese Font Walk Next.** Taiwan: Faces Publications, 2019.

Captan, Lara. and Kristyan Sarkis. "Cyrillic," in **Bi-scriptual Typography and Graphic Design with Multiple Script Systems: Arabic, Cyrillic, Greek, Hangeul, Hanzi, Hebrew, Devanagari, Kanji/Hiragana/Katakana**, ed. Ben Wittner, Sascha Thoma, Timm Hartmann. Salenstein: Niggli, 2019.

Cheng, Karen. **Designing Type.** Yale University Press, 2020.

Christopher Calderhead and Holly Cohen, The World Encyclopedia of Calligraphy. **The Ultimate Compendium on the Art of Fine Writing: History, Craft, Technique.** New York: Sterling, 2018.

Cock-Starkey, Clair. **Hyphens & Hashtags: The Stories Behind the Symbols on Our Keyboards.** Oxford: Bodleian Library, 2021.

Devroye, Luc. "The Schoenfieldian Script Page," accessed November 23, 2024, https://luc.devroye.org/fonts-43554.html.

Ellen Lupton and J. Abbott Miller, **The ABC's of Triangle Square Circle: The Bauhaus and Design Theory.** Hudson, NY: Princeton Architectural Press, 2019.

Garfield, Simon. **Comic Sans: The Biography of a Typeface.** New York: W. W. Norton & Co, 2024.

Garfield, Simon. **Just My Type: A Book About Fonts.** New York: Avery, 2012.

Gladwell, Malcolm. **David and Goliath.** Penguin, 2015.

Hochuli, Jost. **Detail in Typography Letters, Letterspacing, Words, Wordspacing, Lines, Linespacing, Columns.** Paris: Éditions B42, 2015.

Izadpanah, Borna. "Persian and Arabic Printing in Qajar Iran," in **Arabic Typography: History and Practice**, ed. Titus Nemeth. Salenstein: Niggli, 2023.

Kawabe Tsutsumi. and Christine Flint Sato. "Japanese," in The **World Encyclopedia of Calligraphy: The Ultimate Compendium on the Art of Fine Writing: History, Craft, Technique**, eds. Christopher Calderhead and Holly Cohen. New York: Sterling, 2018.

Khoury Nammour, Yara. **Nasri Khattar: A Modernist Typotect.** Amsterdam: Khatt Books, 2014.

King, Kevin, and Peter Bilak. **Indigenous North American Type.** Den Haag: Typotheque, 2023.

King, Kevin. "Syllabics Typographic Guidelines and Local Typographic Preferences," **Typoteque**, January 24, 2022, https://www.typotheque.com/articles/syllabics-typographic-guidelines.

Kudrnovská, Linda. **Building Ligatures: The Power of Type.** Prague: TypeTogether, 2022.

Kuzuoglu, Ulug. **Codes of Modernity: Chinese Scripts in the Global Information Age**. New York: Columbia University Press, 2024.

Kwon, Jeongming. "Hangul," in **Bi-scriptual Typography and Graphic Design with Multiple Script Systems: Arabic, Cyrillic, Greek, Hangeul, Hanzi, Hebrew, Devanagari, Kanji/Hiragana/Katakana**, ed. Ben Wittner, Sascha Thoma, Timm Hartmann. Salenstein: Niggli, 2019.

Leonidas, Gerry. "Greek Type Design," in **Language Culture Type: International Type Design in the Age Of Unicode**, ed. John Berry. New York: AtypI Graphics, 2002.

Lofthouse, Andrew. "Nüshu: China's Secret Female-Only Language," **BBC News**, February 25, 2022, https://www.bbc.com/travel/article/20200930-nshu-chinas-secret-female-only-language.

Malli, Karthik. "Devanagari - The Makings of a National Character," **Typoteque**, March 21, 2022, https://www.typotheque.com/research/devanagari-the-makings-of-a-national-character.

Malli, Karthik. "Malayalam Writing Script, History, Evolution and Changes in Traditional and Simplified Orthography," **Typoteque**, June 25, 2023, https://www.typotheque.com/research/malayalam-scripting-tradition-and-modernity.

Mitchell, Ben. "Thai Italics 1," **The Fontpad**, accessed February 23, 2015, https://www.fontpad.co.uk/thai-italics-1/.

Morlighem, Sébastien. "Modern Handwriting: Introduction Series 4 Cyrillic and Greek Handwriting," **Typoteque**, November 7, 2023, https://www.typotheque.com/articles/modern-handwriting-a-historical-survey-5.

Nemeth, Titus, ed., **Arabic Typography: History and Practice**. Salenstein: Niggli, 2023.

Noordzij, Gerrit. **The Stroke: Theory of Writing**. London: Hyphen Press, 2005.

Ross, Fiona. "An Approach to Non-Latin Type Design," in **Language Culture Type: International Type Design in the Age Of Unicode**, ed. John Berry. New York: AtypI Graphics, 2002.

S. Leelaratne. "Sinhala and Palm Leaf Writing," in **The World Encyclopedia of Calligraphy: The Ultimate Compendium on the Art of Fine Writing: History, Craft, Technique**, eds. Christopher Calderhead and Holly Cohen. New York: Sterling, 2018.

Sadan, Meir. "What Is a 'Serif' in Hebrew?" **Medium**, October 25, 2017, https://medium.com/@meirsadan/what-is-a-serif-in-hebrew-8014f1f63f63.

Singh, Vaibhav. "Devanagari," in **Bi-scriptual Typography and Graphic Design with Multiple Script Systems: Arabic, Cyrillic, Greek, Hangeul, Hanzi, Hebrew, Devanagari, Kanji/Hiragana/Katakana**, ed. Ben Wittner, Sascha Thoma, Timm Hartmann. Salenstein: Niggli, 2019.

Smeijers, Fred. **Counterpunch: Making Type in the Sixteenth Century, Designing Typefaces Now**. London: Hyphen Press, 1996.

Spiekermann, Erik. **Stop Stealing Sheep & Find Out How Type Works**. Berlin: The Other Collection, 2022.

Steinmuller, Robert. **Mono is the New Black: Monospace Fontionary**. Sulgen, SW: Niggli Verlag, 2024.

Todo, Takano. **My Life with DX Dyslexia**. Japan: Shufunotomosha, 2011.

Tsu, Jing. **Kingdom of Characters: The Language Revolution That Made China Modern**. New York: Riverhead books, 2023.

Turkenich, Liron Lav, and Adi Stern, "Hebrew," in **Bi-scriptual Typography and Graphic Design with Multiple Script Systems: Arabic, Cyrillic, Greek, Hangeul, Hanzi, Hebrew, Devanagari, Kanji/Hiragana/Katakana**, ed. Ben Wittner, Sascha Thoma, Timm Hartmann. Salenstein: Niggli, 2019.

Weber, Hendrik. **Italic: What Gives Typography its Emphasis**. Salenstein: Niggli, 2021.

Yazıcıgil, Onur F.. **Pergamon: A Greek Script Typeface Design**. YEM Yayınları, 2023.

Yefimov, Vladimir. "Civil Type," in **Language Culture Type: International Type Design in the Age Of Unicode**, ed. John Berry. New York: AtypI Graphics, 2002.

ar٩(｡•́‿•̀｡)۶ab⊠ic☐arm٩(̄、 ̄ ″)ʃueni♥an⊠bur⊠me
c(-(I)-)əse⊠chт (ʊ 益 ʊ τ)in☐ ☐ese☐cyr♥⊠il﹀(｀д´*)ノ
lic⊠devana⚡o(ㄇㄟㄑo)gari☐⊠ge'ʎ(̄ ^ ̄)ʎez⊠geo⊠rg(ɯ
 ̆ - ̆ɯ)ian♥greΣ(°∆°|||)ek⊠heb 0°☐°)ψ re⊠w⊠jap(つ ̆ω ̆
ç)ane⊠se⊠khm(๑^_^๑)er⊠kor⊠(눈_눈)ean⊠?lao(ʕ̆ᴥ̆)ɔ☐
mon♥go٩(ʏ̆^̆)lia⊠n per☐?٩(′ʊ`*)۶و si⊠☐an♥thๆ(=ω
=)ๆai⊠⊡☐ar٩(｡•́‿•̀｡)۶ab⊠ic☐arm٩(̄、 ̄ ″)ʃueni♥an⊠
bur⊠mec(-(I)-)əse⊠chт (ʊ 益 ʊ τ)in☐ ☐ese☐cyr♥⊠il
﹀(｀д´*)ノlic⊠devana⚡o(ㄇㄟㄑo)gari☐⊠ge'ʎ(̄ ^ ̄)ʎez⊠
geo⊠rg(ɯ ̆ - ̆ɯ)ian♥greΣ(°∆°|||)ek⊠heb 0°☐°)ψ re⊠w
⊠jap(つ ̆ω ̆ç)ane⊠se⊠khm(๑^_^๑)er⊠kor⊠(눈_눈)ean
⊠?lao(ʕ̆ᴥ̆)ɔ☐mon♥go٩(ʏ̆^̆)lia⊠n per☐?٩(′ʊ`*)۶وsi⊠☐
an♥thๆ(=ω=)ๆai⊠⊡☐ar٩(｡•́‿•̀｡)۶ab⊠ic☐arm٩(̄、 ̄ ″
)ʃueni♥an⊠bur⊠mec(-(I)-)əse⊠chт(ʊ益ʊτ)in☐ ☐ese☐